Between the Lines
of World War II

ALSO BY PAUL M. EDWARDS
AND FROM MCFARLAND

*Combat Operations of the Korean War:
Ground, Air, Sea, Special and Covert* (2010)

*Small United States and United Nations
Warships in the Korean War* (2008)

*The Hill Wars of the Korean Conflict: A Dictionary of Hills,
Outposts and Other Sites of Military Action* (2006)

Between the Lines of World War II

Twenty-One Remarkable People and Events

Paul M. Edwards

McFarland & Company, Inc., Publishers
Jefferson, North Carolina, and London

LIBRARY OF CONGRESS CATALOGUING-IN-PUBLICATION DATA

Edwards, Paul M.
    Between the lines of World War II : twenty-one remarkable people and events / Paul M. Edwards.
       p.   cm.
    Includes bibliographical references and index.

    ISBN 978-0-7864-4667-4
    softcover : 50# alkaline paper ∞

    1. World War, 1939–1945 — Miscellanea.   I. Title.
D744.E36   2010
940.53092'2 — dc22   2010025083

British Library cataloguing data are available

©2010 Paul M. Edwards. All rights reserved

No part of this book may be reproduced or transmitted in any form or by any means, electronic or mechanical, including photocopying or recording, or by any information storage and retrieval system, without permission in writing from the publisher.

Front cover image ©2010 Shutterstock.

Manufactured in the United States of America

McFarland & Company, Inc., Publishers
  Box 611, Jefferson, North Carolina 28640
    www.mcfarlandpub.com

To Paula Jean,
delightful and lovely daughter,
of whom I am most proud

Table of Contents

Acknowledgments — ix
Preface — 1
Terms and Phrases — 5
Introduction — 7

PART I: THE MYSTERIOUS AND UNEXPLAINED — 11
  1. The Sitting Duck — 13
  2. The Phantom Four-Stacker — 23
  3. No German Child Should Go Unborn — 32
  4. Bullion for Ballast — 41
  5. Her Name Was *Evergreen* — 48
  6. The Peking Man: Where Is He? — 56
  7. The First Captives — 65

PART II: THE REST OF THE STORY — 73
  8. Beyond the USS *Panay* — 75
  9. The Smoking Cobras — 85
  10. More Ships Than the Navy — 95
  11. Stories from the KPM — 102
  12. Preempting the Flying Tigers — 110
  13. Winston's Special — 120
  14. The Paukenschlag of April 1942 — 132

PART III: EVENTS WORTH REMEMBERING — 141
  15. The *City of Benares* — 142
  16. The Battle of Buna — 150
  17. The Massacre at Palawan — 157

18. The Voyage of the *Li Wo*	166
19. The Saga of Annie Clark	176
20. The Incredible John H. Lang	186
21. The Cave of the Virgins	192
Conclusion	201
Bibliography	203
Index	209

Acknowledgments

As in any work a good many people have been involved in the preparation of this book. Their efforts need to be acknowledged, and appreciation shared. This is not only true of those who have researched and written on the many aspects of World War II, but the many who worked more intensely on behalf of this publication. These include Gregg Edwards, executive director for the Center for the Study of the Korean War at Graceland University; Paula Tennant; Greg Smith; Cindy Roberts; Lisa Hecht; and Susie MacDonald, a longtime friend who finally lost her battle to MS. Acknowledgment must also go, of course, to my ever-present and always-helpful wife Carolynn J. Edwards, and to Bailey, who is asleep in my briefcase.

Preface

While it may sound strange for the writer to complain about the tremendous help electronic cataloguing has been to the researcher, there is nevertheless a complaint to be made. It is simply this: *when the system is too good at giving you what you are looking for, it often fails to give you what you did not expect to find.* This means that the field of research is in danger of losing the one great advantage it has always had, and that is the need to plod your way through a card catalogue in search of wanted materials, whereby you often experience that wonderful serendipitous event of discovering, quite by accident, something you had never heard of before. It is at this point that many of the great stories of history come to light: when you find, hiding just in front of a catalogue card identifying *capitalism,* a card drawing your attention to a book on *Canal, barges* and the opening of a whole new world of research.

Over the years most of the people and events in this book came to my attention in just this fashion, showing up quite unexpectedly during searches for other information. It often happens, as suggested above, purely by accident. Often it is the result of a card discovered in the catalogue, a brief unexplained comment in a text, perhaps a single footnote at the end of a long page, all of which tell just enough that they become the catalyst for further research.

Once the topics were identified, the problem of discovering source material for a better understanding is difficult, for many of these "lost stories" are admittedly not well documented. As in the question of the chicken and the egg, maybe they are not well documented because they are forgotten, or they are forgotten because they are not well documented. But there is information there and generally it is worth the struggle.

A great deal of information has become available through the wonderful selection of articles that have appeared in periodical literature. This is especially true for the last half-century of the *Journal of Military History.* Many of these articles, like Carl Boyd's "U.S. Navy Radio Intelligence During the Second World War and the Sinking of the Japanese Submarine I-52," are often only indirectly related to the story being sought, but still provide valuable information. Thousands of small print efforts have emerged from World War II, which the historian Niall Ferguson calls "the greatest man-made catastrophe of all time."[1]

Helpful as well has been the Internet. Though care must be taken in gleaning information from this source, it is nevertheless an excellent gateway to the small, the minor, and the forgotten in history. But it is also the source of many personal histories, such as those dealing with the life of the hero John Lang or the desperate journey of Annie Clark. Great appreciation is due to those family members who have taken the trouble to make so much of this information available to the public.

There is nothing so helpful as a kind and patient librarian who is capable of turning strange requests into significant documents, and I wish to especially thank the librarian and staff at the Command and Staff Library, Fort Leavenworth, Kansas; the Harry S Truman Presidential Library and Museum, Independence, Missouri; the library staff at the University of Missouri at Kansas City; and the reference librarian at the United States Naval Academy, Annapolis, Maryland, who guided me through the archival maze and connected many of the dots.

As well there have been some excellent, if generally unknown, monographs by participants or survivors, like Glenn McDole's *Last Man Out*. The vast number of these contain wonderful and informative, if sometimes confusing, sources. The papers of participants can sometimes be located in public or private archives. This is true of the materials relating to Admiral Kemp Tolley and the voyage of the USS *Lanikai*. His papers, containing a treasure trove of information, are located at the Chester Nimitz Library at the U.S. Naval Academy at Annapolis.

Some official sources are available and helpful, such as the *Dictionary of American Naval Fighting Ships*, and the less official but still highly important *Blood on the Sea: American Destroyers Lost in World War II* by Robert Sinclair Parkin. Other non-fiction works have been helpful in describing some of the events. These include Thomas Boaz and Russell Ciochon's *Dragon Bones: An Ice-Age Saga of Homo Erectrus* and Ellis M. Zacharias's *Secret Missions*.

Contemporary accounts and newspaper articles in memory or in reference have proven useful, as in the case of Bill Henrick's "Close to Home" in the *Atlanta Journal Constitution* of 14 February 1999; the story on the *Li Wo* found in the *Illustrated London News* of 28 December 1948; the real-time reporting on Colonel Willoughby in *Time* of 25 May 1942; and Tonette

Orejas's "Wreckage of 'Suicide' U.S. Warship found in Subic" from the *Philippine Daily Inquirer* of 14 November 2003.

The events of some of these anecdotes have been discovered by authors of fiction and used as the bases, or background, for their novels. These include James Bassett's fine novel *Commander Prince*, loosely based on the USS *Stewart*, or the lost Peking Man in Amy Tan's *The Bonesetter's Daughter* and Philip K. Dick's *The Crack in Space*. In each case the factual events are somewhat uniquely constructed to meet the needs of the author.

While it was not intentional when selecting which of the potential footnotes on World War II to write about, in looking back on the completed work it is easy to discover some rather interesting threads running through it. If nothing else it suggests how small the world was during those dark, difficult days of World War II.

The historic Allen "Pat" Patterson, a key figure among the American volunteers flying in China before the Flying Tigers, was at Nanking, China, and on board the USS *Panay* when the gunboat was attacked by the Japanese in 1937. He managed to escape by swimming to shore and with little fuss went back to working for the Chinese Air Force.

The commanding officer of the USS *Lanikai* on its mysterious voyage was Lieutenant Kemp Tolley. Tolley, who went on to become an admiral, had been on board the USS *Wake* as executive officer just a few days before she was surrendered. He was quickly given an assignment on the USS *Oahu*, one of the few gunboats that escaped from Shanghai, and the same boat that had come to the rescue of the survivors of the USS *Panay*.

The incredible John H. Lang shows up during his long Asiatic service on both American gunboats, the USS *Panay* and the *Oahu*.

The Lily White girls, who were so concerned about repaying America for the loss of men aboard the USS *Panay* in 1937, were the same as the young ladies discussed in "The Cave of the Virgins."

Many of the Americans taken captive in the Philippines and imprisoned at Palawan POW Camp were members of the famous "China Marines" (the 4th Marines) who had been given responsibility for the Peking Man, and who had been captured in Shanghai, leaving no record of what happened to their charge.

Some of the gold that had to be left behind when the USS *Trout* left, carrying part of the treasure from the Philippine Islands on board, is believed to be a part of the gold that was being sent to Germany on board the Japanese submarine identified as *Evergreen*. The Colonel Willoughby involved in the rescuing and counting of the gold from the Philippines was indeed the same Willoughby who totally miscalculated the Japanese defenses forces during the Battle of Buna.

Some of the ships heading out in "Winston's Special" were also involved in the attempts to evacuate Singapore as portrayed in the stories of the *Li Wo* and Annie Clark.

The KPM *Plancius*, involved in the relocation of German citizens caught in the Netherlands East Indies, was the same ship that Annie Clark managed to catch on her remarkable escape from Singapore.

It is sometimes easy to think of war as the combined efforts of nations, fought out on battlefields and vast oceans, and running continuously from beginning to end. This, of course, is not the case. Most wars, as was World War II, are fought in a series of campaigns, phases, incidents, operations, and missions interspersed by periods of time best described as boredom. And while there are occasions on which massive armies or naval armadas clash, the vast majority of war is fought by small groups in local areas. The most valued history of war, then, is the record of these individuals, each offering their unique contributions. This book is not only about events but also these people, frightened and caught up in war, but heroes and heroines all.

Note

1. Niall Ferguson, *The War of the World: Twentieth-Century Conflict and the Descent of the West* (New York: Penguin, 2006), p. xxxi.

Terms and Phrases

ABDA Command   American, British, Dutch, Australian command, formed in opening days of World War II, which tried to slow Japanese advance in the Pacific.

Asiatic Fleet   United States Far Eastern Fleet created in 1902, and assigned the protection of Philippines and Guam, and the maintenance of the open-door policy with China in 1922.

Blood Chit   A *hu chau*; stitched on an airman's jacket to identify him as a foreign pilot flying for China.

CAMCO   Central Aircraft Manufacturing Corporation, formed for the payment of American pilots flying for China against Japan.

Coast Watchers   Men, often old plantation owners, who were stationed on the numerous islands of the Pacific to report on Japanese naval activities.

Conspicuous Gallantry Medal   United Kingdom medal for heroic action in combat situation.

Federal Malaya States Volunteer Force   Local force of about 2,500 men charged with the protection of Singapore.

Fix   The process of locating a vessel at sea, identifying the location by longitude and latitude.

Flush Deck   Nickname given to the Clemson Class World War I production destroyer that saw service in World War II.

Four Stacker   Nickname given to the Clemson World War I production destroyer.

Hell Ships   Japanese POW ships that were ferrying Allied prisoners to Japan.

HMS   His or Her Majesty's Ship (British).

I-52   Japanese submarine *Momi*.

IJN   Imperial Japanese Navy.

Insular Force Seamen   Local seamen in the Philippine or Guam force.

Kamikaze Planes   Japanese suicide planes flown against Allied forces, particularly heavy against ships at the Battle of Okinawa.

KPM   Koninklijke Paketuarrt Maagsschappij (Dutch Shipping Line).

Malinta Tunnel   Large tunnel complex built on the island of Corregidor and used by the United States first as command and then defense headquarters.

Mothballs   The process of placing a vessel into long-term reserve status.

Nationalist Chinese   Those who supported Chiang Kai-shek and withdrew to Taiwan at the end of the Chinese Civil War.

Navy List   The official listing of all U.S. Navy ships on active duty.

Order of Battle   Identification of all units involved in a particular battle or event.

Paleontology   The study of prehistoric forms of life.

PB   Japanese designation for patrol boat.

POW   Prisoner of war.

PRC   People's Republic of China (Communist), located on the mainland.

Radar   System of locating objects by means of an electronic bounce, used by both the U.S. and Japan on submarines and surface vessels.

RAMP   Recovered Allied Military Personnel; used for USS *Stewart* in 1946.

RCS   Republic of China (Nationalist), located on Taiwan.

River Rats   Nickname for U.S. sailors on the Yangtze Patrol.

RNVR   Royal Navy Volunteer Reserve (British).

Secret Room   Name used to identify the United States system for locating and sinking enemy submarine; also called 10th Fleet.

Sonar   Means of locating underwater vessels by sound reflections.

Subic Bay   Prime Naval base at Manila.

10th Fleet   Highly secret organization with the naval structure, designed to use high-speed radio frequency transmissions to locate and destroy enemy submarines.

U-Boat   German submarine.

Victoria Cross   The United Kingdom's highest-ranking military medal.

War Plan Orange   The United States military plan for response in case of a Japanese attack.

Yangtze River   Major river in China on which U.S. gunboats operated from the early 1920s until the outbreak of World War II.

Introduction

So many wonderful accounts are left untold because the researcher, who is focused on some larger or more immediate target, does not have the time or the space to include them. This is true of all historical research but seems more apparent when studying World War II. Probably this is because there has been so much written, and so many stories told, that we begin to believe we have heard them all. But we haven't. Because it was such an all-inclusive war, large packets of activities have missed recognition. There was so much going on, in so many areas, among such different people, that many of the really interesting people and events are left behind, overshadowed by more prominent ones.

I doubt that anyone who has ever fought in a war would be too willing to define one as a "good war," but certainly to the extent wars can be so classified, World War II meets all the criteria. According to Carl von Clausewitz in *On War*, "The first, the supreme, the most far-reaching act of judgment that the statesman and commanders have to make is to establish ... the kind of war on which they are embarking." In World War II, the description makes sense to Americans because there was, and is, an unquestioned agreement that Nazism was an appalling evil, and that the Japanese aggression was brutal and unacceptable. It is also quickly defined in this way because the clear goals and promised expectations of the war have allowed the media, political analysts, and military authors to treat World War II as a great and triumphal crusade.

Certainly World War II has been portrayed as "romantic military history," against what Max Hastings would define as "non-romantic military history."[1] The first is as much a product of the anticipated reader as it is the author, for those who first wrote the history of World War II wrote it for people who had experienced it, or who knew all about it. There is nothing wrong with romantic military history, for it is primarily a celebration, but its limitations are found in the fact that it does not generally acknowledge the nitty-gritty aspects of the war. Also, both author and reader are more interested in the narrative than they are the analysis of what happened in the larger context.

Clausewitz, in *On War,* stresses that war is more than a sociological constant, but rather that it has the tendencies of a chameleon that alters its appearance in response to its environment. That is to say, the purpose as well as the intensity of war vary greatly and in many ways according to the context: the who, what, when, where, and why of the events. Thus it is often in the smaller story that one sees the variances of war, the distinctive characteristics that alter multiple times within the same war. Movie producers are better at understanding this than are historians. For example, the massive production of *The Longest Day* presents a more meaningful understanding of both the complexity and the uniquely individual nature of the events of 6 June 1944 than a narrative history which tries to explain it in terms of continuity.

Fine historians like Max Hastings have gone beyond the "big picture" approach now and are more and more inclined to look at World War II in terms of telling readers what they do not know — in dealing with the realities of land mines and the complexities of armor and infantry assaults — as well as the desperation and death of battle. At the same time, he tries to describe the localized events in terms of the overall picture. "All history," Darian Cobb tells us, "is local history; it always happens somewhere at some time." The immediate event only becomes a part of the historical package when the ramifications of the event begin to be felt or noticed, and when, looking at it with less romance and more realism, the historian can determine and evaluate the range of events.

Many of the sources in this collection might well be identified as romantic because they are more interested in telling the story, and appreciating its impact on the persons involved, than in placing the events in the context of the larger war. They are not collected to improve on the already excellent works of criticism and analysis; rather, they are collected to portray the actions of men and women under the stress of war.

The twenty-one stories in this book tell of people, events, and realities of World War II that, while maybe outside the mainstream of events, nevertheless were a part of this epic battle. They have emerged from my own research in military history; whenever I ran across such a story, I would promise myself to go back sometime and record its events. These are stories from the backwaters of history. They are not necessarily "unknown," but generally have been bypassed by most storytellers. They are, in their own way, unique and significant. Some of them are a part of some larger, more far-reaching plan; many are simply events in the ongoing process of trying to fight a desperate and varied war.

Among them are stories about events which have never been quite clear, where some mysteries still remain about what happened, or questions about the events and their participants have gone unanswered. For example, the mysterious voyage of the USS *Lanikai* has somehow been bypassed in favor of events taking place at the same time, many more historically significant, but not necessarily as interesting as the story of this remarkable journey from Manila to Australia.

Several of the stories deal with events about which the American public is aware, but about which there is a great deal more to be known and understood. Take, for example, the attack on the USS *Panay*. If asked, most would recognize the attack, but there is far more to the story than is generally recorded.

Some of these accounts reflect events, lives, or memories that time has allowed to fade and which are, in their own right, still well worth remembering. Among these are the story of the HMS *Li Wo* and its successful battle against a Japanese convoy, and the story of the Cave of the Virgins.

As more and more time passes, and especially as those who participated in these great stories reach the end of their lives and take their memories to the grave, it will be harder and harder to find out what really happened. In some cases the memory has been distorted by later events that, in the retelling, provide "better explanations," or by authors of fiction desiring to elaborate on events for the sake of their own agendas. In some cases the perceived romance, as for example in the case of the Flying Tigers, so overshadowed the more interesting but less romantic aspects of the story that many of the lessons that might be learned are missed.

Note

1. Donald Yerxa, ed., *Recent Themes in Military History: Historians in Conversation* (Columbia: University of South Carolina Press, 2008), p. 15.

PART I

THE MYSTERIOUS AND UNEXPLAINED

It is the nature of warfare that much is done in secret, designed to keep the enemy from knowing what is going on. It is also unfortunately true that governments involved feel the need to keep a lot of things secret from their own people. But there are also a lot of mysteries that appear in wartime that are the results of misconceptions, unexplained events, cover-ups and sometimes just plain silence to avoid further trouble, and these often unanswered questions appear to be out of the realm of the ordinary. In the main, most of these can be explained away, some reason found, or evidence uncovered that makes it less a mystery than we thought. Looking back it is important to acknowledge that the justifications for seemingly strange orders may be in the context of the situation, a context that now, in the calm afterlife of these events, we do not comprehend.

Such is the case, for example, with the decision to leave the USS *Wake* behind in Shanghai when she was just as capable of making the run to Manila as the other gunboats that did so successfully. And yet the story remains as one of the more interesting losses of an American warship on active duty to an enemy nation. The unanswered questions seem to be following the story of the USS *Wake* into obscurity.

The same sort of questions surround the destruction, and later reappearance, of the destroyer USS *Stewart*, a mystery that arose out of a bad assumption, as a result of which the phantom four-stacker spent much of World War II as a Japanese patrol boat, and was responsible for the destruction of American submarines.

Certainly every war in history has been the source of myths and legends of lost treasures of gold and precious stones. Edward Michaud, who writes about mysterious treasures, says, "There isn't a country or territory on the face of this earth that doesn't have at least one legend concerning treasure as a result of military conflict." And World War II was no exception, with accounts located in both Europe and the Pacific. The rumors about Corregidor gold and the USS *Trout*'s rescue of Philippine treasures is but one example.

Then there are the rather constant myths about secret weapons, or clandestine deals between friends and enemies. The story of the Japanese submarine *Evergreen* is enhanced by suggestions of early peace efforts between Japan and the United States or, equally as mysterious, the existence of a cargo of uranium for a Japanese dirty bomb. This false information leads us astray and the conclusions drawn are without the benefit of fact.

Some, on the other hand, as in the case of the Peking Man, and the case of the German baby factories, are just plain mysteries. In the first instance there is, despite the times and the situation, just no explanation for what happened. These many myths, rumors, and stories may be little more than smoke, but that would still mean there is at least some fire to be found. Yet, as in the second case, where explanations can be found, the myths are so deeply held that there appears to be little that can be done to address the facts.

Take the stories dealing with how President Roosevelt supposedly set up — or at least had prior knowledge of— the Japanese attack on Pearl Harbor. When war came, both the U.S. and Great Britain expected that the Japanese would attack British Southeast Asia and the Dutch East Indies. The Philippines stood in the way, and if Roosevelt believed — as every evidence suggests — that it was important for the Japanese to strike first, then the Philippines were every bit as good a target as Hawaii. It is this belief that may well lie behind the mysterious voyage of the *Lanikai*.

1. The Sitting Duck

It was a rather anticlimactic death for an old warrior, particularly for a ship that had taken part in one of the more intriguing missions of World War II. Her end came at Subic Naval Base in the Philippines, the last destination of USS *Lanikai*, where she had been sent to undergo much-needed repairs. It was there, in February 1946, that she was caught in a massive storm that hit the area with heavy winds and violent waves, sinking the old wooden warship.

Forty-seven years later, on 5 October 1993, her battered remains were found lying under about 100 feet of water in the remote Nabasan Bay west of what is now Subic Bay Freeport Zone. Divers of the Masterdive, a company hired by the Subic Bay Metropolitan Authority, verified the presence of the wreck that had been suspected because of rumors of artifacts found in the waters by recreational divers. Finally an official inquiry was established to find a wreck of historical importance. But why were so many naval historians so interested in the remains of this old schooner primarily designed for the fishing trade?

Mainly it was because the USS *Lanikai* had an amazing history, including a role in a suicide mission planned at the express orders of President Franklin Delano Roosevelt in December 1941. And why would the president of the United States be personally involved in authorizing sailing orders for an old wooden schooner located in the Philippines? The assumed answer requires some background.

Just what President Roosevelt promised British Prime Minister Winston Churchill when the two met aboard the cruiser USS *Augusta* in August of 1941 will never be completely known. Both participants remember it somewhat differently, each putting his own spin to the agreement. But it is apparent from Churchill's comments that he, at least, believed the United States had agreed to enter the war on Britain's behalf even if it were not attacked itself. Churchill believed that the president had been clear in stating that if the Japanese attacked British possessions in the Far East, America would respond. But there is little evidence to suggest just what Churchill had in mind.¹

Though he did not like it, the president was still bound by the dictates of the Neutrality Act passed first in 1935, then in 1936, and adopted in its final state in 1937. The Act made it illegal for the U.S. to sell arms or war materials to warring parties, or to make loans or run up credits to such nations. The acts also outlawed the use of U.S. ships to transport war materials for warring countries. And while Roosevelt had managed to introduce a "cash and carry" provision, it did not free him to make the sort of decision that was being suggested by Churchill's understanding. In some ways Roosevelt was already breaking the treaty, though not in a manner that would draw much attention. He had approved the arming of merchant ships on the Yangtze River, and had on more than one occasion allowed the use of American gunboats to transport the men and military supplies of the Chinese, who were moving against Japanese intruders.

But the American people were not ready to go to war and at this point did not see the Japanese as the enemy Roosevelt envisioned. The president figured that in order to avoid being caught between his promise to the British and the United States Congress, it was essential that the Japanese initiate some action that would provide a legitimate excuse for entry into a war. Secretary of War Henry Stimson recorded Roosevelt as saying, "The question was how we should maneuver them into the position of firing the first shot without allowing too much danger to ourselves."² It is on this basis that most historians have assumed that the president ordered the mission of provocation. It was our government's intention that if there was to be war, the enemy must fire the first shot.

On 3 December 1941, Admiral Thomas Hart, commander in chief of the frail Asiatic Fleet stationed at Manila, received "top secret orders" that reportedly came directly from President Franklin D. Roosevelt. Already anticipating an attack by the Japanese, and struggling with the arrival of men and ships from all over the Far East, he was ordered to "charter three small vessels ... and send them as soon as possible and within two days if possible after receipt this dispatch ... to stations off the Indo-Chinese harbors," where the Japanese invasion forces destined for the Malayas were then at anchor. The purpose of the mission was clouded in secrecy and preparation was considered a top priority.³

For the first phase of this mission, Admiral Hart sent for Lieutenant Commander Harry E. Shoemaker, captain of the USS *Isabel,* with verbal orders, to undertake the mission. The *Isabel,* built along destroyer lines but never allowed to assume a military posture, had served as everything from a cruise ship to the Admiral's yacht. The USS *Isabel* had sailed for the Far East in 1921 to join the Yangtze Patrol. In the 1930s she served as flagship at Manila and then as the unofficial yacht. She was a trim, nine-hundred-ton yacht acquired by the Navy during World War I. She was still painted a bright white. She was probably selected because she looked more like a Chinese merchant ship than a man-of-war. For some reason the *Isabel* had been identified by name in the president's order. Roosevelt, an old Navy man, may have had his reasons.

In preparation the *Isabel* was relieved of much of her weight, and additional fuel and provisions put on board. Even her charts and codebooks were taken ashore for safekeeping. After loading, the *Isabel* set out on her first "combat" mission, sailing toward the coast of Indochina. Her orders were to be seen, to act as a fishing boat, and if at risk of capture, Shoemaker was to sink the boat. The hope, of course, was that the *Isabel* would draw fire from the Japanese. She had not yet reached her assumed station when she was spotted by Japanese planes, and while they flew around a bit to check her out, she was, after that, totally ignored. What few passing ships she located paid her no mind. So, having failed to draw any fire from either the planes or any of the several Japanese ships spotted on the horizon, she was ordered back to Manila.

But this was not the end of the ploy. The second bit of bait had been selected and was waiting to go. She was the USS *Lanikai,* a 67-ton, 87-foot, wooden two-mast schooner commissioned as an American naval ship on 5 December 1941. By this time she already had a varied history. Originally built by W.F. Stone and Company in California in 1914 as the *Hermes*, she had been completed for a German firm. She was designed for one officer and a crew of eighteen. The outbreak of World War I prompted the United States to intern the ship, and eventually she was commissioned in the U.S. Navy as the USS *Hermes* on 1 April 1918. During the war she served as a patrol vessel about the Hawaiian Islands.

After the war she was decommissioned and finally stricken from the Navy List on 1 July 1926. The Lanikai Fish Company purchased her, changed her name and installed a diesel engine, and from then until 1936 she served several companies within the fishing trade. In 1936 she was briefly stationed in Seattle, Washington, where she was engaged in the Alaskan salmon trade. In 1937 the well-seasoned craft was purchased by Metro-Goldwyn-Mayer for the making of the movie *The Hurricane,* an adventure film staring Jon Hall and Dorothy Lamour. She remained as MGM's yacht until 1939, when she was purchased by E.M. Grimm of the Philippines and used by the Luzon Stevedoring Company as an inter-island trading ship.

As evidence of impending war was gathering in the Pacific, the U.S. Navy chartered the *Lanikai* for a dollar a year and the promise to return her in the same condition when the war was over. She was commissioned the USS *Lanikai* and listed as an unclassified vessel in the Asiatic Fleet's Order of Battle. The commissioning took place on 5 December 1941 at Cavite, Philippine Islands, with Lieutenant Kemp Tolley in command. The ship was armed with a quick firing 3-pounder that was left over from the Spanish-American War, a Lewis gun (.30), and a .50-cal antiaircraft machine gun. She remained painted white.

Once commissioned, all she needed was a proper crew. It had been a point in the original orders that the crews involved should be made up of both U.S. Navy personnel and native Insular Force seamen. Manila was full of sailors with no ships and the *Lanikai* could have been easily staffed, but the rules were followed. The man the Navy had selected to command this odd vessel on its strange mission was Lieutenant (later Admiral) Kemp Tolley.

Kemp Tolley was not the ordinary sort of Asiatic sailor and, when selected, he had only recently escaped from Shanghai. He had been the executive officer aboard the gunboat USS *Wake*, left behind in Shanghai as America's last warship. He had made the trip to Manila on the fleeing American gunboat USS *Oahu*, serving as an auxiliary navigator. Some reports suggest that he was selected for this assignment by order of President Roosevelt, though the written order does not mention him.

A 1929 graduate of Annapolis, Tolley had served, prior to World War II, on the U.S. battleships *Florida* and *Texas* and the heavy cruiser USS *Houston*. Assigned to the Asiatic Fleet, he had been aboard the submarine tender *Canopus*, and then served with the Yangtze River patrol "River Rats" with the gunboats *Mindanao*, *Tutuila*, and *Wake*. A capable linguist, he was one of the few Russian speakers in the Navy. He had also taught French at the Naval Academy and had picked up considerable Chinese and some Japanese from his time in Shanghai. Later he would serve as assistant naval attaché in Moscow from 1942 to 1944.

The key to the crew selection was to get qualified U.S. Navy personnel to be responsible for the running of the ship and supplement them with native crew members. Those selected included Chief Boatswain's Mate Charles Kinsey, who could not believe the poor condition of the ship to which he had been assigned, and Chief Gunner's Mate Merle Pickings, who had no sooner come aboard than he had set to work on the single 3-pounder. As suggested by Roosevelt, eighteen of the crew were Filipino, including Hilario Velarmino; Simplicio Gomez; Crispin Malto Tipay; Vincente Magtulis; Baldomero Belarmino; Marciano Matos Pelarca; Mario Pamero; Prudencio Tumbagahan; Aramdo Alcantara; Demetrio Taleon; Santiago Reyes Profeta; Crispin Guzman Almadin; and six others. They were sworn in as U.S. Navy sailors and given uniforms and equipment. They spoke very little English and were not sure what was going on, but they joined the ship with no hesitation.

With a speed and recklessness unknown in the navy at more traditional times, the ship was made ready, Tolley signed the receipt for "a schooner"— the only paperwork required — and waited as a small cannon was located and installed. Civilians and servicemen from ordnance, supply, communications, and personnel mobilized to get it done. The radio receiver was discovered to work properly, though there was no way in which to transmit, but there was no time to change things. The only other problem was a shortage of water which, Tolley was instructed, he might get from a passing Japanese ship if needed.

While he had been given the larger picture, the mission on which Tolley was being sent was still secret and the full extent of it was not known even by Tolley until he opened his sealed orders after leaving Manila. But in effect it was this: The ship was to sail toward Indochina and to go on station between Hainan and Hue, the first on Cam Ranh Bay and Cape St. Jaques on the far eastern tip of Vietnam, and the other off the Pointe de Camau on the southern tip of Indochina. She was to operate with her running lights on low as if she were a fishing boat. The stations were clearly in the path of the Japanese and would be spotted if so placed. The *Lanikai* sailed out about fifteen miles waiting for dawn before following the minefield channel. She was planning to relieve the USS *Isabel*, which had been on station since 3 December and was heading back.

Fully prepared and ready to go, the *Lanikai* and her somewhat perplexed crew slipped out to sea, moved through the minefields, and lay waiting for the morning in order to move out on her mission. However, as the cool morning of 8 December 1941 dawned, the radioman on duty on the *Lanikai* received new orders which he delivered to his still sleeping captain: "Orange War Plan in Effect. Return to Manila." Orange War Plan was the supposedly secret code to inform the ship that the Japanese had attacked and that war on was on. The *Lanikai* headed back to Manila. At this time even Congress was unaware of Rainbow, the rather elaborate plan for fighting

World War II which, among other things, gave first priority to the war in Europe and the survival of Great Britain over American territories in the Pacific.

This assignment, at least, was called off. The *Molly Malone*, which had been identified as the third ship in the mission, if needed, was relinquished. She would not have had an easy trip. Only half the size of the *Lanikai*, she was equipped with a three-pound cannon and machine guns like those on the *Lanikai*, but was considered sluggish. But she was no longer needed; the Japanese had already made the first move.

With the mission canceled, the schooner *Lanikai* was assigned to the Inshore Patrol, where she conducted missions about the harbor. In the main she was in limbo, spending her time sailing through the minefields on a daily basis, as she provided anti-submarine patrols around the harbor. On Christmas Eve she was called on to aid in the evacuation of Subic Bay at Zambales and the headquarters at Manila's Cavite Navy Yard.

Working with the gunboat USS *Oahu*, the *Lanikai* assumed a search pattern on the lookout for approaching submarines or aircraft. Japanese troop ships were surely on the way, but they had had not shown up yet. Then she moved slowly back and forth inside the harbor entrance waiting to be of help if necessary, and using her machine guns to fire on the occasional strafing aircraft that showed up. Unfortunately the *Lanikai*'s guns could not be elevated more than about 20 degrees and so did not have much chance of hitting anything.

Soon Admiral Hart determined it was necessary for the Asiatic Fleet to move out. The Navy no longer had a role in the quickly deteriorating situation in the Philippines, and they were regrouping. The forces of the sea war were not centering on Java. The evacuation orders for Admiral Hart provided a means to accomplish it, but he was not able to take the entire staff, deciding to take out the most essential individuals only. This coverage did not include his flag lieutenant, Lieutenant Commander Charles Adair. Although a lot of Navy men remained, joining up with ad hoc and mixed military groups determined to carry on the fight, Adair did not intend to stay on the island if he could help it. Locating Kemp Tolley, he asked if he was willing to try to make a run through the Japanese-held waters in search of a friendly port. It would be in keeping with Admiral Hart's having ordered all other ships in the harbor out and leaving for Java on the U.S. Submarine *Shark*. There was no hesitation in Tolley's mind, and with permission from Admiral Francis Warner Rockwell, who had taken command from Hart, and after swabbing on green paint as quickly as possible, the crew of the *Lanikai* departed Mariveles, Luzon, on 26 December 1941 at 1940 hours, carrying one Dutch and three American officers and a Filipino crew, destination unknown.

Sailing with great care, mostly at night, and hugging the islands whenever possible, the *Lanikai* sailed from Manila to Surabaya on Java in the Netherlands East Indies. She participated briefly in the doomed defense of the Dutch island of Java and then sailed to Tjilatjap, where she aided in the evacuation of Allied stragglers trying to get away. She finally departed Java on 26 February 1942 just prior to the Dutch surrender, and arrived at Fremantle, Australia, 18 March 1942. Still flying were the tattered flags of the Philippines and the United States, and the tangled remains of what appeared to be a commissioning pennant. It had been a long haul across dangerous waters.

The plucky ship was transferred to the Royal Australian Navy on 22 August 1942 and renamed the HMAS *Lanikation*. She was outfitted as a boom defense ship and served in that capacity at Australian ports during the rest of the war. The ship was decommissioned 22 August 1945 at the close of the hostilities, and transferred back to the U.S. Navy. The Navy then converted her back to a schooner rig and returned her to Manila in 1946. The Luzon Stevedoring Co. to which she had belonged refused, however, to take her back because she was in such bad shape.

It was while undergoing repairs at the Naval Shipyard at Subic Bay that the tired old schooner/windjammer/warship was hit by the winds of a violent typhoon and sank beneath the waters where she had so long served. There she lay unattended for more than half a century, unclaimed and unsought.

Her assignment in Manila remains a mystery invoking questions never satisfactorily answered. Why was the president involved in what appears to be such a low-level mission? What did he want? To many it was a deliberate attempt to goad the Japanese into firing on American naval vessels — even if the Japanese did not know that is what they were — and thus providing a legitimate excuse for America's entry into World War II. Thomas Fleming calls it one of a "series of provocations, punctuated by American intransigence, that disregarded the desperate last-minute efforts of the Japanese to reach a peaceful settlement."[4] Like many, he believed that the USS *Lanikai* was sent into harm's way where, as a sitting duck for Japanese warplanes, it might well have provided the initiative to begin World War II.

There has been a lot of talk the past seventy years suggesting that President Roosevelt knew about, or maybe even had a hand in, the bombing of Pearl Harbor by the Imperial Navy of Japan. Despite the theories, as well as some confusing evidence, there is little doubt that President Roosevelt believed that if a war was to start, it was in the best interests of the United States for the Japanese to fire the first shot, and that he was willing to encourage such an action. There is some primary and a great deal of secondary evidence that Roosevelt planned the *Lanikai* effort, and that it was the result of considerable preconsideration. The Navy Department would not have ordered it unless specifically told to do so.

As well, there was more than a little reluctance on the part of those higher authorities that were involved. Commander Harry Slocum, Asiatic Fleet Operations Officer, would later suggest that most of those involved understood that time was running out, and that whatever President Roosevelt had in mind "could in all probability never be carried off."[5] Admiral Hart, at least according to Kemp Tolley's later writings, knew that Tolley and the *Lanikai* were being used "as bait." In later testimony about the conduct of the war during those early months, Admiral Ingersoll testified to the suggestion of "bait," as did Admiral Stark, though Stark reported that no reasons had been given. Stark, if he knew more, has chosen not to reveal it.

Was the mission on which the *Isabel* and *Lanikai* were sent a pair of one-way-trips in which it was anticipated (or at least hoped) they would be sunk by the Japanese? This seems to be the case. Certainly the selection of vessels to be involved raised some question, for they were not easily identified as American fighting vessels, but were clearly American vessels, and thus would appear as easy targets, if the Japanese were inclined to attack.

Logically there was no other reason. There was no need for a patrol to seek information about the movement of the Japanese fleet. In fact the Navy was able to tell Lieutenant Tolley just about where to expect to run into the Japanese. At this point in the chronology of the prewar period, both the Navy and Washington knew where the enemy was. In fact, the War Cabinet had met at noon on 28 November to discuss what they should do about the major Japanese naval force that was heading south off Indochina.

Besides, since the *Lanikai*'s radio had no transmitter, there was little hope they could have reported even if they had seen something unusual. Those sending out the *Isabel* and *Lanikai* knew that air patrols in the area would be able to report if the ships were attacked, but at the same time, could well report any unexpected movement of the fleet. There is no rational explanation for the two vessels' sailing as ships of reconnaissance.

There are two other facts to bring into consideration. One has to do with Japanese intentions. At the time, Roosevelt and many of his military advisors believed that the Japanese would be attacking either British- or Dutch-held territory, but not American. If it was the Dutch-held possessions it might be tolerable, but if it was British, then the commitment to Churchill came into effect. But even an attack on British territory still might not be enough to bring America into the conflict. If the Japanese were going to go to war it was essential that they make an attack on American soil or vessels.

The other consideration, which has received less attention, was the president's insistence that the crew consist of a good number of Filipino nationalists. Why? Looking back now, after sixty years of propaganda and good relations, it is hard to remember that there was no assurance that the Philippine government would support the American cause in case of war. The Americans were, after all, an occupying nation and the promise of freedom was still years away. The Japanese call for an area of Asian influence had a good ring to it. Perhaps, it may well have been considered, the firing on an American ship might not make the difference, but Roosevelt was pretty sure that if the Japanese fired on the ship and killed Filipinos on board, it might well go a long way in encouraging President Quezon of the Philippines to join in the fight.

In some ways the *Lanikai* assignment stands as an argument against those still claiming that Roosevelt knew about the coming attack on Pearl Harbor and did nothing. In their book *Deceit at Pearl Harbor: From Pearl Harbor to Midway*, Lieutenant Commander Kenneth Landis and Sergeant Rex Gunn make the interesting claim that Roosevelt knew more than ten days in advance of the Pearl Harbor attack. What would be the point, in such a case, of sending the provocation mission on 5 December? What would be the point of a small skirmish near Indochina when Japan would be attacking America within the next few days?

Perhaps the attitude of the American people had changed by 1941. Maybe they would more easily respond to an insult, particularly a military attack, against their country than they had four years before. Roosevelt had been astonished at the relatively calm reaction of the American people when the Japanese had "accidentally" sunk the American gunboat, the USS *Panay*, on the Yangtze River in December of 1937. Following that attack, which was well documented for the American people in films taken at the time, there had been less response than one would have thought. Americans had not risen up in anger as Roosevelt thought they might. In fact, after a few apologies and payment of compensation, the whole thing was quickly dropped. Most historians assume that the low-key government reaction had to do with the fact that the United States was not ready, at that time, to take on a war with Japan. Why did he think the public would be ready to fight now? Maybe he did not need a reaction, only an excuse.

Notes

1. *Proceedings*, House of Commons, January 1942.
2. Kemp Tolley, "The Strange Mission of the *Lanikai*," *American Heritage* 24, no. 6, (October 1973): on pp. 1–8.
3. "Wreckage of 'Suicide' U.S. warship found in Subic," *Philippine Daily Inquirer*, 14 November 2003, http://www.antiwar.com/justin/pf/p-jo62501.html.
4. Thomas Fleming, *The New Dealers' War: Franklin D. Roosevelt and the War Within World War II* (New York: Basic Books, 2001).

Further Reading

Hilton, James. *The Story of Dr. Wassell*. New York: Little, Brown, 1943.
Hoyt, Edwin. *Lonely Ships*. New York: David McKay, 1976.
Landis, Kenneth, and Rex Gunn. *Deceit at Pearl Harbor: From Pearl Harbor to Midway*. N.p.:1st Books Library, 2001.
http://members.tripod.com/pricegraphicarts/WorldWideTerrorism/id48.htm.
Tolley, Kemp. *Cruise of the Lanikai: Incitement to War*. Annapolis: United States Naval Institute, 2002.

2. The Phantom Four-Stacker

Slipping through the fog lying near the coast of more than a dozen islands, the ship was quickly acknowledged but never identified. To the Air Force men on high flying aerial reconnaissance missions she was an American ship way out of bounds and found to be sailing deep in enemy waters west of New Guinea. To Coast Watchers in their hazardous perches among the island hills she was a recurring ghost ship, constantly showing up in their sightings, but for which they had no explanation to report. To the men of the United States Navy she was a phantom ship that had been spied around the Java Sea, and which conjured up thoughts of *The Flying Dutchman*.

This phantom ship looked American. Some said that she had the silhouette of a Clemson Class four-stacker destroyer, but she also displayed the typical Japanese combined fore funnels. And she was always seen in enemy waters. The stories about her compounded at every sighting, the claims of her illusive nature expanded by every retelling. At once she was believed to be a clandestine American raider responsible for the loss of unreported ships, a supply ship feeding enemy submarines fuel for extended voyages, and the ghost of a dead destroyer seeking revenge for some unknown crime. Lt. Commander Frank E. Haylor of the U.S. submarine *Hake* (256) spied her on one occasion at a distance through his submarine periscope and misidentified what he saw as the old Thai destroyer *Phra Ruang*. But she was none of these.

To the American authorities, to whom she was constantly reported, the mysterious ship was not a subject to be taken all that seriously. The Navy had other things to worry about. Strange sightings were pretty common among sailors and with all that was going on, and in so many theatres, the stories of this appearing and disappearing ship were considered little more than the illusions of fatigued men on watch. But the reports continued to come in. The stories, hazy to begin with, had been given extended credence by rumors among enlisted men — rumors that had been considerably exaggerated in the retelling. Each sighting brought on a whole new set of explanations, but none of them fit. Whatever she was, she continued to appear throughout the war, sighted in strange places, under strange conditions, and on unidentified missions. There was still some doubt if she was friend or foe.

All of these reports of the sighted ship described it from a considerable distance, seen on the horizon or amidst other seagoing vessels. The lack of information did little other than to expand the belief in this seagoing phenomenon. A ship without identification raised the question in many minds: just what was the cause of these sightings?

The answers to the questions about the phenomenon are both simple and complex, but were not available until after the conclusion of World War II allowed some hands-on investigation. While it could not explain all the sightings, most of what had been seen and reported for the past two years was in fact nothing more complicated than the Japanese Patrol Boat #102, which was finally found snug in the harbor when the war ended. But this discovery created a new set of questions, because the patrol boat that was discovered in that Japanese harbor was also the United States Navy four-stacker destroyer USS *Stewart* (DD-224), of the Asiatic Fleet. This was a ship that American authorities believed had been destroyed in the opening phases of the war. So where had she been, and why was she flying the flag of the Imperial Japanese Navy when captured?

First, where had she come from? The destroyer had been originally ordered as a part of America's naval buildup during World War I. She had been constructed by William Camp and Sons in Philadelphia, where her keel had been laid on 9 September 1919. She was launched on 4 March 1920 as one of the many of her class to be too late to be involved in the war for which she was constructed. At a length of 314 feet 5 inches and a 31-foot, 9-inch beam, the *Stewart* had a displacement of 1,215 short tons. Powered by four White-Foster oil-burning boilers, her four geared steam turbines allowed her to reach a speed of 35 knots. She was designed to carry a complement of 101 officers and enlisted men. The original armament consisted of four 4-inch guns, one 3-inch gun, and 12 twenty-one-inch torpedo tubes. She was named after Captain Charles Stewart, commander of the USS *Constitution*, and was commissioned 15 April 1920 by Mr. Margaretta Stewart Stevens, the granddaughter of Rear Admiral Stewart. Lieutenant S.G. Lamb was her first commander.

This class was distinctive with its "flush deck" 4 piped or 4 stacks, and were a product of World War I's mass production. Once constructed, the four-stackers became the backbone of the United States destroyer force. Over the decades the ships had been converted to a variety of duties from minelayers to seaplane tenders, and the *Stewart* had been given tracks for depth charges and mine laying. At the end of World War I these destroyers suffered the same fate as the rest in the arms reduction, and more than sixty were sent to the mothballs. A good many of these destroyers would appear again at the outbreak of World War II and were the source of the 50 lend-lease destroyers that President Roosevelt made available to the British. Old and often outdated, they nevertheless played a vital role in keeping the convoy lanes as safe as possible.

The narrative of her service was mixed, as was true for so many of the old Clemson Class four-stacker destroyers, but unlike many of them she had led a busy and even heroic existence. Since the Great War was over when she was completed and there was no immediate military service required, she reported briefly with the coastal divisions and then joined Destroyer Squadron Atlantic on 12 October 1921. For two years she saw service in the Mediterranean and Indian Oceans and on 26 August 1922 arrived at Chefoo, China. She had been ordered to join the Asiatic Fleet with assignments in China and the Philippines, where she would protect American interests. The Asiatic Fleet was America's presence in the Far East and had its hands full with responsibilities both in China and the Philippines. With the Asiatic Fleet she undertook patrol and anti-submarine missions. From 1922 to 1928 there were dozens of protests and disturbances against the foreigners in the area, and the USS *Stewart* was called to aid in the control of disruptive elements. In January 1925 she ferried Marines to Shanghai in an effort to protect Americans during one of the many outbursts in the city.

In September of the following year she took part at Yokosuka in providing relief to those caught up in the great Kanto earthquake. Later, when the Chinese Communist troops began attacking foreigners at Nanking, and for several months after, she was stationed at a variety of cities in which were located foreign concession stations, including Wuhu, Nanking, Shanghai and Chenglin, to protect American nationals and maintain shipping rights along the Yangtze River. She was at the China coast when the Japanese launched their air attack against Shanghai in late 1932. She steamed in support of Nationalist troops during the 1937 Japanese attacks on Shanghai, and again in January of 1940 she transported elements of the U.S. Marine 4th Regiment sent into Shanghai to safeguard American interests there. She made one final trip to China to the Yellow Sea ports from 7 July to 23 September 1940.

When war broke out in Europe the destroyer *Stewart*, still in the Philippines, was immediately assigned to patrol and anti-submarine duties. She underwent a major overhaul at the Cavite Navy Yard during April 1940.

When the work was completed in June of that year, she acted as a plane guard for seaplanes flying between Guam and the Philippines. In November of 1941, under the command of Lieutenant Commander Harold P. Smith, she sailed from Manila as the flagship of Commander Thomas H. Binford's Destroyer Division 58, which consisted of the *Stewart*, *Parrott* (DD 218), *Bulmer* (DD 222) and *Barker* (DD 213). Admiral Hart wanted his ships out of danger, and he saw danger on the horizon.

She was at station with several other ships of the Asiatic Fleet at Tarakan Roads, Borneo, when news of the war came. Because of Admiral Hart's actions they had escaped the Japanese at the Philippines, but found the situation was not much better in and around the island of Java. The Japanese, it appeared, were closing in on all sides. At first her duties remained rather normal, including the escort for ships that were still able to move between Australia and the Philippines, but the destroyer was soon pulled off for more active service as the Japanese invasion fleets, now sailing toward Australia, grew closer. The Allies determined that some effort, no matter how costly or how futile, had to be made to slow them down. The *Stewart* was then assigned as a part of DESRON 29, along with other U.S. destroyers placed on duty with the American-British-Dutch-Australian (ABDA) Command in defense of Java under Dutch Admiral Karl Doorman.

What remained of the Asiatic Fleet was well aware that they were neither large enough nor well enough supported with air cover to accomplish much against the Japanese fleet that appeared to be coming in never-ending waves. But they went out looking for a fight. The *Stewart* joined with the U.S. cruiser *Marblehead* on the last of January and sortied with her for several days without making contact, returning only for fuel and supplies. On 4 February 1942, in an attempt to intercept Japanese forces in the Makassar Strait, the *Marblehead* suffered tremendous damage. The *Stewart* was assigned the job of escorting her back to Tjilatjap, Java, in hope of repairs. Once there, the *Stewart* was assigned to Admiral Doorman's small combined fleet, which on 14 February set out in another effort to attack and slow down the Japanese forces heading for Sumatra.

The occupation of Java and Sumatra were the beginning of phase two of the Japanese war plan. Once Singapore was taken, Japanese forces were scheduled to move to northern Sumatra. The ABDA was dedicated to at least slowing them down. Over and over again the small ships headed out to take on elements of the Japanese invasion fleet. In most cases their success was limited. During these fateful engagements the *Stewart* was able to hold its own, delivering several blows to the enemy and then managing, when

2. The Phantom Four-Stacker 27

ordered, to withdraw. She was still undamaged and her crew intact on 16 February when she was detached and sent to Ratai Bay in Sumatra to refuel.

On the night of 19 February, near Sanur Roads southeast of Bali, Admiral Doorman once again sent his ships against the Japanese invasion fleet. The joint ABDA Command actually outnumbered the Japanese at this time. In what was later known as the Battle of Badung Strait, the destroyer *Stewart* was assigned as the lead ship in one of the attacking groups. Moving into position at 0146 hours, she became engaged in a duel with two Japanese destroyers, the IJN *Oshio* and *Asashio*.[1]

Despite her constant movement and general fire, the *Stewart* was hit three times during the engagement. The impact of one of the damaging hits had blown her boats away. The second explosion was near the galley and the torpedo tubes, and both were destroyed. This was followed by a third hit, this time below the waterline, that sent floods of water into the steering section. With considerable effort her crew was able to withdraw her from the engagement, and managed her back to Surabaya the following morning. She needed repairs or she could not continue. There at Surabaya, on the northeastern coast of Java, the expectation was that she would be repaired at the large naval base there. The outcome of the battle supported the belief that the Japanese navy was much better at night fighting than were the ABDA Command.

Having achieved the role as the most badly damaged ship of the fleet, the *Stewart* was assigned the first floating dry dock available. The ABDA needed every warship they could keep afloat. Naval command located a 15,500-ton dock operated by a privately owned firm at Surabaya. The crew worked her into the dock on 22 February 1942 to correct damage to the port propeller. The salvage crews were working under strenuous conditions, and at regular intervals the Japanese bombers appeared to raid the area. Those setting up the dock for the ship had been rushed and did not properly set the blocks, so when the dock began to rise, the *Stewart* slipped from the blocks onto her side in 12 feet of water.

An assessment of the damage was most discouraging. It now showed the destroyer was listing at 45 degrees and that the weight of the fall had caused even greater damage to her hull. In addition, both propeller shafts were now bent. The Navy was not sure what to do. With the docks coming under continual attack by Japanese planes, and civilian workers fleeing whenever they could, there seemed to be little chance that the *Stewart* could be repaired. One thing was certain, however, she could not be allowed to fall into enemy hands.

Commander T.H. Binford, commander of DESRON 29, was out of torpedoes and supplies, and was desperately in need of more dockyard space. He decided that his best bet was to withdraw his command through the Sunda Straits to Tjilatjap. But he could not leave the damaged USS *Stewart* behind. Reluctantly he gave orders to scuttle the ship. While this decision was being made a Japanese plane, seeing the docked *Stewart*, flew low over the stricken ship and dropped a bomb that hit her amidships and damaged her even further. As far as the Navy was concerned, this seemed to solve the question of the *Stewart*.

Japanese military forces began to gather from Borneo, the Celebes and the Molucca Islands for their attack on Java and by 26 February a convoy of Imperial forces, including 56 transport ships, were seen heading for Java. With the port under threat of immediate occupation, the responsibility for the final destruction of the ship was given to naval authorities ashore. The last of the embattled crew members, under Lt. Commander H.P. Smith, left the damaged ship on the afternoon of 22 February 1942. Under navy supervision, demolition charges were set under the broken *Stewart* and in and around the dry dock on 2 March 1942, and the charges were blown.

The destroyer's name was stricken from the Navy List on 25 March 1942 and her proud name given to the DD-238, another destroyer under construction. As soon as the explosions were heard, those that were able joined with the hundreds fleeing the island to avoid capture.

So how did this American ship come to be in the hands of the enemy? It is a testament to the Japanese needs, engineering skills, and determination that they were able to save her. After the successful invasion of the island, the Japanese discovered the *Stewart* in the dry dock. While the charges had gone off as anticipated and the dock destroyed, the angle of the ship's tilt had dispersed some of the force of the explosion, and while it had brought the dock down around the ship it had not added a great deal to the damage of the vessel itself. Since the Japanese were increasingly in need of escort craft to maintain patrols around their island conquests, an engineering unit of the Imperial Japanese Navy under Lt. Fukui Shizuo set about trying to salvage her. The Japanese reconstructed the No. 102 Repair Facility and set to work. Though she had been lying on her side under water for more than a year, the Japanese salvage workers were able to raise her in February of 1943, and started putting her back into shape. After considerable work the ship was declared suitable for duty and was commissioned on 20 September 1943 as IJN Patrol Boat No. 102, under Lieutenant Mizutani Tamotsu as commander and Lieutenant (Jg.) Okubo Tsurayuki as executive.

In the rebuilding, the original United States armament had been removed by the Japanese and replaced with two captured Dutch Army 3-inch guns and two 7.7 machine guns. The patrol boat was also fitted with depth charges for anti-submarine warfare. Both for identification purposes and boiler efficiency, her two fore funnels were trunked together in the Japanese naval style. Despite their efforts, however, they were only able to get two of the ship's four boilers to function.

Japanese naval authorities were skeptical about the ship's value, as she was consider far too narrow of beam and was top-heavy. Nevertheless, they needed as many auxiliary ships as they could muster, so to combat the latter problem, the stacks were lowered to reduce her center of gravity. The bridge structure was also altered, and added ballast was provided, all of which made her ride better. In time the engineers were able to get three of the four boilers working and she was able to reach 26 knots. The boilers would continue to be a problem during her service and rarely did more than three operate efficiently. A hanging lantern-type Japanese surface radar was provided and somewhat later sonar was added to increase her capabilities for anti-submarine work.

PB 102 was put to work immediately, and was ultimately assigned to the Japanese Southwest Area Fleet on 23 August 1944 under the command of Lieutenant Tomoyoshi Yoshima. Assigned primarily as an anti-submarine patrol craft, she often traveled with other ships in support of small convoys. At 0630 on 24 August, Lieutenant Commander Frank E. Haylor of the USS *Hake* (SS 256) ran into the PB 102, in conjunction with a trio of Japanese ships. The American officer incorrectly identified her as the Thai destroyer *Phra Ruang*. While the *Hake* broke off, the USS *Harder* (365) continued toward the bay just as the PB 102 and CD-22 turned to come after her. They commenced a series of depth-charge attacks, driving the American submarine deeper and deeper. Working in anti-submarine exercises, and in cooperation with IJN CD-22, the PB 102 was given partial credit for the fifth salvo sinking of the American submarine the USS *Harde* (257).

While records are limited both in American and Japanese archives, the USS *Growler* (SS 215) is also considered to be one of her victims. The *Growler* was on her 11th war patrol and working with the USS *Hake* and *Hardhead* in early November 1944. Sailing near the Philippine Islands, the group attacked a Japanese convoy on 8 November, sinking one transport. The Japanese escorts moved in for the kill, letting go numerous depth charges as they crisscrossed the area where a sub had been seen. The last word heard from the *Growler* was her commander's order to "commence firing." After that, underwater explosions and the sounds of breaking up were heard, and it was believed that Commander T.B. Oakley, Jr., and his crew of 83 were lost. Any attempt after that to contact the sub was in vain. Patrol Boat 120 was there providing cover for the convoy, and had attacked along with other ships, and while the sinking was not verified it is generally assumed she was responsible.

Still limping on fewer than her full number of available boilers, she was sent in November of 1944 to Kure for further repairs. While she was there, the old Dutch armament was removed and replaced with 3.1-inch AA, fifteen 25mm guns and 72 depth charges. The work done there allowed her to briefly operate on all four boilers. She was further trimmed and given a light tripod foremast that changed her appearance considerably. However, it did not make the basic structure less recognizable to knowledgeable sailors.

On 28 April 1945, the converted destroyer was discovered by United States Army planes from Mokpo, Korea, and strafed and bombed. The patrol boat was damaged in the attack, but not enough to stop her continuing with her assigned missions. In May of 1945 she was identified as the flagship of the Kure Guard Force under Rear Admiral Kiyota Takahiko. According to Lieutenant Yoshimi, the PB 102 was also designated as the flagship of the Eighth Special Attack Force, but this claim has not been confirmed. Working both in patrol and anti-submarine duty, she arrived at Hiro Bay east of Kure with a reduced crew in August 1945. The sturdy little ship avoided further damage through several air attacks, and was even able to survive the Hiroshima atomic bomb. She was sitting calmly in the harbor when she was finally located by American occupation troops in Hiro Bay.

Once it was determined that Japanese Patrol Boat 102 was in fact an American destroyer, Vice Admiral Jesse B. Oldendorf, Commander Task Group 53.5, ordered the four-stacker put back on active service. Inspected by Naval officers she was found to be rat-infested and in decrepit condition. Japanese prisoners were ordered to clean her up, fumigate, and paint the ship, and she was taken over by a prize crew on 28 October 1945. Given the circumstances there was little that could be done with her, however. The navy, at this point, had more ships that she knew what to do with. Besides, the *Stewart* was no longer on the Navy List. Nevertheless, while in Hiro Bay she was recommissioned in the United States Navy. Her name had been given to a newer destroyer when the USS *Stewart,* the third with the name, was launched 22 November 1942 and was immediately put into active duty convoy service. Lacking a legal name they could give her, the Navy identified the ex–*Stewart* simply by her old number, DD 224. The crew, however, referred to her as the *RAMP 224*, standing for Recovered Allied Military Personnel; the *Stewart* was considered a liberated prisoner of war. And like all the other released prisoners, she needed to go home as quickly as possible. She was put under the command of Lieutenant Commander Harold H. Ellison.

In tough shape, with only two of her boilers in working condition, she was nevertheless able to leave under her own power as she headed out for the United States. However, her tired engines gave out near Guam with fuel pump problems and she was taken in tow by the USS *Wesson* (DD 184) and pulled into Apra harbor at Guam. There she was repaired and left harbor again on 10 December 1945. The ship arrived in San Francisco in early March 1946. She had done her job, but was no longer needed in the expanded and modernized navy. Time, renovations, neglect, and battle had all taken their toll; it was time for her to be put down. The twenty-seven-year-old destroyer with two battle stars was decommissioned 23 May 1946. There was some discussion about seeing if the *Stewart* could be preserved as a floating museum and as a symbol of her rather unique history, but no location made a bid for her, nor could the funds be raised for such a project. In memory of her faithful service, however, the Navy decided not to sell her for scrap. Rather she was allowed a Viking funeral. The old *Stewart* was sunk off San Francisco by U.S. Navy F6F Hellcat and F4U Corsair fighters. The Phantom Ship had come to rest.

Note

1. *The Maru Special, Japanese Naval Vessels No 49, Japanese Subchasers and Patrol Boats* (Tokyo: Ushio Shobo, 1981).

Further Reading

Alford, Lodwich H. *Playing for Time: War on an Asiatic Fleet Destroyer*. Bennington, VT: Merriam Press, 2008.
"Convoy HI-71: USS *Harder*'s Last Battle." www.militaryphotos.net.
Fukui, Shizuo. *Japanese Naval Vessels at the End of the War*. Annapolis: Naval Institute Press, 2009.
Money, James L. *Dictionary of American Naval Fighting Ships*. Washington, DC: GPO, 1968, 1976.
Whitley, M.J. *Destroyers of World War II*. London: Arms and Armor Press, 1999.

3. No German Child Should Go Unborn

They looked like brothels at first and were often passed off as just one more indication of Nazi debauchery. But these homes located in World War II Germany and German-occupied countries were both more, as well as less, than simply brothels; they were baby factories. These were the birthing centers for the development of the master race. Set up and maintained from the very top of the Nazi hierarchy, the network of Lebensborn homes, as they were called, were the result of a fairly simple but deeply believed Nazi ideology: *No German child should go unborn.* The goal established for this program was to achieve a population of 120 million pure Germanic citizens and to do so quickly. In order to achieve this goal more than 20,000 German babies were born out of wedlock and nearly a quarter of a million kidnapped children were Germanized. This more secret and incredible experiment was all a part of the Nazi plan to create the master race. It is the other side of the Holocaust equation.

In order to understand what was going on, and to see the Lebensborn movement in the proper context, it is important to remember that within the political structure of the Nazi party, blood was the marker of national-ethnic identity. In this ideology the worth for the individual is not determined by his individuality but rather by his membership in what was called a "racial collective nation." What this meant, in the long run, was that most political movements such as Marxism or pacifism were cross-racial and thus anti-nationalistic and reflected a danger to the world. These movements were inspired, the Nazis believed, by the Jewish people.

An integral part of German National Socialism, the more formal name for Nazism, is the belief that all of human history is the biologically determined struggle among different races. Nationalism disassociated from racial endeavor was, they believed, the source of most of mankind's difficulties. In addition, they saw the mentally and physically ill as blemishes on the genetic stream of the master race, in this case the Aryans, including Germany and some other northern Europeans. To allow these "lesser" beings to reproduce was to endanger the race. In 1931 they established a Race and Settlement Office, based on the pseudoscientific support of intellectuals and racists that influenced the 19th century. Adopted as official policy by Hitler and his closest advisors, the program focused on the Jewish people. The Nuremberg Laws of 1935 provided a code by which to determine the biological definition of a Jew. Strange as it seems, the attack on the Jews was not, at least in the early years, so much a hatred of the Jewish people, as much as it was a fear of the anti-racial affirmations they reflected.

This point of view rather naturally led to two basically different responses, both directed at the same goal: the establishment of a pure Aryan race. The first was the destruction of any and all carriers of deficient blood or disabled genes. The second was the promotion of the birth of those with the characteristics of the master race. It is within the second of these larger plans that the Lebensborn program began.

The program, when fully operational, included three phases. The first was a home where unwed mothers of Germanic origin could be housed and receive medical and financial aid needed in order to have a healthy illegitimate child. These children would then be put up for adoption in well-connected Germanic families. The second phase was to encourage the procreation of Aryan "racially pure" children by means of bringing together men and women in safe and secure environments from which anticipated children would become wards of the state. The third segment was to form a collection and education point for the Germanization of children kidnapped from occupied nations. The combined effort was nothing less than an attempt to engineer blond-haired, blue-eyed German children.

The initiation of the first segment of this plan was a follow-up on the 1933 declaration by the German state that outlawed abortions and incurred the death sentence for any doctor who violated the law. This was both a moral and political code, for the National Socialist government was against abortions, but it was also political in the sense it determined to deal with unwed motherhood in such a manner as to serve the state. Reichsfuhrer Heinrich Himmler's solution to the number of unmarried pregnancies was the establishment of the first of the Lebensborn homes at Steinhoring. The home offered Aryan women a place to deliver their illegitimate children, to receive medical treatment and some financial help, and to keep the births secret from the outside world. The children were then turned over for adoption by high-ranking SS officials, or put into the educational program. These children were provided with legal (within the confines of the Nazi interpretation) documents of birth in order to avoid the identification as bastard.

The homes themselves were clean, well-kept, well staffed with medical personnel, and made available to the girls and women housed there a caring community, a source for food and excellent extended care. The centers were usually housed in the homes and mansions taken from wealthy Jewish families whose material goods had been confiscated and the owners taken to camps. They were maintained by the state, protected by the army, and legitimized by the creation of forged documents.

The second segment was more aggressive, and is that aspect of the plan which was the source of most of the moral indignation. In this plan eligible young Aryan women were encouraged to come to the homes in order to have sexual relations with qualified German men. Young women of the League of German Girls were encouraged to do their duty and have a child for Hitler's Germany. The aim was the procreation of citizens of the German Aryan nation. Women who were selected as hostesses in these establishments were very carefully screened to be sure they were pure and lacking in any mental or physical disqualification that might discredit the race. Even then, their offspring were checked again to be sure nothing but the purest genes had been passed on. The homes were opened to the German soldiers, who were urged to father as many children as possible, but they also had to go through extreme screening to be sure they were up to the standards required. In some cases the system even granted military men promotions and other rewards based on the number of children they produced. Later, some of these homes were opened in Norway, primarily because Himmler was impressed with the "Viking blood," and procreation was encouraged between Aryan soldiers and Norwegian women. The children of these unions were made legitimate, and then offered for adoption by German families.

Despite what it sounds like, these were not bordellos, but can be more honestly understood as baby factories. Notwithstanding whatever sexual pleasures might have been enjoyed — and these were expected to be enjoyed — the purpose behind the homes was both more legitimate and more moral than simply providing prostitution. At least this was true as far as the SS was concerned. Granted the extremes to which the SS seemed willing to go, it was nevertheless true that they tended as a group to be rather conservative with a strict, albeit strange, moral code. The idea of strengthening the Fatherland by the production of potentially good citizens was a much stronger motivation than simple "houses of pleasure," and would have been more attractive for the SS.

An additional function of each center was to determine if those children born were, after all, up to the standards required. In the search for the purity of the race, this system gave the SS the opportunity to weed out any of the newborns that did not measure up; any crippled, disabled or retarded children were sent to euthanasia clinics.

The third segment, perhaps the most devastating, took the philosophy of the Lebensborn to the extreme. In this segment SS officers were encouraged to find, kidnap and collect small children from occupied countries that appeared to be pure Aryan and who might be taught to be German. The goal was the preservation and promotion of a racially valuable Germanic hereditary property; that is, a growing collection of persons who were considered to be genetically appropriate. The system literally took children out of their mothers' arms and transported them to Lebensborn centers, where they were to be stripped of the parental nationality and cultural identity, and taught to be little German children. The Lebensborn program had expanded from production to collection.

Under orders from Himmler the "confiscated" were mingled into the system where they were to be "Germanized." It was a harsh program, for the staff of these centers felt they only had a short time to accomplish their assignment. The children were forbidden to speak anything but German, told their parents were both dead, and given stories about their birth that provided the "needed" contacts, complete with forged birth certificates suggesting a German birth in Germany. The transition was difficult, and so many of the children were already old enough to have established national and family identities that only a small percentage of those taken into the program worked out. Those deemed too stubborn to be "reborn" were sent to the camps where a good many of them died without any identity at all.

The exact number of those involved is difficult to determine because a great deal of effort was expended in order to keep it all secret, but the best estimates suggest a figure of about 350,000 children were taken from their homes. The best guess suggests 200,000 from Poland, 50,000 from Ukraine and 50,000 from the Baltic, with smaller numbers from other areas. Most of the children from the Lidice massacre were placed in the program. Among these a large number were found not to be racially pure, or could not adjust to their new roles, and they were eliminated. At the end of the war about 25,000 were finally identified and returned to the countries of their birth.

The records of this program are sketchy for a variety of reasons. Most of the records were destroyed before the Allies occupied the area. In those areas where the records were not destroyed, great care must be exercised because what was found was a mixture of truth and forgeries, with little there to help tell the difference. Many of the staff who were involved in the system have either passed on without leaving comments, or are reluctant to speak if identified. The number of the homes established has been determined, with nine homes located in German, ten in Norway, two in Austria, and one each in Belgium, Holland, Luxembourg, France, and Denmark.

This plan was in operation for more than twelve years. During that time more than half the births that took place at *Lebensborn Eingetragner Verein* (the Spring of Life) took place in Germany itself and a little less than half in one of the occupied countries which supported homes. Even in the last months of the war, when the masses of the German people were finding it difficult just to locate enough food to eat, the homes were well supplied, the best of foods were made available to them, and men and women otherwise needed for the defense of the nation continued to be occupied in duties related to the preservation of the goals of the Lebensborn.

Even during the war, and covered with the umbrella of patriotism, these houses and their Lebensborn children were not popular. Despite their carefully documented credentials and the glowing promise as potential citizens, the children and the mothers were looked upon primarily as illegitimate. It was worse in the occupied areas, where the mothers — accused of giving aid and comfort to the enemy — were identified as whores and traitors. The children in these areas were known as *Tyskerunger*, meaning German Kids or Kraut Kids. Even today, when talking about the system and the children that resulted, the politically correct term, *Krigbarn*, war children, is still reflective of the feeling.

When the war was over the local response to the Lebensborn program was not good. When the details of this grim experiment came to light, and with it the resurfacing of the deep psychological problems it created, the reaction were harsh. While it is understandable that many of the women involved in the Lebensborn were treated as whores and traitors, it is hard to see why this curse was carried over to the children. Among the women, the birthing of a German child was treason, and they paid with public embarrassment and often the loss of all their private property. Like many of the women in the occupied countries that were accused of being prostitutes, some had their heads shaved in public humiliation, while others were beaten, and some, it appears, were even killed.

And the children themselves were not much better off. Though all suffered, consider the problems of the children of the three phases separately. Those children who had been born of unwed mothers in the Lebensborn early program had, to a large extent, been documented, sent out, and adopted into families which they believed were their birth parents. A large number of these young people grew up never knowing any differently, and lived out their lives as might any adopted child. Of the few who became aware of the true situation, and made the effort to locate their parents, it was not too traumatic, and some, like Helga Kahrau, were able to trace them down.

Those children born in the "production" homes had a somewhat different fate, though they were also often adopted out among members of the German elite. In these cases, however, there were few legitimate records kept, and the forged records gave no clue whatsoever as to who the parents were, if in fact anyone knew.

Perhaps the most difficult problems were among those whose identity, nationality, and national culture had been violated. Even among those that had been adopted by German families, the tendency to "keep them" after the war diminished, and most were given to the state to find some way to take care of them. Many of them had no papers at all, and those who did had to acknowledge they were fakes, which meant even the refugee system was not working for them. Many of the children were seen as having been "Nazified" and were not trusted. A good many of them were deemed to be mentally defective and institutionalized. Still others were moved from one internment camp to the other. Countries began to argue about taking back children, once thought to be theirs, who were now more German than anything else.

Very few of these children, now well into their 60s and 70s, have ever become aware that they were Lebensborn children. Some who have figured it out see it as a mark of shame, thought the situation was not of their making. Some see themselves as having been literally "born and bred Nazi," and while their lives were lived as decent and respectable persons, they still find shame in their births. Some, on locating evidence of parentage, have discovered the crimes of their SS fathers and carry those burdens.

Part of the problem for these persons today is the amount of information available. In some respects it is way too much, telling them more than they want to know about pasts they would never have remembered. In other ways it is far too little for them to learn much of their early lives, information that a few of them wanted to know. Some records were found in German and are now preserved when located. In Norway, the Nazis determined that the records would be harmful and destroyed all the children's records there. One account said that they were burned in a large bonfire as the Allies approached, the second that they were sunk beneath the waters of the Isar River. The children from the homes were scattered and left on their own. Most remember nothing but the family — often the family of an SS officer or high civilian authority — that raised them. Of the few who are aware of their heritage, only a handful of those have made any effort to locate their parents.

When the war ended an estimated 500 children were still living in some of the homes. In every case the staff had simply left as the Allies approached, abandoning the children. When the Allies captured the children, they were rounded up and taken care of for a while, but as quickly as possible the military turned them over to the custody of the state. That in itself was difficult, for whatever state services existed were badly damaged and incapable of doing very much. In a good many cases the children ended up in mental institutions, often because they were the only institutions still functioning. For the children that were just left somewhere, it was impossible to tell the difference between them and the increasing thousands of refugees that wandered the city streets of Germany and other occupied countries. There were a few cases in which adoptions were arranged, but those who were not taken remained in state institutions until they were 18 years of age.

There have been some cases of successful research and the ability to trace a mother and locate a father, if the father was even known. Some have been reunited with their earlier families. Today, some of those involved in seeking their parents meet together to help each other untangle their histories, and provide mutual comfort and help. Most that have identified themselves as a part of the Lebensborn program have lived with it, doing little beyond the acknowledgment, and have moved ahead and made lives for themselves. A few have sought monetary support from the governments of the countries involved, or lacking that, have been eager to identify their fathers in hope they could gain support from the men who sired them. But few of these efforts have led to anything. During November of 2006 thirty-five to forty Lebensborn children met in Wernigerode, Germany, for a reunion at which they urged other such children to "go public" and erase the shame involved. Many of them told stories of their long search for identify, and the difficult times they had living with what they discovered. Most of them grew up, one said, knowing that they were living a highly secret life, but they did not know what it was or why they believed it.

One of those who has been successful in her research is Helga Kahrau, one of the Lebensborn children. Her mother, she learned later, had been a secretary in the office of Martin Bormann. She had been involved in a one-night stand with a German officer and became pregnant. Recognizing the ban on abortion and having no other opportunity to avoid the expense and the shame of being on her own, she applied for the Lebensborn program. Helga's mother was accepted into the program and provided with excellent care. Her child was given up for adoption to a good German family, and Helga grew us as the foster child of a man, she later learned, who worked for the secret police.

The German records at the end of the war made it possible for the authorities to locate her mother, and they were reunited. She grew up without her mother ever telling her of the circumstances of her birth, anything at all about her father, or her early Nazi education. But she had some suspicions about her birth, and when her mother died, Helga set out to try to locate some information. She had heard of the Lebensborn program through a mutual friend and was finally able to locate some records that had been kept. She discovered that she was the daughter of a German officer who, at the end of the war, had been tried for war crimes. And her father was still alive.

Helga was able to locate him shortly before his death. The old Nazi showed some interest in her, but not a lot. Nor was he able to tell her much. For him his encounter with Helga's mother had been a one-time experience with little or no contact since. After the war the man had made a considerable fortune, but when he died she discovered that as an illegitimate Lebensborn child, with no "honest identification," she was ineligible to inherit anything.

Some who located fathers or mothers had some contact and in a few cases actually established a relationship. But for the most it was a disappointing experience, leaving them no better off for having learned of the conditions of their birth and the nature of the biological parents. For the most part, they recognized they were not the result of parental love, nor had there been time to develop any association between the parents and the child — in many cases the children had never even been seen. There was little basis for a renewed relationship.

Like any significant event, the existence of the Lebensborn program has led to many myths and theories. Some critics say that the system was nothing more than an effort to disguise houses of prostitution provided for the German military, and that it was little more than another example of the depravity of the Nazi Party. The system seems far too broad and well-defined to be nothing more than that; besides, there was no reason for the Nazis to hide such houses if they had created them.

Other critics say that the women involved in the houses were forced into service, especially those women from occupied nations. Again there is little evidence that this is true, and the general national reaction to the houses suggests that the women were seen more as objects of shame than as victims.

There has been little reconciliation between these women and the children they bore, and the nations that reacted so strongly to them after the war. For the most part the women involved tried to merge back into their own societies, though that was more difficult in the occupied countries. Many went on to marry and raise families of their own, never speaking again of the experience they wanted to keep to themselves.

Perhaps the most lingering myth related the establishment of the Lebensborn program to the need to replace German Jews who were being killed in the Holocaust. The theory goes that the Jews were often Germans, and if their deaths were decreasing the German population, thus weakening the nation, they needed to be replaced. There is no evidence that there was ever any connection.

There is little or no evidence of pride in involvement, and no effort to "memorialize" the experience. What stories have emerged from the twelve years of Lebensborn operation have been the stories of the children, not the stories of the mothers and the fathers. That part of the story is even less well known. One or two books have tried to incorporate the program into the larger ideas behind the Master Race, or the Jewish extermination efforts. But they do not tell us much about the lives of those involved. And, other than a new story carried from time to time — usually when a Lebensborn child comes out of the shadows — there is very little available about the children's current opinions.

Many of the women carried the identification "Nazi swine" long after the war. In some countries the harsh treatment continued for some time. In Norway the police sent 14,000 women and girls who had been participants in the program to an internment camps, where they were mistreated and kept incarcerated for varying and indeterminate times. It was years later that Norway's prime minister finally acknowledged that some great injustice had been done and at least apologized to the children.

Further Reading

Burleigh, M. *Death and Deliverance: Euthanasia in Germany 1900–1945*. Cambridge: Cambridge University Press, 1994.
Clay, Catrine, and Michael Leapman. *Master Race: The Lebensborn Experiment in Nazi Germany*. London: Hodder and Stoughton, 1995.
"The Forgotten Camp." ABC News *20/20*, April 27, 2000.
Hammer, Joshua. "Hitler's Children." *Newsweek International*, March 20, 2000.
Heimannsberg, B., and C.J. Schmidt. *Collective Silence: German Identity and the Legacy of Shame*. San Francisco: Jossey-Bass, 1993.
Hillel, Marc, and Clarissa Henry. *Of Pure Blood*. Paris: Fayard, 1976.

4. Bullion for Ballast

There was way too much money to see it fall into the hands of the Japanese. But the question was, could they get it out in time? The responsibility was given to Colonel Charles Willoughby of Army Intelligence, who was ordered to move the contents of the Philippine National Treasury and the Philippine Central Bank from the twelve member banks onto the island fortress of Corregidor. Corregidor was a rocky, tadpole-shaped island off the coast that was a mile wide at the widest point. The treasure to be moved amounted to something over 51 tons of gold bullion, 32 tons of silver bullion, 140 tons of silver pesos and centavos, and millions of dollars in paper treasury notes, currency, bonds, and corporate stocks.

When the United States occupied the Philippines, the Americans set up a monetary system based on gold with the value of the pesos established at two for one U.S. dollar. Now both national funds and stockpiles from private firms and individuals were in danger. At first there was little consensus about what to do with the treasures. The easiest solution was to take them out into the harbor and simply sink them in expectation that they could be recovered after the war. But this seemed risky. Some of the silver had already been badly dispersed when the area of old Fort Santiago was bombed and bags of silver coins burst and flung everywhere. Most, it was recorded, were salvaged, but this added to the pressure to get them to safety.

But there was a question of how well the treasure would hold up if simply dumped into the ocean, as well as the larger question of what was to stop the Japanese from sending down divers of their own. So the decision was to burn eighty million in paper and store the rest, for a while at least, on Corregidor.

Under the First War Powers Act, Francis B. Sayre, high commissioner to the Philippines, who was also former President Woodrow Wilson's son-in-law, ordered the burning of the soft currency then held in the Philippines. It amounted to a little more than 3 million American dollars, 28 million Philippine dollars, and 38 million dollars in treasury checks. In this action he was helped by Charles Willoughby of intelligence and Colonel Vance of the U.S. Army Finance Corps. Willoughby was given the responsibility of saving as much of the rest as he could.

To accomplish this, Willoughby collected a variety of smaller ships consisting mostly of out-of-date Navy harbor tugs and small civilian boats. Significant among these vessels were the *Don Esteban*, a civilian vessel, and the presidential yacht *Cassiando*. Bars, ingots, coins and other precious metals were stuffed into footlockers and whatever else could hold the weight and taken to the waiting ships. Even with crews working around the clock, the transfer took four days. Once loaded, the ships sneaked out of the harbor and headed for the temporary safety of Corregidor Island. The move took place on the night of 27 December 1941, and was undertaken by a loading party made up of members of the Treasury and Philippine Scouts. Admiral Hart was around, keeping an eye on the procedure. Moving slowly, with an eye out for any intruder, they arrived at the north dock of the island stronghold in the morning. There they started the unloading process. It took them two nights and one day to deliver the valuables from the north dock to the vault locations where they were to be held. The move was considered to be temporary, of course, and they all knew it. If Corregidor was in danger of falling, and it was, then the treasure would have to be moved again.

The 140 tons of silver pesos were placed in canvas bags and were taken to the quartermaster section of the large underground complex known simply as the Malinta Tunnel. Private holdings of gold and deposits were sent to the stockade area located at the Middleside section of the island. Here, it was located in the old jail made out of cement blocks and located under a battery of 12" mortars. In these latter transfers it was getting more difficult to keep straight what gold belonged to what depositor. But temporarily, the gold was located in a former brig and considered safe.

Most of the rest of the treasure was stored in the interior spurs of the Navy tunnel, on the south side of the Malinta tunnel complex. Colonel Willoughby, assisted by his wife and a Colonel Vance, tried to take an inventory at this time. The serial numbers on the notes were carefully recorded so that bills could be burned and the currency reissued.

While the bullion transfer was going on, the U.S. Navy was having its own problems. Its forces, and those of the Army and the Philippine Scouts, were desperately in need of supplies. The Navy was involved in trying to provide some much needed food and ammunition and, as the outcome was increasingly obvious, to evacuate key personnel from the island. The Japanese had taken control of the sea, so about all that had a chance to getting through were submarines. A desperate plea had gone out from the defenders at Corregidor that they needed ammunition. All that was available to help were four U.S. submarines. Of the four, three—*Swordfish, Seadragon,* and *Seaworld*—had left Pearl on the first two days of February and entered Corregidor's San Jose Bay on the south side of the island. They had been redirected from their patrol areas to evacuate key personnel from the island, and did not actually tie up at the dock.

The fourth sub was the USS *Trout*, which had been on a training mission when the raid occurred at Pearl Harbor and had returned several days later. Once there, she was basically disarmed, leaving only the torpedoes that were in the tubes, and stripped of all unnecessary equipment. The USS *Trout*, now turned into a cargo vessel and carrying several tons of ammunition, departed Pearl Harbor on 12 January 1942. She ran on the surface as long as she could, and then, on 27 January, conducted an unsuccessful attack on an enemy ship. When the attack failed, the intended victim turned on the *Trout* and it was forced to dive in order to get away. The submarine arrived 3 February 1942 at Corregidor, where it was met by a torpedo boat (PT-43 under John Duncan Bulkeley of *They Were Expendable* fame) that escorted it though the mine fields to the island's south mine dock.

There the crew found the island was a mess: the troops were suffering from lack of proper food and water, and were exhausted from the constant bombardment the Japanese maintained. Their needs far exceeded what little could be brought in. Captain Fenno also discovered that while morale was not as bad as might have been assumed, there was very little information about what was going on in the rest of the war. It was here that a curious event took place. The Japanese had been dropping leaflets informing the Americans and the Filipinos that the U.S. fleet had been destroyed at Pearl Harbor. General MacArthur apparently did not believe the report, or was giving the impression that he did not believe it. According to Lieutenant Frederick Gunn, the *Trout*'s engineering officer, MacArthur was startled when the naval personnel verified the news.

Once the submarine made it to the shore, the crew began to unload their cargo of 3,517 three-inch high-attitude anti-aircraft shells, and over 500 cases of food and medical supplies. They had come directly from the Naval Base at Pearl Harbor. Her commander, Fenno, had been told to deliver the supplies and then continue on with his assigned patrol area. But, after the unloading of a significant amount of heavy supplies and equipment, the submarine had risen precariously in the water. Fenno needed considerable ballast so that the sub could dive quickly. He asked for 25 tons of rock and sand, but the request was denied on the grounds that whatever the defenders had was being saved to build fortification. This appears to be a somewhat strange response considering the make-up of the rocky island fortress. Then it dawned on someone that the situation might provide one way to get at least some of the treasure off the island.

In response to the opportunity, two trucks were sent to the vault at the stockade to bring back two tons of privately held gold ingots. The private gold apparently had been given priority over government stakes. When the trucks arrived at the *Trout*, the sub rested several feet below the level of the dock. It was necessary to literally throw the bars from the dock to the deck of the submarine. As they were caught, the bars, weighing about 40 pounds each and worth 23,000 dollars (at the time), were stored in the *Trout*'s forward battery, after battery, and amidships armory compartments.

A small portion of the silver pesos were then added and packed in and around the gold bars for additional ballast. All in all a total of two tons of gold ingots and 16 tons of silver pesos in canvas bags were loaded. Also taken aboard were four torpedoes provided from the Navy tunnel. At 0300 hours a total of 320 gold bars worth $7 million, and 630 bags of silver coins worth $1,000 each, had been inventoried as being aboard.

As daylight approached, Captain Frank Fenno took the *Trout* out into the bay to sink the submarine for the day. This was necessary to avoid the many Japanese planes that constantly flew over the area. Later a small boat met them in the harbor and transferred a large number of treasury securities. Captain Fenno discovered, as well, that President Manuel Quezon and nine bags of his possessions were also on the transport. The president was under the belief that he was to be leaving on board the *Trout* with his gold. The arrival caused considerable confusion, but on the basis of having no orders about the removal of the president, the American officer did not allow the Philippine leader on board, and he returned to the docks.

Upon leaving the harbor, the USS *Trout* continued on her regular wartime patrol of the Philippine Islands, paying little attention to the fact she was being ballasted by millions of dollars. During the extended patrol she managed to sink two small Japanese vessels. At she approached Pearl, after completing her tour of patrol, the authorities were anxiously waiting for her. She was met by the USS *Litchfield*, which escorted her into the harbor. There she docked near the USS *Detroit*, to which she was to transfer the treasure for reshipment. The *Detroit* took it as far as Guam, where it was transferred to the USS *Michigan*, and on to the United States for safe keeping. In time the rescued treasure was delivered to the U.S. Mint in San Francisco.

Even now, after so many years, it is hard to get a clear picture of just how much of the Philippine National Treasury was actually saved. Up to this point there seems to have been a lack of clarity as to how much was taken out, what was left behind, and what fell somewhere in between.

The accounting for much of the treasure that was used as ballast is fairly clear. The rest of the securities, however, are not so well noted. Once the *Trout* left, there were still over 125 tons of silver and at least 51 tons of gold on the rock, which soon fell into Japanese hands. Most reports later state that the majority of the silver deposits were taken out and dumped into the deeper waters of San Jose Bay during the final days of April and the first week or so of May. Among those ships involved were the tug USS *Pigeon* and minesweeper *Harrison* which, each towing a barge full of silver pesos and centavos, made several trips out of the south mine dock, eventually dumping 115 tons of silver. The accounting for the rest of the treasure is not complete.

Today it is generally assumed that most, if not all, of the unaccounted-for gold and the missing silver dumped into the harbor has been recovered, either by rather elaborate American efforts or by the natives. According to Edward Michaud, an occasional silver peso or centavo would be discovered, having washed up onto the shore, but there seems to be little evidence of any significant remains, though occasional diving efforts are still undertaken.

Edwin Kiefer, who was aboard the USS *Trout*, and was decorated with the Army Silver Star at MacArthur's recommendation, wrote in *The End of the Rainbow* about his patrol. In it he says very little about the unexplained loss of bullion. After the war, however, he was offered a job at the Baguio Gold Mines owned by John W. Hausserman, who owned a good piece of the gold that had been saved, and who continued to lay claims to a significant amount that had been lost.

Over the next year or so Captain Fenno would make a series of half-hearted efforts to claim salvage on the cargo, claiming that what they had taken out was private gold and not that of the government, and thus subject to rules of salvage. The Navy suspiciously changed these regulations only a month after the successful evacuation. The Navy finally ruled it was an official government-to-government transfer, and thus there would be no salvage award.

Undaunted by the rebuff, *Trout* commander Frank W. Fenno of Massachusetts would eventually rise to the rank of rear admiral. He would receive the Distinguished Service Cross, the Navy Cross with two gold stars, the Silver Star medal, the Legion of Merit with one gold star, and the Bronze

Star medal. He died in August 1973 and is buried at Arlington National Cemetery.

All of the seventy officers and men aboard the *Trout* were given Siler Stars for their actions during the fifty-one-day run that included bringing out the gold. The USS *Trout*, then commanded by Lieutenant Commander Albert H. Clark, was lost at sea, along with her crew of 81 men, on or about 17 April 1944. Her fate is not known. During her service she had sunk 23 enemy ships.

When the treasure was transferred from the banks in Corregidor, and then loaded on board the *Trout*, the funds were inventoried by the wife of Colonel Willoughby. At that time there were 320 bars. When the ships unloaded the *Trout* at Pearl Harbor, a new count placed the number received at 319. The assumption was that one of the crew had managed to sneak off a bar for his own retirement, or that it was simply lost in the confusion, and little was done. However, when Colonel Willoughby turned up in San Francisco, he produced the bar, saying that somehow it had gotten in with his things during the transfer.

That much money and that little accounting will inevitably lead to a variety of theories about what actually happened. After the successful delivery of the treasury funds in Pearl Harbor, there remained approximately 125 tons of silver and 51 tons of government gold unaccounted for. The belief persists that the gold from the Philippines — either the national treasury or valuables brought to the Philippines from Japanese conquests elsewhere — remains hidden on the island. Many believe that the vast majority of the Philippine treasure, as well as hoarded Japanese wealth said to be on Corregidor in unsupported stories, were discovered by the U.S. shortly after they recaptured the island. This view holds that since that time the unaccounted fortune has been used to support a good many of America's clandestine activities, and the remainder continues to be hidden from the public by a conspiracy between the Japanese and Americans.

There remains a cloud over these events, and whether or not there is the evidence to support them, the conspiracy theories remain. Carol M. Petillo, a professor at Boston College, had reported in the 11 February 1980 *Time Magazine* that five hundred thousand dollars had been transferred from the Philippine treasury in New York City to General MacArthur's personal account on 19 February 1942. The events surrounding the story suggest that it was only after the transfer that President Quezon of the Philippines, the source of the transfer, was put aboard an American submarine and taken to safety. It was Commander Frank Fenno who reported that Quezon had tried to board the submarine *Trout* that was taking out some of the bullion, but was refused.[1]

There were significant reasons, other than military, to explain MacArthur's desire to get back to the Philippines. He had a considerable financial stake in a wide variety of industries, as well as numerous shares in several of the mines still in operation there. Ten years after leaving Manila, MacArthur sold his stock in the Consolidated Mines, Inc., in Manila for just over a million dollars. Several others among MacArthur's "staff" also had meaningful investments in the Philippines, and sold them for significant amounts after the war. These would include General Courtney Whitney and Colonel Charles Willoughby.

Willoughby was a very interesting man. Born Adolf Tscheppe-Weidenbach, Willoughby was a somewhat insignificant man who seemed to end up bungling positions of considerable responsibility. Colonel (later General) Charles Willoughby, as MacArthur's chief intelligence officer, played a pivotal role in the loss of the Philippines, the failure to anticipate Japanese numbers or determination in the Battle of Buna, and later the failure to comprehend Chinese intentions during the Korean War. (For further information see Chapter 16, The Battle of Buna.)

Note

1. Sterling Seagraves and Peggy Segraves, *Gold Warriors: America's Secret Recovery of Yamashita's Gold* (New York: Verso, 2005).

Further Reading

Thomas, Lowell. *The Escape of the Treasure: These Men Shall Never Be Forgotten*. New York: John C. Winston, 1943.
"Mystery Money." *Time Magazine*, Monday, February 11, 1980.
Seagraves, Sterling. *The Marcos Dynasty*. New York: Harper and Row, 1988.
www.tribune.net.ph/commentary/20080930com4.html

5. Her Name Was *Evergreen*

The salvage plan had been simply to locate the lost Japanese submarine I-52 and retrieve her lost cargo. The Nauticos Corporation's Operation Project Orca, launched in 1994 and directed by Paul Tidwell, finally found evidence of the large cargo submarine in 5,200 feet of water, and some distance from where she was reported sunk. Though it had been submerged more than half a century, the submarine's conning tower was still intact and divers were able to read the hull numbers. Plans were made to raise the Japanese imperial submarine from World War II, and to recover the cargo — primarily the 146 bars of gold. How did she get there, and what was she doing in these waters?

The ship was the IJN *Momi*, the Japanese word for "evergreen," and she was given the naval identification of I-52. The keel was a type C-3 cargo submarine and was laid on 18 March 1942. There is not a lot said in the narrative histories about the Japanese submarine force, but at the beginning of the war the Japanese had one of the largest and the most diverse submarine fleets in the world. The variety included manned torpedoes, midget submarines, and long- and medium-range submarines, as well as a fleet of cargo and supply submarines. The Japanese built the largest submarines in the world, and even had subs that could carry one or more aircraft.

The I-52 was commissioned on 28 December 1943, and she was assigned to the 11th Submarine Squadron. She was not simply another submarine, for she was built by the Mitsubishi Corporation as a long-range cargo carrier. She was very long for a submarine, about 357 feet, with a displacement of 2,564 tons, and had a two-shaft diesel and electric motor that could produce 4,700 horsepower on the surface. She carried a crew of 94 and could maintain a speed of 12 knots for a range of 21,000 nautical miles. Twenty of these submarines had been envisioned as an underwater cargo system, but only three were ever actually constructed.

The question is: how did she get where she was found? Upon commissioning, she was placed under the command of Commander Kanmeo Uno, an experienced officer. He and his sub were a part of the growing use of the underwater boats for the transportation of cargo. The success of American submarines and the increasing losses among Japanese merchant ships made it necessary for the Japanese to take advantage of their larger supply submarines for transporting some of their more necessary cargo. Such trips were becoming fairly common, though they were not without their own danger. The I-52 was selected to run an exchange mission to the Keromon Submarine Base at Lorient, France, on the south coast of Brittany. At the time Lorient was the home of the large German undersea force. Five other submarines had made this transcontinental voyage during the Second World War, three of which had been sunk by either British or American submarines. So even this method of moving men and cargo was growing increasingly dangerous.

What the I-52 was doing there is yet another issue. The *Evergreen* began her maiden voyage on 10 March 1944, sailing from Kure via Sasebo for Singapore. Her cargo at this time consisted of 9.8 tons of molybdenum (an element used in alloys for its high corrosion resistance, primarily for airplane parts); eleven tons of tungsten (for forming high temperature alloys), 2.3 tons of opium to be made into morphine for use by the wounded, 54 kg of caffeine, and 146 bars of gold packed into 49 metal boxes. The gold, it was explained, was in payment for German optical technology and had an estimated value today of 61 million dollars.

On board the submarine as well were several unidentified passengers. It was not unusual for a submarine to carry civilian passengers, both in terms of an engineering and technological exercise to test and maintain the ship, and also in order to provide them transportation. The speculation around the passengers on board the I-52 suggests that some segment of the Japanese government had decided to try to make peace with the Allies, and that the passengers aboard were involved in it. It is not clear if this was the military acting without the knowledge of the Emperor, or the other way around, but there is very little to suggest that any sort of peace mission was afoot. Certainly the Japanese were not a defeated nation at this time, so such a proposal would appear to be incongruent under the circumstances. Also, of course, there were other, equally efficient means of communication if such a plan was underway.

The first stop on their journey was Singapore. There the I-52 took on an additional load of 120 tons of tin, 59.8 tons of raw rubber, and 3.3 tons of quinine. There was no mention of any items or personnel being unloaded at this time. On leaving Singapore, the I-52 moved through the Indian Ocean and into the Atlantic. So far the journey had been smooth and uneventful and there were no cause for alarm. But she was in far more trouble than she realized.

The Allies already knew where the I-52 was, where she was heading, and just about what she was up to. The Japanese submarine was being tracked by means of what serves as an excellent illustration of how high speed radio traffic intelligence was being used by the Allies to locate, down, and destroy enemy submarines.

Intercepted Japanese radio traffic first identified the I-52 shortly after she was commissioned, and again in March when news of her mission to Germany was sent out in January of 1944. Carl Boyd, a military historian writing about the services of the radio intelligence network, wrote, "We knew well in advance that this submarine was coming around through the Indian Ocean, around the tip of Africa, and into the Atlantic."

Sailing on toward its destination, the I-52 was contacted by its own people in Germany when, on D-day, 6 June 1944, they transmitted the news of the Allied invasion at Normandy. The Japanese naval attaché in Berlin also sent information warning that the Allied landing might necessitate a change in destination. The record at this point is confusing since some indications are that the Germans changed the ship's destination, but the Japanese records the ship was still heading to the docks at Lorient. It was important to the Japanese that the I-52 continue to the original port for, in addition to delivering and picking up supplies, the Japanese submarine was to be fitted with the German invention, the snorkel, in order to increase her underwater time.

At this time the I-52 received the first instructions that she was to rendezvous with a German submarine. In advising them of the coordinates the Germans, of course, also informed the Allies where to wait for them. The meeting between the submarines was to take place at 2145 hours 22 June 1944. The information was specific.

Unknown to the Japanese command and unfortunately for the crew of the I-52, these messages and others like them had been intercepted and interpreted by American radio intelligence personnel for some time while working out of the "Secret Room" of the 10th Fleet. This was the American version of the British Admiralty's Submarine Tracking Room.

One of the lesser-known activities of the U.S. Navy during the war, 10th Fleet was a very effective submarine fighter. It was set up in part as a response to the successful German *Paukenschlag* attacks on the east coast of the United States. While it had no ships and only about 50 personnel, 10th Fleet was responsible for the sinking of a significant number of submarines.

Under command of Admiral King and run primarily by Admiral Low, his chief of staff, it was housed in a Navy Department building in Washington, D.C. Those at 10th Fleet were responsible for the coordination of antisubmarine efforts in the Atlantic.

The "secret room" was fed information that came to it by high frequency direction finding stations ("Huff-Duffs") that operated from the Shetlands in Britain down the east coast of the U.S. to Brazil and Africa. The Huff-Duffs were used to monitor German radio transmissions between the U-boat commanders at sea and Admiral Doentiz's headquarters. The information was often very clear and specific. This information was fed into the "Secret Room," where it was compiled and analyzed, and the results sent out as "recommendations for action" to Allied forces in the Atlantic. While not as simple as it might sound, the information nevertheless led to many an attack on an enemy submarine, and the "fix" provided usually got the hunter to within a few tens of miles of his target.

In order to take advantage of the information provided, special naval task forces were established. Such a task force was created to go after the Japanese submarine. It was built around the escort "jeep" carrier USS *Bogue* (CVE 9), especially capable of conducting ASW operations. Also in the group were the destroyers *Francis M. Robinson* (DE 220), a Bulkeley Class destroyer with Lieutenant (Jr.) J.E. Johansen in command; Lieutenant R.E. Peek on the USS *Swenning* (DD 394); the USS *Willis* under Lieutenant G.R. Atterbury; and Lieutenant Commander H.E. Cross's USS *Jannsen*.

Task Force Casablanca sailed on 15 June under the command of Captain Aurelius B. Vosseller. On board the carrier were 9 FM-2 Wildcats and twelve TBF-1-C Avengers from VC 69. This force was one of the best at tracking and had a good record, having accounted for 13 German and Japanese submarines between February 1943 and July 1945.

On the night of 22 June, some 830 nautical miles west of Cape Verde Island on the coast of Africa, U-530, under the command of Kapitanleutnant Kurt Lange, met the I-52 and transferred to the Japanese sub provisions, fuel, a Naxof FuMB7 radar, an Enigma coding machine, and two radio operators, Petty Officers Schulze and Behrendt, to help them make the entry into France.

The task force, which had been guided by Ultra to the point, arrived in the vicinity of where the I-52 was steaming on the surface during the night of 23 June 1944. At 2300 hours the task force sent planes into the air but they arrived too late to catch the U-530. It had pulled away just about an hour before they arrived. The plane flown by Lieutenant (Jg.) Hirsbanner reported at 2303 hours that he was receiving disappearing radar signs from the retreating German submarine, but he did not pursue.

The trap was sprung nevertheless. The planes had no more than lifted off the carrier when Ed Whitlock, the radar operator in Lieutenant Commander Jesse D. Taylor's Avenger, identified a target. Flares were dropped and Taylor brought his plane in low, first dropping depth charges and then releasing a Mark 24 acoustic anti-submarine torpedo (called Fido, because it followed the target around), the first of the Allied acoustic torpedoes. Following their explosions, sounds of a ship breaking up were received, along with a series of smaller underwater explosions. It was Taylor's assumption that he his Mark 24 had hit the I-52. Another pilot in the air at the time thought he had picked up propeller beats.

Captain Vosseller was increasingly concerned that the elusive submarine might have gotten away and he ordered his planes out on a second round of attacks. One of the Avengers, under the command of Lieutenant Gordon, again circled the area and dropped another M-24. In Gordon's plane with him was Price Fish, a civilian from the Underwater Sound Labs in London, who listened closely for any further information, but said that nothing more was heard. Later it was reported that flotsam had been discovered, consisting of quantities of rubber and silk and even parts of some human bodies.

On 30 August 1944 the Kriegsmarine officially declared the I-52 as having been sunk by Allied bombing in the Bay of Biscay on 25 June 1944 with all the crew on board. The Imperial Japanese Navy declared the submarine sunk on 2 August 1944, but did not remove her from their Order of Battle until 10 December 1944.

Waiting at the docks for the arrival of the I-52 was 800 kg of uranium. The understanding is that it was to be used by the Japanese to develop a radiological weapon ("dirty bomb") for use against the Americans. This was probably not enough to create a weapon, but it was known that the Japanese had some other resources.

Now, more than half a century later, the I-52 having been found in more than 5,500 meters of water, questions mostly unasked during this period have now begun to come up. Some interesting things have come to light about the ship and her voyage which perhaps do not mean much individually, but collectively they do raise some unanswered questions. In any case, there is more to the story.

The persistent myth accompanying the sinking of I-52, as well as a supposed explanation for the quick Allied action, is that the submarine carried a secret peace proposal. The story is that Yoshikazu Fujimura, a leading naval officer and the assistant naval attaché in Switzerland, had been conducting highly secret talks with Allen Dulles, concerning a possible peace initiative. The agreement, being sent from Japan to Switzerland, was supposed to be on the I-52 when she was sunk. It was being delivered via occupied France. The story is that when the I-52 failed to show up, Fujimura returned to Switzerland empty-handed, and the effort failed. It makes a good story. However, there is little evidence that, at this point in the war, the Japanese were giving serious consideration to a peace settlement. Also interesting is why the Allies would want to destroy such an effort if it were being made. But more telling is that, as far as is generally known, the Fujimura-Dulles discussions did not happen until June and July of 1945, a year after the sinking of the I-52.

Making the secret-negotiation theory all the more believable is the fact that for several years after the sinking of I-52, much of the information about it was still being classified as top secret by the National Security Administration. The belief was that this effort was made in order to hide information about the secret offer. Chances are that this is not the case; more likely, the government was interested in keeping secret the highly sophisticated cryptological activities involved in the locating of the submarine.

Yet another of the myths associated with the story is that the I-52 was intended to return to Japan with a load of uranium. This may well have been true, but the implications might be easily misconstrued. By this time the Japanese were already working on some sort of nuclear weapon, and the means to deliver it. Richard N. Billings's somewhat dramatic book *Battleground Atlantic: How the Sinking of a Single Japanese Submarine Assured the Outcome of World War II* makes the case that the primary mission of the I-52 was to purchase U-235, that is, the lethal element of a "doomsday weapon." A dirty bomb, composed of this element mixed with ash, could kill millions and contaminate a vast area. According to Billings, the Germans had the capability of such a weapon, but Hitler, fearing retaliation from the British, chose not to use it. Japan, however, was willing to do so and had arranged to purchase the elements from the Germans for gold. In anticipation of this purchase, the Japanese were prepared to attack the United States along the California coast. Phillip Henshall argues that one reason the U.S. used the atomic bomb so quickly was that it feared Japan was in the last stages of preparation of their own weapon.[1]

Another interesting fact is that the manifest of the I-52, upon leaving Singapore, does not list any gold as being aboard. There could be several explanations for this, but none of them fully explain why, if it was meant to be delivered to Germany, it was taken off, or if not taken off, why the manifest does not list it. To add to the mystery, when the submarine was discovered one of the diving teams removed and brought to the surface one of the metal boxes in expectation of locating some of the gold it contained. However, when the box was opened there was no gold. Instead, it was filled with opium.

Who is to get credit for the sinking the I-52, if in fact it was sunk? Though it is assumed that the I-52 had been sunk by the Avenger flown by Jesse D. Taylor, some questions remain. The claim was that after his attack there was no further communication with the submarine. But it is also true that, on the night of 30/31 July, a mysterious QWF signal was received and was believed to be from the I-52. The source of that communication has never been identified. Lieutenant (Jr.) William "Flash" Gordon, who was Taylor's relief pilot, and who was accompanied by the civilian underwater sound expert Price Fish, reported that about 0100 hours on 24 June, a faint underwater propeller noise was detected in the area. While most authorities at the time made the assumption that the submarine was sunk by the torpedo launched by Taylor's Avenger, the Navy was not sure enough that it was willing to give him credit. Instead, they credited the sinking to both Gordon and Taylor, uncertain about the outcome of the first attack.

And just to add a little to the confusion, the I-52, when located, was in a spot more than twenty miles from the point where the Navy listed they had intercepted and sunk her. The wreck was located via a process called Renavigation (RENAV), which uses contemporary accounts to reconstruct the events of a battle and correct the navigational errors that might have crept into such accounts.

The strange story gets even stranger. After the war the German U-530 did not surrender as ordered, but went undetected for more than two months. Under its commander, Oberleutnant Otto Wermuth, the submarine disappeared for more than sixty days during which it kept no record of its movements. When the submarine finally appeared on the lower coast of Argentina to surrender, it was discovered that the boat had jettisoned its deck gun, the ships' log had disappeared, and no member of the crew carried any identification whatsoever. When news of the sub's arrival on the lower Argentine coast reached the Allies the rumors began immediately, including the claim that it carried Adolf Hitler and Eva Braun. Brazil's Admiral Dudal Teixeira believed that the U-530 had been so long in coming because it had first made a visit (delivery?) to Japan. The boat was taken to the United States and the crew interned, later to be dealt with as all German POWs.

A second would-be treasure hunter, Larry Barbernell, also from Texas and also in search of the *Evergreen*'s gold, has also indicated an interest in trying to raise the I-52 from its depths. He claimed that much of what Paul Tidwell knew had been taken from him, and there were suggestions that a restraining order had been issued.

After a great deal of trouble and preparation, on 21 November 1998, Tidwell and two Russians pilots, in a hulled submersible (MIR 2), descended to the wreck. They could not see much nor was recovery fruitful. Nevertheless a Japanese Ensign was returned to the I-52 and a box, which they believed contained gold, was brought up.

Extreme pressure at its 3-mile depth meant that, for the moment, it remained unreachable and that the gold, or whatever it is that is down there, may well never be recovered.

Most of the questions surrounding the I-52 can be answered, it is assumed, if and when Paul Tidwell is able to raise the submarine and recover its gold. He made trips to the site in 1994 and 1998, but was unable to recover much at all. His continued interest in Operation Rising Sun suggests an interest in raising the gold, but also as many other artifacts as can be saved.

Note

1. Phillip Henshall, *Vengeance: Hitler's Nuclear Weapon: Fact or Fiction?* (London: Sutton, 1995).

Further Reading

Billings, Richard N. *Battleground Atlantic: How the Sinking of a Single Japanese Submarine Assured the Outcome of World War II*. New York: Penguin, 2006.
Boyd, Carl. "U.S. Navy Radio Intelligence During the Second World War and the Sinking of the Japanese Submarine I-52." *Journal of Military History* 63 (April 1999): p. 339.
Gardner, W.J.R. *Decoding History: The Battle of the Atlantic and Ultra*. Annapolis: Naval Institute Press, 2000.
Hamilton-Paterson, James. *Three Miles Down: A Hunt for Sunken Treasure*. New York: Lyons Press, 1999.

6. The Peking Man: Where Is He?

A shooting war was nothing new to the 4th Marines, known as the China Marines. During their fifteen years of occupation duties in China, they had been involved in a variety of wars, insurrections, rebellions, and civil wars. In China to protect American civilians and trade interests, they had done their job well, all the time trying to keep from getting too involved in the politics, or the military activities, of the time and place.

But in late November of 1940 the situation changed dramatically, and it became a whole new situation. The Imperial Japanese Army, with lightning speed, was moving toward Shanghai, and the American government had decided to pull out, leaving only the minimum of diplomatic connections. The Marines, scrambling to get out of the way of the advancing Japanese Army in the highly dangerous China of December 1940, suddenly discovered they had yet another assignment, one more responsibility among a series of disasters. It was not another rescue mission for missionaries coming in from the hills in hope of being last-minute evacuees. It was not the preparation of fortifications for the making of one last stand. It was, instead, the care of a man who had been dead nearly a million years.

Concern for the bones of the prehistoric man led the Chinese authorities to request American ambassador Nelson Johnson to offer them safekeeping; that is, that the remains somehow be shipped to the United States in the diplomatic pouch. This seemed unworkable, and Johnson was worried about the legal implications of dealing with items of antiquity, so he arranged for the U.S. Marines to take on the job. They were to take the bones with them when they left China.

To the Marines it may well have been one more unnecessary pain, but to many in the scientific community it was a last-minute effort to prevent the loss of the Peking Man. As it turned out, the loss, when acknowledged, was listed as "single greatest loss of original data in the history of paleontology." The loss remains just as significant today as it was when it was first discovered. The disappearance of this treasure has remained not only a mystery among the international community, but the inspiration for the plots of more than two dozen novels and movies.[1]

When the initial discovery was made, it was considered the most important evidence concerning man's early evolution ever uncovered, and the source for many of the theories both for and against the creation of man. For what had been found was evidence of a fire-making, stone-sharpening being that lived more than a million years ago. But as much of a controversy as the discovery was when it was found, it has since become one of the most baffling mysteries in the scientific world. What happened to the fossil remains of the prehistoric human ancestor known as the Peking Man?

The discovery took place at Dragon Bone Hill in the mountainous regions of Zhoukoudian, in the Fangshan District, some 49 miles southwest of Beijing. The area got its name because bones found there were believed to be from dragons. The bones were said to have magical properties, were ground up and made into medicines used by people in the area. It was there, on 2 December 1929, that the remains of a human skull were uncovered. The area in which it was discovered was at the time the most comprehensive site of archaeological findings that represented the early Paleolithic Age. The search, which had been going on for several years, was first under the direction of Davidson Black, and then was later funded by the Rockefeller Foundation and was conducted under the Chinese archaeologists Yang Zhonglian (C.C. Young) and Pei Wenzhong (W.C. Pei).

The species represented by the skull and teeth fragments was called the Peking man (*Sinanthropus pekinensis*/*Homo erectus pekinensis*), and was believed by many to be the "first man." Under the circumstances of the find it appeared to be the earliest species yet uncovered that had the use of fire. The Peking Man was small, about 5'1", and the Peking Woman about 4'8", with brains approximately 20 percent smaller than modern man. They were considered invaluable to the world of paleoanthropology. The search for additional materials continued to turn up significant artifacts until July of 1937, when the Japanese occupied Beijing and the site was temporarily abandoned.

Among all the fossils found it was acknowledged from the beginning that the most significant were the skull and teeth of the Peking Man. Fearing they might be in danger from the Japanese who were advancing into China, they were taken to the Peking Union Medical College, a Baptist teaching college. There Dr. Henry Houghton, president of the college, agreed to save the fossils. They were kept safely until September of 1941, when it was determined that the danger posed by the advancing Japanese was too large to ignore. At that point it was determined that they should be crated up and removed, the idea being to send them temporarily to the United States. Dr. Franz Weidenreich, who led the Cenozoic lab at PUMC, a lab for the analysis of two- to sixty-five-million-year-old artifacts, made plaster casts of the fossils and kept them, along with the notes of those early finds, at the college. Elaborate plans were then made to get them out of China.

Despite the efforts of the scientific and military communities, some time during the final days of December 1941, during what the Chinese now call the War of Resistance Against Japanese Aggression (1937–1945), the Peking Man's skull and all the other related fossils mysteriously disappeared from the face of the earth.

The disappearance provoked a new series of questions about what had actually been found. Some scientists, as well as anti-evolutionists, claim that it was all an elaborate conspiracy from the very beginning. The early facts — or more actually the lack of facts — led many to consider that the "disappearance" was simply an easy way to conclude a story that had been generated with little or no factual evidence at all. It focused first on the amount of materials that had been located. The *New York Times* and the *London Daily Telegraph* of 16 December 1929 both report that ten bodies (skeletons), or at least significant pieces of skeletons, had been discovered. *Nature* magazine, while not as clear as the newspapers, reported the incident as the location of "the remains of ten individuals." Noted environmentalist and Jesuit priest Pierre Tielhard de Chardin reported in a letter that there were "traces of at least ten individuals." So while there were reports that parts of ten skeletons had been found, the official records of the dig make reference to only one partial skull, and that is all that was ever exhibited. While newspaper accounts are sometimes notoriously exaggerated, there seems to be some support for the suggestion proposed by critics that the other relics were either hidden, or more likely destroyed by scientists, because they were too much like modern human beings, and did not provide the evidence for evolution they were seeking.

An effort to trace the source of the reports of the ten bodies leads to a cable reportedly received but for which there is no record. At a scientific and administrative conference called on 28 December 1929 to discuss the find, there was no mention of the ten skeletons, nor did any of the scientists questioned ever provided adequate answers about the missing skeletons.

This claim has hung on, however, despite the fact that there is little hard evidence to support it. There were numerous persons involved in the dig, English and French anthropologists as well as Chinese scientists, who would certainly have known what was located. And even if they did not prove certain theories, the discoveries alone would have been career-building. Why, anyway, would anyone do such a thing? The answer may lie in the conflict surrounding beliefs about the nature of creation. The creationists, of which there were many, hold that the relics were destroyed by the scientists involved because they did not provide the evidence which they were seeking to support theories of evolution. They persisted in the belief that the Peking Man was in fact the remains of an ape eaten by humans, and thus found next to the fire. They maintain the position that the remains were destroyed, and that the supposed casts made prior to their disappearance were not casts at all, but models, and thus untrustworthy. Both the skull remains, and the mysterious ten skeletons, have fed the argument despite the fact the first evidence is mysteriously gone.

So where is the Peking Man? The records tell us this much. True to their promise to keep the fossils safe, authorities at the medical college removed them from storage and prepared them for transit. The items in question consisted of six skulls, a half-dozen lower jaws, about 100 teeth and some fragments of arms and legs. They were carefully packed into two large unpainted wooden crates and then returned to the safe in the Cenozoic Laboratory awaiting transit. Here the contradictions begin. Clair Taschajian, a German worker in the laboratory, claims she was the one who boxed them up. Two others, Hu Chengzhi and Ji Yanqing, also lay claim to having boxed the remains for the Cenozoic Lab. In late November, as time seemed to be running out, the college administrator, Dr. Trevor Brown, drove the crates to the United States Legation in Peking, some three weeks before the Japanese bombed Pearl Harbor. At this point a group of Marines from the 4th Marines (China) were given the responsibility of ensuring the safe transit of the crates. The precious boxes were supposedly then taken with the troops on a train that was bound for Tientsin, China.

Once there, the crates were to be delivered to the U.S. Marine compound in Tienstin, and from there were to be taken aboard the USS *President Harrison*. She had been hired on a day-by-day contract by the military and was under the direct orders of Admiral Hart. The first segment of the Marine departure, 2nd Battalion and half the headquarters and staff personnel, had left on the *President Madison*. The rest were to be taken off on the *President Harrison*. The ship had been contracted to take American military and civilian evacuees home to America, and was due to leave on 8 December 1941.

However, the *President Harrison* never arrived as promised. She had been at sea when war broke out and was immediately followed by Japanese naval vessels. The captain, who had been heading to the Chinese port city of Chingwangtao determined that the Japanese would not get her, finally ran her aground.

On 8 December, the Chinese date of the Pearl Harbor attack, members of the Marine detachment to which the crates were supposedly delivered were all taken prisoner by the Japanese. There is no record of the crates' ever having been delivered to the Marine compound, nor were they ever found there.

The area was in shambles, and most men were thinking more of escape or resistance than of treasured artifacts. It is at this point in the story that any reliable records cease to exist. In fact, there is no real evidence as to the sizes of the boxes, how many boxes were in question, and if they had been delivered. So, what happened to the Peking Man?

The theories of the loss of the relics are about as numerous as there are persons looking for them. Some explanations are based on fact and have led to further inquiries and explorations; all have been fruitless. Most of the theories, however, seem somewhat implausible and a lot are pure speculation. There is some evidence that the Japanese military, forewarned by their scientists, had been on the lookout for the bones. If that is the case, and if the Japanese found them, there has never been any acknowledgment of the fact.

The earliest possibility is that the cases that had been collected at Tensing never got on the train. The Marines, who were serving as embassy guards at Peking, Tensing, and Chingwangtao, were taken by surprise during the quick Japanese advance. The plan had been for them to gather and be taken out on 10 December 1941. But on 8 December (7 December in the States) the Japanese took the Marines prisoner. One view is that the boxes were simply left there as the Marines were hauled off, having never been put aboard the train.

At this point there is at least a bit of evidence that they arrived, for one Marine, in describing the Marine detachment's preparation for battle, seemed to remember resting the mount of his light machine gun on one of the crates. How he knew what it was, or if the crates were marked in any specific way, is not explained.

Perhaps one of the more plausible of the theories is that the crates containing the fossils did make it aboard the train bound for Tientsin, China. Along the way the Japanese, who were advancing faster than the evacuees could escape, stopped the train and ransacked the luggage aboard, looking for treasures. Here the story varies. One version says that the Japanese, not knowing what they had found, scattered the bones once they discovered what the crates contained. A second version is that the Japanese, alerted to look for the Peking Man, had taken the crates and put them under military guard. When the war began to draw to a close, the Japanese, trying to save what booty they could, put the crates on board the Japanese merchant ship the *Awa Maru*, bound for Japan.

The *Awa Maru* was a "hell ship" that was carrying Allied prisoners of war to Japan to be put to work. If this theory is true then the story ends at this point, because the *Awa Maru* was located and sunk by the Allies in 1945 on the way to Japan. After considerable searching, the wreckage of the *Awa Maru* was located after the war. Deep-sea divers were able to move through the remains. While some valuables were located and brought up, no sign of the Peking Man was found.

But this did not end the continued belief that the Japanese held the Peking Man. In 2006 this suspicion increased when a group of international paleoanthropologists made an effort to establish a foundation and search committee in Japan, in the hope that the fossils could be located there. But the efforts were stymied when the Japanese government turned them down. Whatever reasons the Japanese had, it was nevertheless taken by many as an admission of guilt.

Another theory is based on the testimony of two ex–Marines who acknowledged in 1945 that they had been assigned to the detail that delivered two crates which they believed, at the time, to be the fossils of Peking Man. The cargo had not been delivered to Tientsin as planned, but rather to a Swiss warehouse in the port city of Chingwangtao. This makes some sense, as this was the port to which the *President Harrison* had been sailing when sunk. This may, in fact, have been the original plan. The crates were to be held there awaiting shipment to the United States. It was the Marines' belief, and for many the generally held assumption, that the crates were then delivered to the United States Marine compound for shipment. But there are no records of shipment or arrival.

One of the more interesting theories, and one that keeps coming up in the argument over whether Taiwan is an independent nation or a province of China, is the belief that the remains of the Peking Man are on Taiwan. After the war a Chinese soldier said he had seen them being loaded aboard a military plane which was then flown from Beijing to the city of Kaohsiung, Taiwan, during the early phases of World War II. He claimed the crates were unloaded there, and that they had been buried so deep in an undisclosed place that it had taken three days to accomplish the task.

A variation on this theme comes from a farmer in the Henan Province of China, who reported that his grandfather, a Chinese soldier, had told him of watching a military unit bury an entire truck with crates in the back. It had been buried at the crossroads of his village. This story created enough interest that efforts were made to locate the buried truck, but they were unsuccessful. One theory is that the fossils were buried in China and that after the war they were recovered by the Americans and smuggled out of China. The United States, it is believed, has had them all along, but has denied their existence ever since. The explanation for why they would do so has never been offered.

In 1999, during the controversial debate over evolution that was taking place in the Kansas legislature, *Time* magazine reopened the Peking Man discussion, and there quickly followed several new attempts to locate the lost remains. Among these was a renewal of the story about America hiding them.

A retired construction worker who once worked for the United States Embassy reported that the fossils were hidden in Tianjin. According to him the Americans, trying to keep the fossils safe, had hidden the crates in a secret basement compartment under the Embassy, just days before they had fled China ahead of the Japanese. Efforts to locate the spot and the fossils have been unproductive.

Some Marines reported that the fossils had been buried in Chou K'ou Tien (same vicinity as the Zhoukoudian find), or at the Marine compound nearby, in an effort to save them. At this point some maintain that the fossils were located and taken by the Japanese when they overran the Marine barracks in December of 1941. There are two endings to this version: one is that the Japanese returned them to the mainland and they are now hidden there; the second is that the Chinese found them in Japanese hands after the war and, for whatever reason, have not disclosed the find.

In 1951 Dr. W.C. Pei, one of the fossils' discovers, who apparently espoused the Communist creed, announced that the Japanese had taken the relics when they invaded China, but that agents of the Americans had moved in directly after V-J Day and taken the fossils to the United States.

In 1970 one of the strangest situations surrounding the Peking Man was the appearance of an American woman who said that she was the widow of one of the Marines who was supposed to guard the crates. She said she had a box of items left to her by her husband, and that among the items were some of the fossils. She contacted a wealthy Chicago businessman by the name of Christopher Janus. They met; she showed him some photographs and asked for $500.000. The pictures she left with him were examined and provided a mixture of opinions about their authenticity. It made no difference, however, for once she agreed to further discussions, and left the Empire State Building where they had met, Janus never saw or heard from her again. One needs to take this story with a dash of salt since the same Mr. Janus was convicted, shortly after this episode, of fraud. In 1975 he wrote a book about his search. A Chinese diplomat a few years later claimed the same mysterious woman had set up a meeting with him, but in this case the woman never showed at all.

In September of 2005 the Communist government in China set up a committee of scientists and non-scientists to seek known fossils that were lost or missing. The list included the skull, teeth and bone fossils of the Peking Man. This effort has given the Chinese and Americans even greater interest in locating the materials and a good many interested persons believe they can still be found. The *Chinese Daily* reported that Gao Xing, deputy head of the Institute of Vertebrate Paleontology and Paleoanthropology under the Chinese Academy of Science, believes that they could still be located intact. He reported that since they had started looking once again, more than sixty-three credible tips had been received.

One of the recent clues comes from a man named Ren, who said that his father had been a physician at the medical college where the fossils were stored. He said that his father took a piece of the skull back to his home and buried it in a spot that had since been covered up by a high-rise residential building. It was deemed not worthy of an additional evacuation at that time. "But, as long as there is a glimmer of hope, we will never give up the search," reported Yang Haifeng, the head of the search team in July 2005.[2]

On 3 November 2003, the *People's Daily* reported the exhibition of a skull that the government claimed had been found recently in new excavations at the original site. While the newly discovered skull was dated at only 200,000 years old, rather than the much older original, hope was expressed that further digging might lead to more discoveries.[3]

The search goes on today with several parties involved. The scientific communities, as well a good many adventurers, are not willing to give up the search. Whether their interest is scientific or they hope to gain financial reward from the discovery, they still believe that the Peking Man is still around somewhere, and that in time he will be found.

The interest in the Peking Man got a boost when in 1989 the Chinese government issued a postage stamp to celebrate the 60th year of the Peking Man. The stamp showed a female version of the Peking Man, and in the background, fire and wooden tools.

Whether the fossils will be found or not, the mystery has caught the fancy of many who are more interested in the story of the disappearance than they are of the actual value of the fossils. As such, the case has stimulated numerous answers and inspired the plots for short stories, novels, movies and plays. Among these is the Shaw Brothers' film epic of 1977, *The Mighty Peking Man*, which is a beauty-and-the-beast story to match *King Kong*. In this film, the Peking Man, a giant creature found in the jungle, has little to do with the fossils or their disappearance.

Even Clive Cussler's *Flood Tide* weaves the lost Peking Man into his plot, the villain being in possession of the treasure. It seems that Chiang Kai-shek had the Peking Man, but it was lost — or so he thought — when the ship he used in 1949 to smuggle out valuables prior to the takeover by the Communists was lost. Another of the better-known stories was provided in the first novel by Nicole Mones, *Lost in Translation*, which is more a story of cultural identity than fossils, but which uses the search for the lost Peking Man as the current on which to float several individual stories. The mystery also appears in the plot of Katherine V. Forrest's *Sleeping Bones*, as well as in Robert J. Sawyer's famous short story "Peking Man," in Amy Tan's *The Bonesetter's Daughter*, Philip K. Dick's *The Crack in Space*, and Carolyn G. Hart's mystery *Skullduggery*. In 2001 the Japanese produced *The Peking Man*, a movie in which the DNA of a found Peking Man is nurtured and becomes a problem as the nations of the world try to copy it.

From the desperate attempt to withdraw American forces in China during the early days of December 1941, to international intrigue and literary significance, the Peking Man continues as one of the many unresolved stories of that desperate time and place.

Notes

1. Thomas Boaz and Russell Ciochon, *Dragon Bones: An Ice-Age Saga of Homo Erectus* (Oxford: Oxford University Press, 2004).
2. *Chinese Daily*, 6 September 2005.

Further Reading

Aczel, Amir. *The Jesuit and the Skull*. New York: Riverhead Books, 2008.
Lanpo, Jia, and Huang Weiwen. *The Story of the Peking Man: Archaeology to Mystery*. New York: Oxford University Press, 1990.
Shapiro, Harry. *Peking Man: The Discovery, Disappearance and Mystery of a Priceless Treasure*. New York: Simon & Schuster, 1974.
Taschdjian, Claire. *The Peking Man Is Missing*. New York: Felony and Mayhem, 2008.

7. The First Captives

A fog still hung on the harbor, the few lights from the moored ships appearing as a distant glow. It was 0400 and not quite light yet, but the noises of the river were beginning to grow. On board the American gunboat USS *Wake*, the light guard and radio operator were groggy and ill-tempered from the long night. They had made a mad dash down river from their normal station and now, anticlimactically, they sat on the river waiting through the night. Then, suddenly, one of the sounds became louder and the deck watch jerked up, alert to something happening, only to see an officer of the Imperial Japanese Navy arrive on board. The officer had slipped on board from his launch with only that one brief sound. He was quickly backed up by several members of the Special Landing Force troops, with guns drawn. They had come up on the *Wake* by motor launch, arriving slowly through the darkness from the Japanese destroyers in the harbor.

"The Japanese have declared war on the United States," Captain Otani Inaho said, quite matter-of-factly, "and I am here to take the surrender of this boat." He had no more finished his comment than the radio operator bounded up onto the deck, screaming out the news that the Japanese had attacked Pearl Harbor. One man, further up on the deck, figured out what was happening and dove into the water seeking to escape. The others, having no time to react, were taken prisoner. "Where is your captain?" the Japanese asked, again demanding a formal surrender. The captain, Lieutenant Commander Columbus Darwin Smith, as it turned out, was ashore asleep in his apartment, unaware of the danger to his ship, or the events that had occurred.

The surrender of the *Wake* occurred without a shot. It was the first and only surrender of an active duty American warship during the war. While the crew had spent considerable time the previous couple of days rigging it with explosives, just in case something like this happened, there was neither an attempt nor opportunity for them to scuttle the ship. It all happened too fast and there were too few on board to offer any resistance. This was the morning of 8 December 1941 (Shanghai time).

The American gunboat, USS *Wake,* was built at the Kiangnan Dock and Engineering Works in Shanghai in May of 1927. She was one of six sister ships that had been designed especially for duty on the Yangtze River and was fully adapted for it, with a length of 159 feet and beam of 27 feet. Flat-bottomed, she drew little draft and was heavily powered to move her against the currents of the river. Lightly armed, she nevertheless could deliver fire from a 3-inch gun and several machine guns.[1] Originally named the USS *Guam,* she fulfilled her assignment moving up and down the Yangtze, protecting American interests in China. Following the Boxer Rebellion, the Chinese had granted trade concessions to the Western powers, which turned out to be little less than small sovereign states located along the Yangtze River. For the next fourteen years the *Guam* was the symbol of American interests and power in China. Involved in numerous moments of terror when warlords or bandits decided to fire on them from the shore, or troops in the Chinese civil war made demands the U.S. could not fulfill, there were also hours, days, and weeks of incredible boredom. Very little in the day-to-day routine ever changed, the scenery grew old and dull, and the duties were light and undemanding. In 1941, with little official notice, the USS *Guam* was renamed the *Wake,* in order to free her name for a larger ship just being built.

In the later part of 1941 the *Wake* was sent upstream, where she was assigned as the station ship at the Chinese city of Hankow. This was a particularly difficult assignment as the Japanese Army had already taken the city from the Chinese, and maintained a strong presence in the area. Until recently Hankow had been a large embassy and replacement area, and there were still some embassy civilian personnel in the area. The *Wake* provided the basic link to the American political authorities. However, even as the war was raging about them, part of the job of the gunboat remained social functions and public relations.

While the role of the *Wake* and its crew was to protect American citizens, it found itself in all sorts of scrapes trying to keep peace with the Japanese. Their war with the Chinese had been going on for some time, and while in most areas the Japanese were getting the best of it, large portions of the country were still free and fighting. Finally, as it became increasingly apparent that there was going to be a war, the United States decided to take action. The fleet was moving to Manila. The USS *Wake* received orders that she was to close the station at Hankow. Her job was to sell off what she could of the Navy supplies there, then give the rest away to the missionaries in the area or destroy it. The decision was to leave nothing for the Japanese to use.

7. The First Captives 67

Once this was accomplished, the *Wake* was ordered to return to Shanghai as quickly as possible. The Navy had orders to pull out and all the gunboats were instructed to gather in Shanghai for what they assumed would be a run to either Manila or Australia. Returning, however, was going to be far easier said than done, as the Japanese were in complete control of the river, even to the point that the *Wake* needed to obtain most of her supplies through the Japanese. At this point the Japanese were very correct and polite, and respectfully provided much of the fuel required.

The Japanese had informed all foreign boat captains that they needed to notify the authorities and get permission if they wished to leave. But under the circumstances the captain of the *Wake* had decided that he should simply move out without announcing it. The trip before them was about 600 miles and the Japanese controlled every mile of it. Keeping her movement a secret was impossible, and as soon as the *Wake* pulled up anchor and started heading out, she was stopped by a Japanese officer and told they could not go without an escort. Resorting to boldness, the ship's captain, Lieutenant Commander Andrew E. Harris, informed the Japanese officer that they were leaving and that if he did not want to go with them, the officer should leave the *Wake*.

It worked and the officer retreated. The *Wake* was on her way. However, within a few minutes of clearing the harbor the men on the *Wake* discovered that they were being accompanied by two Japanese naval vessels that followed them, one on each side. There was no harassment — in fact, the officers of both nations even dined together on the American gunboat one of the evenings — but the Americans' every movement was watched on the five-day trip to Shanghai.

The other gunboat up river was not to be so lucky. The USS *Tutuila*, a sister ship, was stationed at Chungking, too far up river for there to be any hope of escape. Realizing that she could not get out, the Navy ordered the officers and crew to abandon her, and to seek another way out of China. The ship was turned over to the Republic of China Navy, where she served throughout the war.

When they arrived in Shanghai, the crew of the *Wake* discovered the city was in chaos. The other gunboats, the USS *Oahu* and the USS *Luzon*, were closed up and waiting to go. Some of the crew on board the *Wake* were transferred off onto other boats, doubling up their complement. In return a few, mostly radio operators, were transferred to the *Wake*. When the rearrangements were complete, the *Wake* was left with a crew of fourteen under a naval reserve officer who had been a Yangtze River pilot, Lieutenant Commander Darwin Smith. Captain Harris and the executive officer, Lieutenant Kempt Tolley, were given other assignments that would get them to Manila. The trip was to be their last assignment as a unit, for with the arrival of the *Oahu* and *Luzon* at Manila Bay, Admiral Glassford dissolved ComYangPat. The *Wake* was now an orphan.

On board the captured *Wake*, its crew, including some who had been rounded up from where they had spent the night's leave, were forced to witness the attack on yet another gunboat. Unlike the USS *Wake*, the HMS *Peterel*, which was stationed just upstream from the *Wake*, chose to fight rather than surrender. The last commissioned British Naval vessel on the Yangtze, she had been moored at Shanghai, stripped of most of her weapons, and assigned as a communications vessel with a skeleton crew. Aware that they had no chance in a battle with the Japanese warships in the harbor, the gunboat had been rigged with explosives in case it became necessary to destroy her.

As the crew of the *Wake* watched, a Japanese naval launch approached the British ship and their officers. Once given permission to board, the Japanese officer demanded the ship be surrender. Lieutenant Stephen Polkington, commander of the small gunboat, refused, and demanded that the Japanese "get off my bloody ship." They did, but soon afterwards, they directed their guns against the *Peterel*, hitting it numerous times. The badly damaged gunboat rolled over and sank, taking some of the crew with it. It had not been much of a fight.

Lieutenant Commander Smith had been notified and by this time had arrived at the docks; however, they would not allow him to board his boat. He had not been captain of the USS *Wake* very long, having only come back into the Navy a few weeks before. Smith was a commercial Yangtze River pilot. His assignment to the gunboat was more a matter of intelligence than it was naval skills, for the *Wake* crew was informed that it had been left behind to provide highly significant radio communication for the few officials who were to remain in Shanghai after the American fleet had gone.

When the capture was complete and the crew hauled off to become the first American POWs of the war, the Japanese took command of the *Wake*. In a quasi-official ceremony, the little gunboat was commissioned into the Imperial Japanese Navy and renamed *Tatara*. U.S. naval officials, not really sure of her disposition, but well aware she was no longer under American control, struck the USS *Wake* from the Naval Register on 25 March 1942.

Commander Smith, after having witnessed the capture of his boat, quickly returned to his office at the American embassy, where he maintained radio contact with dozens of agents all over China. Just what his duties were, or who the agents were, is not clear. But several men from the *Wake*'s crew were there at the embassy, working the radio and informing the agents that they were now on their own, when the Japanese finally arrived and took them into captivity.

The crew of the *Wake*, and the surviving crew members from the *Peterel*, along with military and civilian personnel in Shanghai that the Japanese considered enemies, were placed in camps. Not all lived to be released in August of 1945.

The Japanese upgraded the armament on the *Tatara* and sent her back to duties on the Yangtze River. She patrolled off Nanking and Hankow, and occasionally moved troops to upriver stations. While the Japanese controlled large portions of the mainland, they did not control it all, and the need to keep men and equipment on the move required much of the service the *Tatara* could provide. The *Tatara* was reported as being seen on several occasions, usually on patrol along the Yangtze, on the sea side of the rapids. As the war wore on she was fired on by American bombers flying ship harassment missions over the Yangtze River, and while she was hit once or twice she was not badly damaged.

In August 1945, when the war came to an end and the Allies returned to Shanghai, they discovered that the USS *Wake* was there. In poor shape and showing signs of its hard life with the Japanese, the little gunboat was nevertheless capable of active service. Back under American command it continued its interrupted duties on the Yangtze, patrolling in an effort to keep Americans safe from the increasing hostilities among the Chinese people. For a brief period she was reinstated on the Naval Register. But conditions in China were changing rapidly. While the war with Japan was over, the conclusion of hostilities in that arena marked the return of the Chinese civil war that had been put on hold for the duration. In this case, the United States backed the Nationalist Chinese under Chiang Kai-shek in their bid for control of the mainland. One of the concrete actions taken by the U.S. was first to lease, and then to give the USS *Wake* to the Nationalist Chinese Navy in 1946. In this new role she was renamed once again, this time as the RCS *Tai Yuan*.

The *Tai Yuan* supported the Nationalist movement, primarily on the Yangtze River, and took increasing fire from the Communist forces advancing along the shores. The communist control of the countryside increased, however, and it became more and more evident that the Nationalists, if they were to survive, would end up in a defensive position on Formosa. The *Tai Yuan*, however, did not last that long, for it was finally overcome by troops attacking from the shore and was captured by the Communists in 1949. Taken under control, she was incorporated with other patrol vessels and put to work along Yangtze River. She also took on a new name, which at this point is unfortunately unknown.

Few Americans today are aware of the role played by gunboats on China's Yangtze River for more than forty years, and even fewer have heard the story of the *Wake*. In all the time since her capture, and eventually numerous owners, there remains some interesting questions about what happened and how. Few are making any effort to understand them and they may never be answered. But the questions remain nevertheless.

The questions start with the captain, Lieutenant Commander Darwin Smith. Why was he picked to captain the *Wake* if, as it now seems, there was every intention to let her be captured? While a capable naval officer in World War I, he had only been recalled into service a few weeks before. At the time, he also maintained an office at the American Embassy, where he communicated by radio with agents located all over China. Who were they and what were they were doing is another story, and one full of questions. What was intended by his last-minute appointment as captain, since he was not even aboard her? The indications are that he had other primary responsibilities, and those lay with the United States rather than with the USS *Wake*.

Second, if war with Japan seemed imminent, and America's actions at the time seemed to indicate that it was, then everyone would know that the USS *Wake* was in danger of being taken. One must wonder why neither the captain nor the vast majority of the crew were aboard. Why there was so little preparation for just what happened?

Also, there has never been any good explanation offered as to why the USS *Wake* was left behind. Despite what was being said about providing radio communication to the outside world for the embassy, it needs to be remembered that the embassy had all the necessary radio equipment to keep in touch, and that it was at the embassy, not the ship, where the radio operators were found by the Japanese.

Besides, the *Wake*, while older and certainly battered by years of service, was in just as good a shape as the other gunboats that were deemed worthy of making an escape to Manila. It was a long shot, obviously, but better chances than she was given. Why didn't the *Wake* go with them? Or if she was considered too fragile to make the trip, and then why not tow her out to sea and scuttle her? It would have seemed a more fitting end for a ship that had provided such great service.

And why was the ship not blown up as had been planned? The crew had worked a good many hours to rig her with explosives that could be set off with a moment's notice. Why weren't they? How could the Japanese have come up on them so swiftly that the prearranged scuttling could not occur?

After the event, the commander of the *Wake,* Darwin Smith, successfully escaped from a Japanese prison and in an incredible story of survival, managed to get out of China. In fact, when United States forces returned to Shanghai, it was Smith, acting as a Yangtze River pilot, who brought the ships into the harbor.

The other gunboats involved managed to survive for awhile. The *Oahu* (PR 6) and *Luzon* (PR 7) left Shanghai in the early morning hours a few days before the war began. Harassed and followed by Japanese warships, they finally broke into open sea. They then undertook a long and perilous voyage in boats never designed to see duty on the open sea, but finally arrived in Manila just a week before the outbreak of war. There they joined up with the naval forces preparing to defend the island.

The *Oahu* continued to provide service, patrolling, running men and supplies for those on Bataan and later Corregidor, until, on 5 May 1942, she was sunk by Japanese naval fire. The *Luzon* was scuttled in Manila Bay to avoid being captured. However, the Japanese managed to salvage her and she was part of the Imperial support fleet in and around the Philippines until 3 March 1944, when she was sunk by the American submarine *Narwhal* (SS 167).

The officers and the crew of the USS *Tutuila* managed to get flights out of China and by a long and time-consuming route were finally returned to territory under Allied control. The ship, turned over to the Republic of China in 1942, was in service throughout the war. The *Mei Yuan,* as she was called, was finally scuttled to prevent her capture by the Communist Chinese forces moving toward Shanghai.

Most of the crew spent the war as prisoners both in the Philippines and on mainland Japan, where they worked as slave labor. Those who survived were finally released in September 1945.

Note

1. Technical descriptions of the USS *Wake* from the *Dictionary of American Naval Fighting Ships* online.

Further Reading

Cable, James. *Gunboat Diplomacy, 1919–1991: Political Applications of Limited Naval Force.* New York: St. Martin's Press, 1994.

Clark, George B. *Treading Softly: The U.S. Marines in China from 1840s to 1940s.* Pike, NH: Brass Hat, 1996.

Edwards, Paul M. *Under Four Flags.* Yardley, PA: Westholme Books, 2009.

McKenna, Richard. *The Sand Pebbles.* Annapolis: United States Naval Institute, 2008.

Saqqal, George. "A Short Philatelic History of the Yangtze Patrol." *Log*, March, April, and May 2004.

Tolley, Kemp. *Yangtze Patrol: The U.S. Navy in China.* Annapolis: United States Naval Institute, 1984.

Part II

The Rest of the Story

When telling some of the more popular stories to come out of World War II, many historians and popular authors end the stories way too soon. That is, the meat of the story has been put forth and explained, leaving a good deal of the story, often the more significant part of it, untold. In the initial years of historical reporting there was a tendency to "skim" off the best or more dramatic information, hitting only the highlights, and often neglecting the best part of the story. In the first place this is the waste of a good story, but more important the remainder of the story is often even more interesting and illustrative of the multifaceted events of the war, as is that limited part we have chosen to remember.

Take, for example, the American tendency to forget that the Allied cause in World War II was supported by many, many nations, some not too large nor powerful, but all of which made significant contributions. Some, like the Dutch or the Brazilians, played highly significant roles but have generally gone unnoticed; some of the most interesting stories come out of their involvement. Also, while there has been a lot of talk about the successful amphibious landings of World War II, it is generally assumed that this was the role of the Navy, when in fact, in many cases, both the majority of the ships and their crews belonged to the Army.

Somehow most Americans failed to detect the fact that the country of Japan had risen from a feudalistic state the size of Montana to an international power that had, among other things, attacked and destroyed a U.S. warship at sail, and had done so with near impunity. Despite what the attack on the USS *Panay* should have told us, there was little understanding of its wider implications.

A partial explanation of the bifurcation of American thinking about Japan and its intentions came from the failure to acknowledge the wider degree of America's early military commitment to friendly nations. An excellent example of this was the nation's military involvement in the early fighting of World War II. In terms of direct support there is no better example than those young Americans who flew with China well before the creation of the well-known Flying Tigers.

It is in the individual stories, the smaller but perhaps more common incidents, that much of the larger reality is understood. An example is the grotesque manipulation of the Japanese soldier, who was led to believe that spiritual purification arrives through dying a meaningful death, and who therefore approached war with a fanaticism generally unseen before. By a large margin, World War II was the most violent conflict of modern times, and particularly in the Pacific, where Americans and Japanese fought with an intensity rarely equaled. The Japanese belief in the necessity of an honorable death is displayed in a variety of ways in these stories: the aggressive ruthlessness of the *Panay* incident; the meaningless deaths attributed to the "Cave of the Virgins"; or the dire mistreatment of American POWs, as in the case of the Palawan massacre.

A less direct Allied involvement, but a blatant act of aggression nonetheless, was Roosevelt's involvement in the creation of a convoy designed to carry British soldiers to a war zone in American ships, contrary to both the Neutrality Act and the wishes of the American Congress.

8. Beyond the USS *Panay*

Gunfire on the Yangtze River was not unusual, nor were death and destruction. But in December 1937 they came to the river in an unusual way. On that day warplanes of the Japanese Empire bombed, strafed, and sank the USS *Panay*. The American gunboat was in China, and on the river, as a part of the United States Asiatic Fleet. On this date the *Panay*, an aging gunboat under the command of J.J. Hughes, was located approximately 28 miles upriver from the Chinese city of Nanking. She was anchored at the Hohsien Cutoff in about 45 feet of water.

During October and November of 1937, preceded by the victory at Shanghai, the Japanese moved toward Nanking. The Japanese, who had expected a quick victory over the Nationalist forces, had run into a determined enemy. In the prolonged battle the Japanese timetable was disrupted, and the frustrated Japanese soldier was seeking some sort of revenge. When the Shanghai forces were relieved, the Japanese moved over 50,000 strong toward Nanking, where the Nationalists waited, poorly organized and poorly led. As the tension increased, American gunboats had evacuated most of the Embassy staff from Nanking. As the Japanese army approached, Commander in Chief Tang-Shengzhi issued a bulletin saying that he could not guarantee the lives of any foreigner who remained in Nanking. The *Panay* was assigned as the station ship to guard the rest of the staff and several journalists, and bring them off when it was necessary.

The *Panay* was one of six U.S. gunboats that had been built at Kiangnan Dockyards in Shanghai especially for the Yangtze Patrol. She was only lightly armed, with 3-inch guns behind steel splinter shields, and two light .30 caliber machine guns. She had just recently evacuated U.S. Embassy personnel, as well as some journalists and filmmakers, just ahead of the Japanese attack on the city.

The day before, and despite the fact the Japanese had been given advanced warning of their arrival, the *Panay* was fired on as she arrived about 1400 hours. Incredibly, not one of the forty or fifty shells fired hit the ship.

Commander Hughes, nevertheless, decided to move the small flotilla away to avoid trouble, so he moved about twelve miles upstream from Nanking. When shelling began again the next morning he moved again, another ten miles or so upstream.

Steaming toward their second stop, the ship was halted about 0940 hours and searched by a Japanese gunboat under the command of Lieutenant Isoble. The action was done with all formality and proper protocol, and when the Japanese discovered no Chinese soldiers aboard, the *Panay* was allowed to go on. All the ships, the USS *Panay* as well as the three tankers sailing with her, bore huge American flags on their canopies and painted on the sides of their hulls. Both the Americans and British were neutrals in this conflict between the Imperial Japanese and the government of China. Japan knew this, and also had been notified that the ships were coming in an effort to remove citizens still trapped at Nanking. Nanking, a city in eastern China, had become an important place after the Treaty of Nanking (1842) that opened up China to foreign trade.

The Japanese were also forewarned that sailing with the *Panay*, for protection, were the three Standard Oil ships. Earlier, in a move reportedly designed to prevent any trouble on the river, the Japanese had assigned neutral zones where ships could anchor and not be subject to ground fire or air harassment. They did not work.

The Japanese planes, including Yokosuka B4Y Type 96 bombers and Nakajima A4N Type 95 fighters, attacked the American gunboat as well as the three American oilers that had been moving "oil for the lamps of China." The *Panay* was hit by at least two of the 18 counted bombs dropped. On the first pass the bombers ignored the oilers, but the fighters took the opportunity to strafe the ships. The captain of the *Mei Ping*, which had suffered some immediate damage, had run his ship aground as the firing intensified.

When the attack occurred, on a Sunday afternoon, many of the crew and passengers were mingled together. Whenever possible, the Americans would retire to the civilian ship, where an alcoholic drink could be located.

In the early 1900s almost a hundred percent of the American kerosene delivered to China came through the Standard Oil Company (Socony). This was challenged by both British and Dutch companies, but in 1937 Standard was still delivering a majority of the much-needed oil to light the lamps and heat the food of many of the Chinese. The Japanese obviously saw them as "helping the enemy," and made them targets as well. Alice Tisdale Hobart, the wife of the Socony Oil Company manager in Nanking, had made a point of this significance in her 1933 study of the company.

On 9 December 1937, the three Standard Oil (Socony Vacuum Company) tankers were at Wantun, anchored astern of the *Jardine*'s hulk. Traffic on the river was becoming more and more dangerous, and the three, though anxious to be on the way, did not dare it alone and were waiting for the *Panay* to provide them some bit of protection. The three, the SS *Mei Ping*, the SS *Mei Hsia*, and the SS *Mei An*, were typical oilers, with American officers and Chinese crews. Now they found that their proximity to the *Panay* was proving to be a disaster.

The *Mei Hsia* had a rather long history of interfering in Chinese business, having smuggled Szechuan river pilots upriver to Chungking to break a strike by rival Huaeh pilots. Her presence was often a matter of tension when docking at the wrong port.

For those on board the *Mei An*, things were not going well. A tobacco merchant named Vines reported that he could not believe that they were actually being attacked. "American flags were flying everywhere," but it made no difference. A bomb hitting the *Mei An* moved through the wardroom, killing the captain and everyone else in the room. Marshall, a writer for *Colliers*, had jumped from the stern of the *Panay* to the *Mei An*'s top deck, thinking it might be safer. But he was no sooner on board than he was hit by gunfire as the Japanese planes returned to strafe the ships. Nevertheless he made it to shore with others of the crew of the *Mei An* as she was beached and then hit again and destroyed. Captain Carlson, her skipper, was killed.

The *Mei Peng* and the *Mei Hsia*, secured to pontoon at the Kaiyuan wharf, continued to be attacked. Several small boats from the *Panay* carried a major part of the crew to the far river bank. Three men had died on board during the attack and 27 were injured. As they watched from the shore, a Japanese launch arrived. After it pulled up alongside the sinking ship, some men went aboard for a few minutes, probably looking for code books. The launch then shoved off, peppering the *Panay* with heavy machine gun fire. As her survivors watched, the USS *Panay* rolled over to the starboard and sank into seven to ten fathoms of water.

Most Americans know something of this part of the story. But it does not end here, either for the Americans or for the British, whose vessels were struck as well during this time. Much of the information about the continuing story has been kept from the public.

The day had been one of several attacks even before the Japanese planes hit the *Panay*. As the American gunboat moved upstream, she ran across the remains of a burning British freighter that had been attacked from the air by Japanese planes.

The Japanese rampage was not limited to the American gunboat and Standard Oil ships. On the 13th, the day after the *Panay* incident, the British ship HMS *Ladybird*, a gunboat, was at Wuhu. While there she was fired on and hit six times by Japanese artillery shells coming from the shore. During the bombardment one seaman was killed. The *Ladybird* was badly holed below the waterline and it was necessary for the men to wrap a tarp around her to stop the water from coming into the hull. Feeling it was all a mistake, the British consul from Nanking left the *Ladybird* in the midst of the firing, rowed to shore, located the battery commander, and ordered him to stop. He did.

The day before, the SS *Wantung*, under the command of Captain Donald Brotchie, was sailing under the protection of a small British convoy. She and her escorts, the HMS *Scarab* and HMS *Cricket*, both insect gunboats, reported on the 11th that artillery shells had been fired from the shore and apparently were directed at them, even though there were no hits. The shells had landed in the river between them and the shore, causing no damage. The next day, the 12th, three Japanese planes, coming in out of the sun, moved in close and discharged several bombs at the anchorage where the ship was located, with fire certainly directed toward the *Wantung*. During their first pass there were no hits and so the planes came around again, this time coming in close for a second effort. The fierce gunfire of both the *Cricket* and *Scarab* drove off the planes.

For awhile following the attacks Japanese aggression continued. When the naval boat appeared at the sinking *Panay*, boarded her briefly, and then raked her with machine-gun fire, the Americans hiding in the reeds along the river banks found it difficult to determine if the Japanese were trying to help rescue the remaining American sailors from further harm, or if they were anxious to locate the survivors and kill them.

J. Hall Paxton, second secretary at the Nanking embassy, went ahead of the rest in order to find a radio so that Captain Hughes could get a radio message through to Nelson T. Johnson, the American Ambassador at Hankow, about 200 miles upstream. The message was sent, and the rescue effort was under way. Most of the survivors made it to Hohsien, where they were picked up by the *Panay*'s sister ship, the *Oahu*.

As soon as they could be rounded up, the survivors were brought to the USS *Augusta* in Shanghai. When Lieutenant Commander J.M. Sheehaw, captain of the *Oahu*, pulled alongside, officers and men stood on the deck of the capital ship in silence. A temporary wooden bridge had been constructed between the two ships to allow the survivors to come on board.

They were greeted with considerable joy as well as food, clothing, and medical treatment. Admiral Harry E. Yarnell, a man known for his calm under extreme emergencies, sat in his cabin waiting for the participants' report of the incident.

At some point on 12 December, almost as if following a script, the Japanese either suddenly discovered the error of their ways, or they had fulfilled the elements of their mission, for suddenly the attacks turned into a recovery effort. With seemingly sincere apologies and contrite comments, the Japanese military set out to be of help. The American and British military responded immediately, and upon hearing the news a small Anglo-American task force, consisting of the British gunboats HMS *Ladybird* and *Bee* and the U.S. gunboat *Oahu*, sped to the scene in order to be of help. The HMS *Ladybird* was a British gunboat with a long history on the Yangtze. At the time she was located about twenty miles from the *Panay* and responded quickly.

Also arriving was the HMS *Bee*. The third ship with this name, it was launched in 1915, as an Insect Class gunboat. At the time she was servicing as the Yangtze flagship for RAY (Rear Admiral Yangtze). The *Bee* had been damaged by the same shore batteries that fired on the *Ladybird*, but the damage was not reported until much later. Many historians believe that this was in hopes that the hostilities created would pass over.

About two hours after the attack, the Japanese appeared in the search for survivors. Immediately planes were sent out to search for members of the crew who were still afloat. A launch from a Japanese destroyer approached the *Oahu* with two doctors aboard who came to help. They were led aboard, and were watched carefully. Most of American and British officers involved believed they were there to take notes on who had been hurt rather than to offer aid.

Even more dramatic than the military response was that of the Japanese citizens. Regardless of the military intention, the average Japanese citizen seemed to feel the need to make some sort of acknowledgment, and did so on numerous occasions. The populace appeared, at least, to reflect serious concern over the incident. Tokyo schoolchildren contributed $10,000 in pennies to go to the families of the victims. Hundreds of individuals brought gifts to the American embassy, so much so that it became a problem for the Navy as to what they were to do with them.

The incident came close to igniting a war between Japan and the United States, a war that had been brewing for a long time. Yet even from the beginning, cooler heads were involved. The first response came from the Americans. A dispatch was sent to Foreign Minister Koki Hirota on the afternoon of the 12th to remind him that "American vessels were on the Yangtze River by uncontested and incontestable right and were engaged in legitimate and appropriate business."

The official Japanese arm was quick to respond. Either they were forewarned of the event and thus prepared for a response, or they were quickly and deeply aware of the danger that the attack presented. The American military in China were offered "profound regret" locally, and informed of the Japanese Empire's sincere apology for the unforgivable accident.

The Japanese ambassador in Washington sought an immediate audience with Secretary of State Cordell Hull to present a formal and most sincere apology. Hull delivered a letter of protest to the Japanese and demanded a formal apology. The well-formatted and official apology was delivered on 24 December 1937.

In Washington, President Franklin D. Roosevelt was furious and immediately considered an embargo or even some limited naval action. While many supported the idea, most knew that the U.S. was not ready for a war with Japan, and they played down the incident in hopes that an apology would suffice. Without a doubt, Congress wanted to avoid a war with Japan if at all possible.

Four months after the incident both the oil company and the U.S. Navy recorded their expected payments. Standard Oil Company demanded compensation for the ships, the loss of cargo and lives to the cost of $1,594,435.99. The cost to the Navy was billed at $1,211,355.01.

In the end, as far as most people are concerned, the Japanese assumed full responsibility, claiming the attack was an accident and totally unintentional. They provided a formal apology, as well as several less formal ones, and the promise to pay indemnities.

So what happened after that? First of all was the sharing with the world. Never, possibly, was a war crime more carefully documented than the attack on the *Panay*. On board were several newsmen and journalists. Among them were Norman Alley of Universal Newsreel and Eric Mayell of Fox Movietone News, both of whom were able to film the entire attack. In their escape they managed to protect the film, slipping it out of China to the United States, where it was processed and viewed. As a result the film was widely seen in American theaters during January of 1938. It was censored somewhat, as Washington thought it necessary to remove some of the more graphic scenes, including shots where the Japanese pilots' faces could be seen. It was believed this would add to America's discomfort.

The documentary film of the attack was released in Los Angeles along with the premier of *Damsel in Distress*. Many, after looking at the film, believed that the Japanese were fully aware of what they were doing. It seemed obvious that no one could have missed the American flags painted on the *Panay* and the tankers. It also appeared, because of the way the film was shot, that the attack was done was a sense of vengeance.

Nevertheless, the Japanese citizens, particularly the schoolchildren, felt the need to compensate for the unfortunate accident. In Tokyo, girls representing the White Lily Day Schools — special schooling for privileged Japanese girls — delivered money they had collected to aid the wives and children of those who had been on board. Hundreds of citizens contributed money, or sent letters and gifts.

Finally, on 18 December, memos were sent explaining that money could only be accepted by American ambassadors in China and Japan. The gifts were becoming an embarrassment for a variety of reasons, not the least of which the government did not want the money that had been donated to affect the judgments in terms in indemnities. And second, the simple fact of recording the gifts and responding to them was becoming a burden. Admiral Harry Ervin Yarnell, Commander in Chief Asiatic Fleet, was offered a large sum of money by the men of the Japanese Third Fleet, who felt the Army had overstepped its authority, but he declined, accepting the apology as enough.

Most of the men and the ships involved went on to serve, most for a limited time, in their scheduled capacity. The HMS *Scarab*, which had been in service since 7 October 1915, went on to serve in the Orient. She was finally scrapped in Singapore in 1948 after thirty-three years. The HMS *Bee*, also launched in 1915, was finally sold in 1939 for 5,225 pounds. The HMS *Cricket*, also of the same vintage, was destroyed by a floating mine near Mersa Matril, Egypt.

The British gunboat HMS *Ladybird* was never quite the same after her shelling, but when war broke out she was sent into the European theater. She was eventually sunk in the harbor at Tobruk on 19 May 1941. The *Ladybird* did not completely sink, however, and much of her bridge and superstructures were out of the water The British used it as an platform for an antiaircraft station in the defense of Tobruk until the end of the war.

A year after the incident occurred, navy divers dared the murky waters of the Yangtze River, eventually discovered the safe from the *Panay*, and rescued more than 40,000 dollars in notes, vouchers, and pay stubs. At long last this enabled Lieutenant Geist, the *Panay*'s purchasing officer, to finally be "cleared of his accounts." However, the *Panay* itself has never been raised.

Geist, as well as eleven other survivors from the attack on the *Panay*, were present at Pearl Harbor on 7 December 1941. One of the *Panay* survivors, Coxman Morris Rider, was killed at Pearl Harbor. The wounded captain, Lieutenant Commander J.H. Hughes, recovered from his wounds and went on to command the USS *Electra* through much of the war. The executive officer, Lieutenant Arthur Anders, though badly wounded, took command of the *Panay*'s evacuation.

Captain Donald Brotchie remained in Shanghai and was captured and interned by the Japanese during World War II. Following his release he was assigned as captain of the *Shengking*, and became famous running the "Taiwan Trolley," helping Nationalist Chinese evacuees escape from the mainland to the island fortress in the late 1940s.

Several of the Japanese pilots who flew in the attack were sent back to Japan and were reportedly punished for "reckless flying." Most would go on to serve during World War II, with only one or two surviving. Lieutenant Masatake Okumiya, in command of 13th Air Group, the only one of the four flight leaders involved in the *Panay* incident, later wrote of the event. He suggested that the Army had asked for their help, claiming that there were several ships on the Yangtze, loaded with Chinese soldiers trying to escape from Nanking. He reported seeing four or more ships and, believing Army intelligence, he was sure they were loaded with enemy troops. After the war he continued on with the Japan Air Self Defense Force, rose to the rank of admiral, and published several histories of World War II, including *Zero! Story of Japanese Air War in the Pacific*.

Colonel Kingoro Hashimoto, who was responsible for the machine-gunning of the *Panay* as she lay dead in the water, was "withdrawn" from public eye. This incident, even more than the bombing, had disturbed Americans because there could be no doubt it was intentional and malicious. He was recalled in 1938 and lost from sight, but 59 days after the bombing of Pearl Harbor, he appeared and was awarded the Kinshi Medal for his "audacity" in action on the Yangtze River. After the war he was tried and found guilty of war crimes. He was released from prison after contracting terminal cancer.

By 22 April 1938 the Japanese paid an indemnity to the injured parties in the amount of $2,214,007.36. The formal apology was made, as well as numerous less formal ones, and with the payment of the settlement the incident was considered closed.

Since the war fiction has picked up the events both of the *Panay* sinking and the post–*Panay* activities. The events were used in the novel *The Man in the High Castle* by Philip K. Dick and in Douglas Galbraith's *A Winter in China*.

It is hard to see how the attack on the *Panay* and the other ships involved was not deliberate. Many on the spot felt the act was intentional. John Pradoa, navy cryptographer, said that they were intercepting and decrypting radio traffic all during the attack, and that it suggested the Japanese planes were acting under orders. Even at the time it would have been hard not to see a pattern. There had been a wide variety of "accidents" on the river. In 1937 the British ambassador's home had been bombed. At the time of the *Panay* attack there were gunboats from half a dozen nations on the Yangtze, but all of the attacks were on English-speaking ships. The Japanese grew increasingly arrogant as their influence in China grew.

As it was, the American reaction to the attack appears a little strange. The reactions of the government and the people were different, but led to the same results: very little to nothing. The government felt the need to make a lot of noise about the incident, but at the moment their military options were limited. A United States Naval Court of Inquiry operating in Shanghai provided what they assumed was evidence that the attack was deliberate; however, the last thing Roosevelt wanted at this time was a war in the Pacific. This was in part because of, as well as the cause of, the public reaction.

Other than the immediate feelings when seeing pictures of the bombing, most of the anger and concern displayed by the American people was directly primarily toward the American government. Citizens had suddenly become aware that American ships guarded the Yangtze River, and were asking what they were doing there in the first place. Just a few months earlier a poll of American voters showed they preferred a complete withdrawal of all Americans from China, including not only military personnel but missionaries and medical teams.

The British reaction was quick and concerned, but also lacked the bite that might have been expected. A couple of interesting things occurred. One was that though the HMS *Bee* had obviously been hit and badly damaged, as shown in the photographs taken at the time, no report of the incident was registered or compensation asked from the Japanese. There is some hint that the British, who were not in the position to take on the Japanese at this time, having major military concerns in Europe to contend with, may well have played down the hostilities.

All in all, the reasons behind the attacks may have been far more complicated than previously suspected. Strong feeling existed between the Imperial Army and Navy, and the actions displayed in Nanking may well have been seen by the more radical of those within the Army. These men saw war with the United States as inevitable and wanted the United States out of China once and for all. The decision to attack the *Panay* may well not have been a decision by the high command of the Imperial Japanese Army or Navy.

Further Reading

Grover, David H. *American Merchant Ships on the Yangtze 1920–1941*. Westport, CT: Praeger, 1992.
Jellison, Charles A. "A Prelude to War," *American History* 34 (December 1999).
Koginos, Manny T. *The Panay Incident: Prelude to War*. Purdue: Purdue University Press, 1967.
Marino, James I. "Prelude to Pearl Harbor." *America in WWII*, February 2006.
Sawyer, Frederick Lewis. *Sons of Gunboats*. Annapolis: United States Naval Institute, 1946.

9. The Smoking Cobras

Images of clandestine meetings, spies, assassins, war criminals, and Nazi sympathizers, all involved in plots against the Allies, are often what come to mind when one thinks of Brazil during World War II. Even after the war, suspicions continued that ex-Nazi officers had gone to Brazil to find refuge, and perhaps even to continue their efforts at world domination. These, as well as stories of large concentrations of Germans in Brazil living off their ill-gotten treasure, are of course totally untrue.

For reasons never totally understood, most Americans are completely unaware that the nation of Brazil was one of the Allies during World War II. It is a rare combat narrative of the war that even mentions Brazil's contribution, or that the United States maintained air and naval bases there during the war. The indexes of the majority of histories of World War II do not list Brazil's participation, and otherwise knowledgeable people are unaware that air, naval, and ground forces from this, the largest country in South America, fought alongside Americans in combat against the Axis powers. Memoirs or celebrations of World War II very rarely include Brazil as a significant participant. Periodical literature is equally unrepresentative of the contribution of the Portuguese-speaking nation, or of its postwar efforts to become a major player in the United Nations. In fact most Americans, if asked about it, are inclined to suggest that Brazil had supported the German cause, and even more would list Brazil as one of the places where Nazis were able to escape and find refuge after the war.

Some have suggested this misinformation is the result of a combination of limited memories, poor timing, bad publicity, and a series of films and novels that came out after the conclusion of the war. In 1946 Brazil played the villain in the movie *Notorious*, in which Ingrid Bergman and Gary Grant fought it out with Claude Rains, a German agent who was trying to steal atomic materials. Perhaps an even more blatant, and totally unfounded, plot was from 1978's *The Boys from Brazil*, based on Ira Levin's novel. In this latter work, a genetically cloned young Hitler, masterminded by Dr. Josef Mengele, awaited with Brazilian foster-parents to reintroduce Nazism to an unsuspecting world.

Maybe it is just that most Americans are geographically challenged and have a hard time telling the difference between Brazil, which was a strong and helpful ally, and Argentina, which was, to some degree, pro–German. The nation of Argentina did not join the Allies in declaring war on Germany until late March 1945, at a time when Germany was in a virtual state of defeat.

It is also the case that the Brazilian forces fought much of the war as a part of a multinational force, which likewise has been poorly remembered by historians of the war. This wildly diverse unit included the American all-black 92nd Infantry, the Japanese-American 442nd Regiment, British units that combined men from New Zealand, Canada, India, and the Gurkhas, along with black Africans, both Jews and Arabs from the British Mandate in Palestine, and South Africans. The unit also included French Moroccans and Algerians, as well as units from Poland, Greece, and Czechoslovakia, plus some anti-fascist Italians. It was an amazing force, well worthy of a history in its own right, but unkindly relegated to the backwaters of history.

As the war clouds in Europe unleashed their lighting on the world, the nation of Brazil had a population of about 40 million. Many of them had ties to the old country, and they had always had economic and trade connections with Germany. There were large German sections in many of the towns and cities. Yet they were also tied geographically, and to a degree economically, to the United States. Certainly some would have favored one side or the other in the mushrooming war, but most of them, as reflected by their government, preferred to remain neutral. At least in the early stages it was not Brazil's war, and she managed during the early years to maintain a position of neutrality. She traded equally and openly with both the Allied and Axis governments. Since 1930 Brazil had been ruled by Getulio Vargas, who seized power in a military coup, and who was openly quasi–Fascist. As such, he was also fiercely nationalistic, and very much aware of the political and commercial ties his nation had with the United States. He did little that he thought might upset the delicate balance he was trying to maintain. Neither his control over his own country, nor his nation's role on the continent, were all that secure and there was little motivation for him to lead Brazil one way or the other too quickly.

Hitler's Germany was interested in ties with South America, especially with Brazil, and mounted and maintained a well-organized and aggressive propaganda campaign in Brazil. At one point (1935) there were an estimated

3,000 members of the Brazilian Nazi Party, but in the long run this was at best a mixed blessing for the Germans. It certainly suggested support for the German cause, but at the same time it was seen as a potential threat to the government of Brazil. In 1938 Vargas outlawed the Nazi Party in his country and a year later banned the speaking of German, under penalty of imprisonment. This order extended not only to individuals but was also prohibited at public meetings, including religion. The latter was most likely seen as necessary because an estimated half of all the Lutheran ministers in Brazil were pro–German.

Aware of growing German influence in the area, Franklin D. Roosevelt established the Office of the Coordinator of Inter-American Affairs (OCIAA). He saw the need to establish stronger ties with other nations on the hemisphere. He put Nelson Rockefeller in charge of the operation. His job was to change what many saw as an unfriendly attitude between Americans and Brazilians. The American military, if no one else, was aware of Brazil's potential importance. Not only was the east coast of Brazil the closest point for an invasion of America, but the nation itself was very rich in essential deposits of iron ore, manganese, and rubber.

Roosevelt's plan was to enhance good relations between the American and Brazilian people, and to sway Brazil's military and political support to the Allies. Brazilian historian Antonio Pedro Tota said the plan was an "ideology factory." It was Rockefeller's office that was behind such efforts as the rising popularity of Carmen Miranda, and those famous Latin-American heroes the Three Caballeros, and while these were not sufficient to alter attitudes, they went a long way toward improving them.

While the history of trade relations between Brazil and Germany, Great Britain, and the United States is a complex one, it is generally considered that a significant turning point in moving Brazil toward the American position was the decision by Roosevelt's administration to aid in the funding of the Volta Redonda steel mill. The mill was both the "symbol and the substance of Brazil's industrial coming of age," and the decision gave America an advantage in its relationship with Brazil. It was only four days later, on 26 September 1940, that the Vargas government made the decision to cast their lot with America and to make Brazil's rather significant resources available to the Allies. In a strange twist of events, the United States also convinced Great Britain to drop its naval blockade of Germany long enough for German arms, destined for Brazil, to be delivered.[1]

Several other military decisions were made that would quickly tie the Brazilian people to the Allied cause in World War II. Since military planners held the belief that any attempted invasion of South America would be directed toward the northeastern tip of Brazil, which was the closest to the Axis powers, the U.S., with Brazilian approval, worked out a secret treaty in November 1940 with Pan American Airways to begin building a series of airfields in the area. These airfields were presented to the public as new commercial fields but they were designed as well for military traffic. In January 1941 the Vargas government acknowledged the danger of invasion and gave its permission for the construction, and in time gave America control over the bases.

As the ties with the United States increased it became harder and harder for the Brazilian government to remain neutral. Finally, in January of 1942, Brazil severed its relations with German, Japan and Italy. The German reaction was immediate and steps were taken to reduce, if not prevent, war supplies going out of Brazil to America. German U-boats were ordered to begin sinking Brazilian ships, and between the time relations were broken and July of 1942, thirteen unarmed Brazilian merchant ships were sunk. In August of that year, German intensity picked up, and five vessels were lost in two days at the cost of more than 600 Brazilian merchant marines. These sinkings included the *Baependy* with 270 lost, the *Araraquara* with 131, and the *Arara*, hit while stopping to pick up survivors from the *Itacib*, with a loss of 20. All in all a total of 36 merchant ships and nearly 2600 lives were lost during the war.

A public outrage followed as the citizens' anger began to wear down any government reluctance to get more involved. Thus, on the heels of these maritime losses, in late August 1942, Brazil declared war on Germany and Italy. It would be another year before Brazil would declare its adherence to the Atlantic Charter or declare war on Japan. In September, in an almost immediate act of support, President Vargas gave American Admiral Jonas Ingram authority over the Brazilian navy and air forces in order to provide immediate defense for the long Brazilian coastline.

But Brazil's contribution was to be far more tangible than the use of land or resources. Despite its own domestic problems, and the nation's always unstable relationships with some of its South American neighbors, Brazil had every intention of being a significant participant in the war effort. So after some difficulty in the identification of troops, the location of qualified officers and NCOs, and arrangements for equipment and training, the Brazilian Expeditionary Force (*Forca Expedicionaria Brasileira*) was established. The force consisted of 25,334 men. Once organized and trained, they were sent to Italy, where they would fight as a division of the U.S. Fifth Army, first under British Field Marshal Harold Alexander and then later under American General Mark Clark.

Their participation was delayed at first by the difficulties in organizing the Expeditionary Force. And there was some feeling among Brazilians that the government was not at all that anxious to rush into battle. The last time the Brazilian Army fired a shot in anger had been in 1870, in a border war against Paraguay. Her experience was severely limited and her equipment was primarily World War I leftovers. Her inability, or perhaps unwillingness, to move too quickly soon led to the popular saying at the time that "it is more likely for snakes to smoke than it is for the Brazilian Expeditionary Force to set out." From this criticism emerged the phrase "when snakes will smoke," used much in the same way as the phrase "when pigs fly." When the force finally entered the war they did so with considerable pride, and quickly took to calling themselves the Smoking Snakes, *Cobras Fumantes*. Before long there was a division patch created, to be worn on the shoulder, that showed a snake smoking a pipe. Organized as a standard American division with all the services, even mail, it was made up of the 1st, 6th and 11th Regimental Combat Teams with about 5,000 men each in three battalions.

During their time of deployment the 1st Brazilian Division made numerous patrols, chased retreating Germans, and guarded untold numbers of emplacements. Fighting alongside other units they participated successfully in several serious engagements throughout the Italian campaign, fighting at Camajore, Monte Prano, Monte Acuto, San Quirico, Gallicano, Barga, La Serra, Castelnuovo, Soprassasso, Montese, Paravento, Zocca, Marano su Panaro, Collecchio and Fornovo.

Interestingly, the Brazilians remember the battle of Monte Castello as their most significant and respected effort, giving almost a romantic aura to the fight for this elevation during the winter of 1944. While certainly significant, it was not an unqualified success, and was more a prolonged effort than a single battle. But the Brazilians found and maintained the battle to be a symbol of their involvement, their determination, and their eventual success.

The fight at Monte Castello lasted from 25 November 1944 to 12 February 1945. Here the Brazilians confronted a hill that stuck out from the top of Torraccia Ridge, where the Germans were able to fire down from well-prepared positions. As a part of Task Force 45, the Brazilians were given the order to take the hill, and moved forwards. During this first attack the Germans were able to repulse the Brazilians, leaving them with 34 dead and 134 wounded. The assaults continued on the 24th and 25th, but again they were unable to move the entrenched Germans. They struck again on 29 November, once more having to fall back as the German defense intensified. Then, on 12 December, in what was supposed to be a surprise attack, they were given away by poor communication with the artillery outfits. Finally, on 21 February, the Brazilians were able to mount a successful attack, taking the area from the 1043 Regiment of the 232nd German Division. Perhaps the victory was so satisfactory since they had spent more than four of their nine months at war under the German guns. The cost had been high: 145 casualties, compared to 5 Germans killed and 13 wounded.

However, military historians have tended to be far more impressed with the Brazilian victory at Montese on 16 April and during the battle that immediately followed. There the Expeditionary Force took the town in a four-day battle while suffering 426 casualties. The next couple of days they defeated the German 148th Division and the Italian Monte Rosa, San Marco, and Italia Divisions. These units surrendered to General Mascarenhas on 29–30 April, making the catch for the week 2 generals, 800 officers, and 14,700 troops. It was a remarkable event by anyone's reckoning.

As the winter continued, the Brazilian division, along with 5th Army, kept putting the pressure on the retreating German army. The main activity during the cold months was patrolling, which was done exceptionally well by the division, so much so that many received American, British and French decorations for their services during this period. The effectiveness of their involvement can be illustrated by the fact that the Germans took the trouble to direct propaganda directly at them, speaking in Portuguese through a radio outlet known as Goldgreen Hours.

Most historians would agree that the role of the Brazilian Expeditionary Force was a tactical one with the majority of its action performed on the platoon level. This is not to suggest that they did not make a significant contribution, for in fact they did, but rather that they played out a wide variety of assigned roles. It is wise to remember that the heroic soldiers of this division had overcome terrible odds regarding both training and leadership. Most of the soldiers were conscripts from poor rural backgrounds. They were uniquely multinational, having Polish, Russian, African, German, Italian and Portuguese backgrounds, but the units suffered no segregation. The vast majority of their action was in Italy, where the fighting was brutal and where much of it was literally an uphill battle against German troops in elevated and well-fortified positions atop hills and mountains.

The Brazilian Navy was not large but in time it delivered more than 7,000 sailors to the war effort. During the war some five hundred of them lost their lives in action. Their primary assignment was to ensure the safety of ships sailing from Trinidad in the Caribbean to Florianopolis, a city in the south of Brazil. While the significance of this contribution goes far beyond what is suggested by statistics, it is nevertheless true that the Brazilian Navy conducted 574 operations, protecting a total of 3,164 merchant ships. During this time the German subs were only able to sink three of those under their protection. The German Navy later reported that their subs had been attacked 66 times by the Brazilian ships.

Writing of their participation, the naval historian Samuel E. Morison said that looking back at the early days of the war one realizes that Brazil's entry into World War II was "an event of great importance in naval history." Other military units quickly took advantage of Brazil's willingness to provide help, and by the end of 1942 the United States Army had located its South Atlantic Wing of the Air Transport Command at Natal. Also, the Armed Forces South Atlantic established a location at Recife, the same place that Rear Admiral Jonas Ingram's Fourth U.S. Fleet was stationed.[2]

The Brazilians also invested their limited air force in the war effort. The primary unit was the 1st Fighter Group (*1 Grupo de Aviacao de Casa*), which was organized on 18 December 1943 under Lt. Colonel Nero Moura. It consisted of four flights: Red, Yellow, Blue and Green. The command consisted of 350 men, 43 of them pilots. The group took its advanced training in Panama and first became active in defense of the Panama Canal. They flew the American Republic P-47D Thunderbolt. Once ready for combat, they arrived in Italy on 6 October, at which time they became a part of the American 350th Fighter Group. They soon began their own operations, flying from Tarquinia and replying to the call sign *Jambock*.

Quickly reduced to 25 pilots by combat losses and illness, the group disbanded the Yellow flight and divided its pilots among the other three. With this change, pilots were now expected to fly no less than two missions a day. On April 22, 1945, the group flew 44 individual missions, during which it destroyed hundreds of vehicles and barges south of Mantua; it was to be the greatest sorties display of the war. All in all the Brazilian pilots few 445 missions, 2,550 individual sorties, and 5,465 combat flights from 11 November 1944 to 6 May 1945. While it flew only 5 percent of the total missions (under the XXII Tactical Air Command), it accomplished 85 percent of the ammunitions depots destroyed, 36 percent of the fuel depots, 28 percent of the bridges, 15 percent of the motor vehicles and 10 percent of the horse-drawn vehicles.

At the war's end Brazil had lost 1,889 soldiers and sailors, 312 merchant vessels, three warships, and twenty-two fighter aircraft. Most of the soldiers are buried in the Brazilian Soldier's Cemetery in Toscana, Italy.

The Brazilian government expected more recognition for their efforts, but the Potsdam Conference in July 1945 was monopolized by the big three, all of which tended to feel indifferent toward Brazil. In addition, the priority given to rebuilding the war damages in Europe meant that the Latin American countries, including Brazil, were often neglected. So, while relations remained cordial, there is still some feeling their efforts were unappreciated. As well, the Brazilians had hoped that they would be a permanent member of the newly created United Nations Security Council, but that did not work out as desired. Nevertheless, Brazil was a different country after the war, and in a major part because of the Brazilians' contribution. Their war participation served as an engine of economic and political growth, and allowed Brazil to be seen as an actor on the global stage.

There remain some old tales that keep coming up as the historical record of World War II continues to be written. One is the ongoing story of Nazi gold and treasures. In this tale, questions are raised about whether German (if not Nazi) treasure was brought to Brazil toward the end of World War II. The evidence is limited, and often circumstantial, but the fact behind many of the stories is the realization that during the latter part of the war Brazil's metric gold reserve grew. It rose from a reserve of 45 metric tons in 1940 to 314 metric tons in 1945. No one has estimated how much Nazi gold ended up in Brazil, but there was enough concern at the government level that Brazil joined eleven other nations in the setting up of a historical commission to investigate, and if any was located, to return it to its rightful owners.

And there are the many stories that surround Jens Gluessing's account of a German settlement in Brazil, plotted in 1930–36. In his book, *The Guyana Project: A German Adventure on the Amazon*, he described an expedition of German scientists who were sent to explore areas of Brazil with the intention of creating a series of outposts there prior to the war. Among the evidence he provides is a wooden cross he uncovered. The cross stood nine feet high and was covered with swastikas. It was located on an island on a tributary of the Jari River. The inscription on the cross reads: "Joseph Greiner died here on 2.1.1936, a death from fever in the service of German Research Work." This was not the only grave at the site, however, for it appears that at least a dozen others had been buried there. The site also contains other ruins and Nazi paraphernalia. Greiner, it turns out, was one of three Germans, led by Dr. Schulz Kampfhenkel, an SS officer, who had been sent into the region by Heinrich Himmler. According to locals, who call the area the

"Nazi Graveyard," the Germans financed the expedition in the hope of establishing a settlement that could serve as a bridgehead against American influence in the area.

There is no doubt, at least according to Stanley E. Hilton, that the Germans made a concentrated effort to establish espionage units in Brazil, primarily to report the movement of troops and merchant ships. Concern was so high in Washington that in 1940, when the rumor hit that Germany was about to send troops to Brazil to "support their citizens," President Roosevelt ordered the preparation of 10,000 to go by air and 100,000 by sea, to prevent such a thing. It turned out to be false, with no record of any such German intention, but it played into the American fear about Germans in South America.

Contrary to popular opinion, most German soldiers, even most Nazis, did not go into hiding at the end of World War II. In the main they simply took off their uniforms, turned themselves in and, when allowed to do so, went home and tried to regain their lives. The stories of Nazis sneaking out of Germany at the last minute in submarines filled with their pilfered treasures are exaggerated. And even if it was the case elsewhere, there is very little evidence they went to Brazil.

Nazis in Brazil were not unheard of, however, for in the late 1960, Franz Stangl, commander of Sobibor and Treblinka extermination camps in Poland, was discovered by Nazi hunter Simon Wiesenthal and arrested while hiding in Brazil. As late as 2007 the *Los Angles Times* reported that Israel was reissuing its call to Brazil to help them locate Aribert Heim, and about the same time, received assistance in trying to locate Nazi criminal Alois Brunner.

So, contrary to American memory, Brazil was one of the good guys during the war, as she has been since. It is worth remembering the extent to which the Brazilians joined the U.S. and the Allies in their cause.

Notes

1. John D. Wirth, *The Politics of Brazilian Development, 1930–1954* (Stanford: Stanford University Press, 1969).
2. Jens Gluessings, *The Guyana Project: A German Adventure on the Amazon. World News*, 25 October 2008, Webindia123.com.

Further Reading

Clark, Mark. *Calculated Risk*. New York: Harper and Row, 1966.
Hilton, Stanley. *Hitler's Secret War in South America, 1939–1945: German Military Espionage and Allied Counterespionage in Brazil*. Baton Rouge: Louisiana State University Press, 1999.

McCann, Frank. "Airlines and Bases: Aviation Diplomacy: The United States and Brazil, 1939–1941." *Inter-American Economic Affairs* 21, vol. 4 (Spring 1968): pp. 35–50.

Medal, Doris Ann. "The Smoking Cobras: The Brazilian Expeditionary Force in Italy During World War II." Research Project, San Jose State University, 1976.

Ready, J. Lee. *Forgotten Allies: The Military Contribution of the Colonies, Exiled Governments and Lesser Powers to the Allied Victory in World War II.* Jefferson, NC: McFarland, 1985.

10. More Ships Than the Navy

Even if they have seen Jack Lemmon and Ricky Nelson in *The Wackiest Ship in the Army* (1960), most Americans are generally surprised to learn that the United States Army has maintained a general naval, seagoing force, and that this was particularly true during World War II. And, unlike Lemmon's ill-fated ship, most of the Army's vessels were ship-shape and well manned, and served in highly specified functions. The question for most persons, then, is why did the Army maintain a naval function? Why a duplication of effort? The answer has always been rather simple, but the explanation and justification have often become matters of considerable controversy, and have resulted over the years in a wide variety of agencies and responsibilities.

The answer lies first in the concept of use. For the Navy, ships are vessels of combat, and for the Army, vessels of transportation. For the navy the vessel is primarily the weapon, whereas for the Army, vessels are extended trucks. This leads us to the first answer. Without adequate transportation to move men, supplies, and equipment, the best of all military strategy is meaningless. The best plans by the best military minds are without meaning if they do not have the means and the methods available to execute them.

"Effective and efficient transportation involves movement control and the use of all modes of transportation: human and animal, transoceanic and inland water transport, rail, motor, air, and such other methods as pipelines and aerial trams."[1] And because neither the civilian contractor, the Navy, nor the Maritime Commission was able to provide the massive amounts of transportation that the Army needed, it got its own.

Throughout history most field armies have provided most of their own transportation, even over the water. To stay afloat, they have relied on civilian contractors, confiscated vessels, captured ships, or the willing help of civilians joining in on the action. Illustrative of this latter resource were the Marblehead men taking Washington's troops across the Delaware in the dead of winter to attack the German mercenaries during the American Revolution. And while the problem had existed as long as there were military movements about, for America it was during the Spanish-American War that the problems became acute and a solution to Army transportation began to be sought more deliberately.

The difficulty came to a head when the Army was called upon to take the war to the enemy. This greatly increased their need. What they discovered was that ship owners, even those who had already signed a contract, refused to allow their ships carrying men and supplies into danger zones where they had a chance of losing their means for a livelihood. A good many of the owners just stood their ships offshore, refusing to go into shore or to try to land their supplies in high-risk zones.

A related problem was focused on the civilian crews who, understandably, were not interested into going into hot zones when they did not have to. Often, on the last phase of a voyage, the crew would simply refuse to act, or in some cases even jumped ship. In order to be sure that the ships and the crew would go where they were needed, when they were needed, it was felt the crews had to be loyal to the army.

The third problem, and the one that finally required the most attention, was the fact that there simply were not enough ships available to meet the Army's needs. Obviously, the outbreak of war put a sudden demand on transportation, and the nation had never been good at anticipating these needs. The Navy's ships were focused on their own nautical agenda, and their ships, in the main, were constructed for specific naval assignments. The Maritime Commission was responsible for meeting the nation's other requirements, and was quite reluctant to assign ships to Army needs either permanently or on a long-term lease, especially when the needs often arrived without warning. They also believed that the services, primarily the Army, were guilty of operating a less than economic endeavor.

A problem related to having enough ships was the difficulty of scheduling them. Ships were always in the wrong place and going in the wrong direction. Many a vessel steamed forward half full while supplies and equipment waited at another location for transportation. The Army needed, or felt they needed, ships at their beck and call. As they were quick to point out, more than one operation was hampered, or even canceled, because of the lack of adequate shipping in the right place. The demands of the service, not the location of ships with contrarily scheduled agendas, was what should determine availability.

The solution for the Army was to get itself into the transport and shipping business, and it began to do so just after the Spanish-American War. It had some trouble once again during World War I, not only with civilian contracted ships, but with ships of its own manned by civilian crews who were not willing to undertake the more dangerous assignments. In this case the Army arranged for the Navy to provide much of the needed personnel to operate their ships, but transportation difficulties plagued the Army throughout the war.

In order to understand both the confusion and the Army's determination to float its own boats, a quick lesson in American government is in order. Particularly, one must consider the nature of its organization, for the military is, among other things, a huge bureaucracy. Until the reorganization in 1949–1950 there was no Department of Defense, but instead two distinct cabinet positions: the Department of the Navy and the Department of War. Combination of the two was attempted and to an amazing degree it worked, but not in all things. What was considered necessary was for the Army to create and maintain its own naval facilities.

The Army Transport Service (ATS) was organized in 1898 as a part of the U.S. Army Quartermaster Department. It emerged primarily for the reasons given: the lack of vessels as well as the frequent unwillingness of ship owners and civilian crews to take their boats into harm's way. Both Army-owned and -operated and time-chartered ships were in operation during the Philippine Insurrection and the Relief Expedition to Peking. This was true, as well, during much of the occupation duty in China. From then on, and during World War I, the Army moved to take over the function of its naval duties, and did so though the fleet was small and engaged in serving American holdings primarily in the Pacific.

As World War II broke out and the demand for shipping manifested itself, the shipbuilding industry took on the task of producing craft for the Army as well as the Navy. As shipyards miraculously turned out ship after ship, the Army began to build up a large fleet of transports, oilers, and numerous other vessels from close-in watercraft to thousands of landing craft. Few are aware that both the Army and Navy developed, contracted, and operated their own landing craft during the war. The Higgins Company, for example, was building nearly identical landing craft for both the Army and the Navy, under different contracts, until late in 1949 when the Army decided to get out of the landing craft business.

In 1942 the Army Transportation Service was absorbed by the larger and more formally organized Army Transportation Corps, Water Division. The ATS operated with both military and civilian contract employees. The ships, taking on a distinctive color scheme, avoided the Navy's gray on gray. While it is not clear when the ATS began to distinguish its ships by color, by 1943 most Army transports were painted a four-color combination with white for the superstructure, buff for the masts and beams, brown for the decks, and a gray for the hull.

The command situation aboard these ships was sometimes confusing, but well described in the regulation *Army Field Manual* (FM) 55–105. Each of the Army vessels had a master in command and a transport commander, as well as lower utility ranks both for the operation of the ship and the control of the troops on board. The master was in command of the ship with the exception of the armed guard units that were under U.S. Navy command. The transport commander was responsible for loading and unloading, for all military personnel aboard — as well as civilians who were not involved in the operation of the ship — and eventually responsible for everything that did not pertain to the actual operation of the ship. The relationship of control was always confused by the fact that a USAT ship might well be Army owned or leased, or a commercial vessel manned by a civilian crew on contract to the War Shipping Administration.

As the demands of war increased, the Army acquired additional ships, often paying very little attention to the niceties of ownership. To be found among the vessels they operated were Liberty Ships, coastal freighters, Great Lakes ships, a few side-wheelers — one of which was built in 1910 — as well as ships from occupied nations like China and Italy. There were also foreign ships, such as British-owned freighters that were called into use for short periods. One of the lesser known of the Army's shipping operations was the Southwest Pacific Area (SWPA), where largely Australian vessels, flying the American flag but manned by Australian sailors, sailed under orders from the Army Transportation Corps, Water Division, Small Ships. These vessels were the backbone of General MacArthur's campaign through his Philippine invasion.

The transportation problem was tackled as well, by the Army's increasing willingness to have its ships used in the short term; for example, troop ships returning from a delivery might pinch-hit to carry needed raw materials back to the States. The Army also worked on cutting the turnaround time needed, and by the end of the war was operating on a time of three to four days, down from 10 to 14. They also made an effort to use new means for packaging and transit in an effort to increase speed of turnaround.

At its high point the Army was maintaining more than thirty-five large troop transports, sixteen cargo ships, 55 inter-island ships, two cable-laying vessels, a news and communication ship, 23 hospital ships and more than 36 floating, self-propelled warehouse and repair ships. Of the smaller vessels, those less than 1000 gross tons, there were 510 freight suppliers, 104 Y-class tankers, and 746 tugs. The majority of these ships were operated by civilian seamen from the Water Division. The crews necessary to man these ships came either from the Army rolls or were members of the Coast Guard, the latter operating under Army control. Yes, it is true: one could receive sea pay while serving in the U.S. Army.

The Naval historian David H. Grover provides some interesting information that is somehow hard to believe. He counted 111,106 Army vessels in comparison to 74,708 Navy vessels, even when including the Navy's auxiliaries. The Army figures he provided included 88,366 assault landing craft maintained by the Army (compared to 60,974 in the Navy) and the Army's 1,665 oceangoing vessels. The Army's fleet was primarily for transport or supply, while the Navy was primarily combat directed. This being the case, then the Army really did have more ships than the Navy.

In 1949, after the end of World War II, the Military Sea Transportation Service (MSTS), under the naval structure, took control of what had previously been the fleet of Army transports. On 15 December 1948 it was announced that "all military sea transports including army transports would be placed under Navy command." The effort was a part of the military reorganization efforts under President Truman. The transfer included 417 Army ships with a total tonnage of 3,390,000 tons. Not all of the ships had been owned, though, as some had been on charter or some sort of lease arrangement. Under the new arrangement the U.S. Navy, under the Department of Defense, would operate all oceangoing transport and the Army would give up all its vessels and related functions. It is estimated that at the time the Army was operating fifteen oceangoing ships, about half cargo and half troop transport. By the time of the transfer most of the ships had become old and worn out. But this was not the end of the Army fleet, for during the Korean War, just five years later, more Army-owned ships appeared in a wide variety of functions. They tended to fall into groups distinguished by their markings: FP for freight and passenger, FS for freight and supply, FA for cargo vessels, F for steel cargo boats, and Y for tankers. These included some 1,114-foot inter-island freighters built in World War II for the Army, which had never been turned over to the Navy.

The best information suggests that during World War II, 59 Army ships were lost to enemy action. The Army employed about 20,000 civilians who saw service outside the continental U.S. The crews of these ships were mixed and varied; merchant mariners, who have been the most forgotten of World War II heroes; Army and Navy personnel; and even some Coast Guard. During the war the Corps, Water Division, Civilian Branch, lost 519 men due to enemy action.

One way to determine how well the nation remembers a historical event is the amount of fiction that is built around the event; that is, how much the particular episode has captured the imagination of the nation. The amount of fiction built around the Army's naval service has been very limited, and when it is done it tends to be presented more as a comedy than as a serious understanding of this vastly important service. In addition, what is presented is often based on poor information or misunderstandings, for example, the designation of Army ships as USS when they were officially United States Army Transports (USAT). Many a soldier, in looking back on his service records, or seeking to find the ship on which his father or grandfather sailed, is astonished to find out that they sailed to and from their overseas assignment in vessels owned and operated by the Army. The Army Transport continued its service well up to the formation of the Military Sea Transportation Service (MSTS) that took over control and responsibility for ships both Army and Navy. For some time afterward, it was hard to determine the status of an individual ship.

Still alive to some degree, however, the Army's watercraft restructuring plan scheduled for 2013 includes 148 vessels. They operate out of the 7th Transportation Group based at Fort Eustis, near Newport News, Virginia. Undoubtedly, those involved will continue to perform their service in the backwaters of public knowledge. In his 1987 book *U.S. Army Ships and Watercraft of World War II*, David Grover notes with sadness the lack of interest shown in these vessels and in the men who crewed them, especially many ships crewed by the Army itself. Perhaps this is why the Army's fleet of watercraft and oceangoing vessels is known as the ghost fleet.

The Army does not go to any great lengths to announce that it has a naval unit, nor are these units ever widely publicized. This is partly true became the Army has always considered them to be secondary, even auxiliary, to the much more obvious branches: the infantry, armor, cavalry, and artillery. The water units certainly have never received any attention as fighting units, even though many of the water-based units were often in harm's way. For many in the Army, the vessels in question were simply considered "floating trucks," and even if that is the case, the record of this phase of the military has been an efficient and gallant one.

Perhaps some sort of conclusion can be drawn about the success of these Army-owned and -operated vessels. Some historians are very critical, suggesting that Army personnel were no more prepared to deal with ships of the sea than were Navy men able to operate tanks. The Army men might well do the job adequately, but they did not have the feel for it. The Army was, many believed, way out its element and doing a job that was paid for in inefficiency and waste.

Admittedly, few Army officers would not have seen a stint as captain of an inter-island vessel as career-promoting. And some have noted that the Army personnel displayed a lack of feeling or identification with the ships on which they served. Offered as an illustration is the fact that while there are numerous Navy "ship reunions" going on even 50 years later, this is not true for Army watercraft. On the other hand, while the evidence is there that Navy men did not get along very well with their counterparts from the Merchant Marines — professional jealousy, perhaps — the same was not true of the relationship between Army personnel on sea service and the Merchant Marines they worked with.

Perhaps the final evaluation is found in the fact that the job was done, the supplies and men delivered, and the military effort highly successful. And in this context, many critics see the Army's waterborne efforts as highly significant and professional.

Note

1. Charles R. Shrader, in John Whiteclay Chambers II, ed., *American Military History* (Oxford: Oxford University Press, 1999), p. 733.

Further Reading

Army Ships, The Ghost Fleet. http://patriot.net/eastln2/Army.htm.
"The Army's Navy." *Yachting*, May 1944.
Coakley, Robert W., and Richard M. Leighton. *United States Army in World War II: The War Department, Global Logistics and Strategy 1940–1943.* Washington, DC: Center of Military History, United States Army.
Edwards, Paul M. *Small United States and United Nations Warships in the Korean War.* Jefferson, NC: McFarland, 2008.
Grover, David H. *U.S. Army Ships and Watercraft of World War II.* Annapolis: U.S. Naval Institute Press, 1987.
Lunney, Bill, and Frank Finch. *Forgotten Fleet: The Small Ships Section of the U.S. Army Transportation Corps, Water Division.* Medowie, New South Wales: Forfleet Publishing, 2004.

11. Stories from the KPM

The Japanese believed that if they could pull off a quick and complete conquest of the essential American, Dutch, British Commonwealth, Philippine, Siamese, Malayan, Chinese, and Dutch East Indies strongholds, they would be able to secure the vast supplies of raw materials they needed. Perhaps as important, they believed the conflicted nations, including the United States, would sue for peace rather than face a long hard war halfway across the world. It was a daring plan and was carried out with determination and courage by the Japanese military. However, it did not work out as planned, and while there are as many reasons given as there are historians writing about it, in the main the failure came about because of three things: (1) The Japanese did not understand the impact made on the American people by the bombing at Pearl Harbor, nor did they take full advantage of what they could have accomplished in follow up attacks; (2) the Japanese did not anticipate, nor properly appreciate, the determination of the military forces of the Dutch East Indies, and their prolonged resistance; and (3) they were not able to make the adjustments needed to compensate for the delays in their schedule, caused by the Allied success in the Battle of the Coral Sea and Midway.

It is the second of these reasons, the resistance of the Dutch East Indies, that requires some additional look at the rest of the story. Few are aware of how deeply involved the Dutch people were in the battles raging in the area of the Dutch East Indies. Because of the dramatic opposition they presented in Europe, the tendency is to think of the Dutch in World War II in terms of the occupation of their homeland, and the stiff resistance offered by the Dutch people. Few remember that during the early days of the war, the Dutch navy in the Pacific put up a terrific fight in the face of overwhelming odds and in a significant way was in part responsible for delaying the Japanese timetable. Those dramatic final days in the Dutch East Indies were well illustrated in the 1944 film *The Story of Dr. Wassell*, featuring Gary Cooper and Lorraine Day, in which a navy doctor managed to get his badly wounded men from the USS *Marblehead* safely back to Australia. But even in this case, the heroic defense of the men and women of the Dutch East Indies, and their contribution of their Navy and Merchant Marines in the Battle of Java Sea, are almost unknown.

Even as the German Army was sweeping through Europe, occupying the Dutch homeland in late 1941 and early 1942, as many as forty KPM ships escaped ahead of the Japanese advances in Dutch East Indies. Here, vastly outnumbered and with incredibly limited resources, their officers and men joined the Allies for every point of land, every strait, and every nautical mile.

As far as the Japanese plans of conquest, Java was the ultimate goal, the crown jewel of their expectations. Their adversary, at this point, was the South West Pacific Area, under the command of the British General Waverell, which was organized on 2 January 1942. These forces were outnumbered in the air and at sea, but the Allied forces still acquitted themselves well. They were fighting a losing battle from the beginning and they all knew it. In a desperate air battle, 19 February 1942, they lost seventy-five fighter planes in a day of dogfights, leaving much of the area uncovered.

Nevertheless, it was Dutch ships, primarily under Dutch command,[2] that provided the only stumbling blocks to the Japanese as they rapidly moved toward Java and Australia. In a series of attacks, many led by the Dutch Rear Admiral Karl Doorman, an effort was made to slow down the advance of the Japanese juggernaut. In small fleets made up of combined forces, low on equipment and supplies, and with very poor communication—aggravated by the lack of a common language—they attacked the Japanese time after time. The Dutch Defense Forces, supported by elements of Allied forces, managed to prevent the Japanese occupation for three weeks following the fall of Singapore on 15 February 1942. This delay in the Japanese timetable would pay off with major advantages in the Battles of Kokoda Trail and Coral Sea.

In the middle of all this confusion, three incidents went primarily unreported, all regarding ships of the Dutch Forces, and each illustrative of the desperate times involved. One ship's story is representative of the Dutch fears and frustrations, one a story of endurance, and the other of a heroic if unsuccessful attempt to continue the fight.

But first some background. Following the invasion of Norway, Holland, Belgium and France, rumors quickly spread of the creation of a fifth-column movement within those countries. It raised concern among the military authorities that such action might occur in the Netherlands East Indies

(NEI), still unoccupied and with a surprising number of German nationals living and working in the area. In addition to these citizens, the Dutch had also collected an estimated 3,000 German crewmen, both merchant mariners and sailors, from the more than twenty German ships that had been impounded by the authorities when the war broke out.

At first the citizens were simply watched, but when the Japanese declared war and joined the Axis, it was feared that the Germans might well organize and operate as a fifth column in support of their allies. Several plans were considered, but the most immediate one, and the one quickly adopted, was simply to get them out of the area. While at this point the government was not interested in harming them, they were concerned about the impact of their presence. There was already evidence they were causing trouble, if only in the form of negative talk.

The Dutch government in the East Indies looked for a nation that might be willing to take them in, and finally they convinced the government of India to accept them as refugees. Once this outlet was identified, the government began rounding up all the German nationals they could. It was very much like the American internment of Japanese-American citizens during the war, as little effort was made to distinguish between those who remained pro-German and those who did not. This group, plus the sailors who had been previously collected, were divided into three groups, and arrangements made for them to be taken aboard Dutch merchant ships for the trip to India. The situation in the area had quickly grown desperate.

The first group, primarily civilians, was loaded aboard the Koninklijke Paketvarrt Maatschappij (KPM) ship *Plancius,* a 5,953-ton cargo and passenger ship built in 1924. She had only recently returned from delivering 987 troopers from the 18th Division, taking them from Bombay to Singapore, arriving there on 5 February. Later, she served as a floating hotel for British evacuees coming out of Singapore and eventually was used to transport them to safety. For a brief time she served as the headquarters of the Commander Eastern Force.

The second group was also made up primarily of civilians. They were assigned to the cargo-passenger ship KPM *Ophair,* built in 1929. The KPM *Ophair,* having escaped the Japanese net, was later converted into a hospital ship and saw service in the Bombay area during the rest of the war.

A third ship was selected to take off a group that consisted of some civilians and the more aggressive collection of restricted sailors. The ship selected was the KPM *Van Imhoff,* and it is the voyage of the *Van Imhoff* which we will follow.

At this time both the Dutch and British authorities in the area were under considerable strain. There was no way anyone could envision how they could avoid the fairly immediate invasion of Java, and if that happened it was only a matter of time until Australia would be under siege. The Japanese invasion fleet was literally on the horizon. The passengers of these three ships were enemies of the state, and their countrymen in Europe had already caused the Dutch people a good deal of pain. The instruction given to the captains of these three ships were not clear other than to get them out of the area.

Captain Hoeksema, commander of the KPM *Van Imhoff*, received his orders on 15 January 1942 while he was in Padang, the capital and largest city of Sumatra, Indonesia. The instructions simply told him to travel to Sibolga and pick up his load of evacuees. It is not clear if he knew that this group of evacuees was not the usual mix of men and women trying to get away from the island before the Japanese arrived.

The *Van Imhoff* was the second ship by that name. She had been built in 1914. She was old, tired, and ill prepared, with most of her safety equipment either missing or outdated. She was also unarmed. Captain Hoeksema had radioed the commander in chief of the situation, suggesting it was not safe for them to be sailing, but the return instructions were short and simple: "Embark them anyway." When he arrived as ordered, the captain discovered more than five hundred German and NSB internees waiting, as well as a detachment of 62 servicemen acting as a guard unit. There was also a load of 100 tons of barbed wire to be used to secure the evacuees.

Despite the captain's reluctance, the crew began to put together some bamboo rafts in order to process the loading of the men and equipment. As they came aboard, the evacuees were locked in a couple of the dirty holds. The vast majority of them were older business and professional persons who had lived in the Indies for a good many years. They were primarily passive, and more confused than disturbed by the events taking place. With them, however, were the much more aggressive seamen, who had been impounded off German ships. They were all thrown together.

The next morning, loaded and moving slowly toward its destination, the KPM *Van Imhoff* was sighted by Japanese planes that were in the area in advance of their invasion fleet. The planes dropped down onto the *Van Imhoff* and unleashed their bombs. The attack was well executed and the ship began to take on water. Captain Hoeksema moved quickly to save his crew and ordered that they launch the existing lifeboats. He then ordered both his crew and the military guards stationed on the ship to get on board the lifeboats. One of the lifeboats was not operating properly, so, feeling they did not need it, the crew left it dangling on its davits.

Realizing the danger they were in, the sergeant of the guard unit, operating on his own, released the German prisoners from the hold. He explained what was happening and told them to get off the ship and away from it as quickly as possible. He shouted out to those in the lifeboats to pick up as many as they could.

It was at this point that Captain Hoeksema intervened. He identified these men as prisoners, as the enemy, and said they would have to take their chances with the few bamboo rafts that had been taken aboard, and what few lifejackets they could find. He then ordered the lifeboats to row away from the ships, leaving the water full of struggling sailors. Following his orders, the crew of the ill-fated KPM *Van Imhoff* finally made it to shore, where they were taken care of. Most of the crew had escaped, but most of the Germans taken on board, an estimated 413, were lost at sea.

It took some time for the news of the event to get out, but when it did the German authorities identified it as an atrocity. They arrested the members of the KPM staff who were working in occupied Holland and sent them all to labor camps. In addition, they forced the government to pay four million guilders as compensation to the relatives of the men who had been drowned. For many years after the war, relatives and survivors made several attempts to get criminal proceedings started. Some of these efforts continued well into the new century, but it never came to pass.

The second story deals with the KPM *Rooseboom*, also the second ship with that name, built in 1926 by Koninklijke Paketvaart Maatschappij (KPM) of the Netherlands East Indies. She was a small 1,035-ton inter-island ship under the command of Captain M.C.A. Boon. She left the bombed-out port of Tanjung Proik on 22 February 1942 with the intention of making it to Bombay via Colombo. But before leaving the area she was ordered to stop at Emmahaven (Padang) to pick up a significant number of refugees, both military and civilian, who had managed to escape from Malaya.

These desperate people had managed to get out of Malaya and had crossed over the narrow Malacca Strait in small coasters, motorboats, canoes, or just about anything that would float. Under the most difficult of conditions they managed to make their way up the Indragiri River in Sumatra as far as possible by water, and then had worked their way across the mountains on the west coast. Having arrived in Emmahaven, they were looking at their last chance of rescue.

Among these evacuees were several highly placed military leaders. These included men who had been ordered out in the hope they would be able to fight again. Among them were Lieutenant Colonel Geoffrey Charles Douglas Woollcombe, Lieutenant Colonel George Archie Palmer, Major Angus MacDonald and Captain Mike Blackwood. The highest ranking of those aboard was Brigadier Archie Paris, commander of the Indian 12th Infantry Brigade. His brigade had played a major role in the protection of the Singapore garrison. But when it was obvious that Singapore was falling, General Arthur Percival tried to save some of the command staff who had proven successful in fighting the Japanese. Paris was one of those chosen and was heading back to train troops.

Having arrived without occurrence the KPM *Rooseboom* spent 27 February taking on board all she could carry. A significant number of those making their way on board were doing it for the second time, having already been through the experience of a sinking ship. Forever hopeful, they were making one more effort for safety. The ship having loaded up, she was moving smartly and well out into the Indian Ocean to the west of Sumatra. There she was spotted by a Japanese submarine riding below the surface. Without warning, at 1153 hours, the KPM *Rooseboom* was hit by a torpedo launched by the submarine I-59, under the command of Lieutenant Tamori Yoshimatsu. Yoshimatsu would later fight at the Battle of Midway.

The force of the explosion did considerable damage, holed the ship, and took out most of the lifeboats. Taking on water, it began to list almost at once, and within just a few hectic minutes she sank below the waters. During this time the crew was able to launch a single lifeboat.

With daybreak came the sight of nearly eighty people in the single lifeboat designed for less than half that number. Surrounding the lifeboat were another fifty or so floating nearby, clinging onto the gunwales, waiting for their turn to come aboard. Sergeant Gibson, the only survivor who was able and willing to tell the story of the events, said that at one time there were probably 135 survivors in all. Among this number of survivors were the injured Captain M.C.A. Boon and Sergeant Gibson, who had a badly broken collarbone and a shell fragment in his left side. In the boat as well were Brigadier Archie Paris, and the ship's engineer.

Unknown to those in the lifeboat, there were two other survivors. Both were native crewmen who had managed to pull away from the sinking ship, and were located nearly two weeks after the sinking. They were found by the KPM *Palopo*, still clinging to wreckage from the disintegrated *Rooseboom*. They were taken to Bombay but quickly disappeared from the public eye. Counting them, the loss at the time was believed to be just at 500 persons.

For the next three weeks, those tied to the single lifeboat struggled to survive. Over that time, and often in groups, they succumbed to their injuries or died from the heat or lack of water. A good many simply perished from sheer exhaustion. As they fought to stay alive, the lifeboat, with no one controlling it, drifted in an easterly direction, generally heading back toward the west coast of Sumatra. On board the lifeboat, conditions went from bad to worse, as the thirst began to drive men and women mad. There was even some suggestion of cannibalism, but the evidence is not clear. Gibson, in his book about the event, does not give a clear picture of how he survived in his wounded and weakened condition. The Dutch captain was apparently killed by the ship's engineer for some unnamed reason. Brigadier Paris finally died, first falling into a coma after a day of hallucinating.

At one point a group of renegade soldiers took control of the lifeboat and pushed some of the weaker persons overboard in an effort to make the rations go further. Supplies available consisted of forty-eight 12-once cans of bully beef, ten seven-pound cans of fried spiced rice, 48 cans of condensed milk, and six quarts of fresh water. Finally, the aggressive group was attacked themselves by another group, headed by Gibson. They were flung overboard and allowed to die.

Three and a half weeks after the sinking, the lifeboat washed up on Sipora Island. The small boat and its passengers had drifted for more than a thousand miles and had arrived at a point only a hundred miles from Padang, where their voyage had begun. On board there were four persons alive, but then only barely. These included Sergeant Walter Gibson, a young soldier from a Scottish regiment; Doris Lim a young Chinese woman; and two native crew members. There is some confusion here, as Gibson later described five persons alive when they arrived on the island.

At first the natives of Sipora Island managed to nurse them back to health. One of the natives remembered — and this may explain Gibson's calculations — that one of the native crewmen had died while trying to get the lifeboat ashore. The two others, once regaining some degree of strength, took to the jungle and disappeared. In time, the sergeant and the Chinese girl, Doris, were discovered by the Japanese. Doris Lim, it turned out, was considered to be a spy for the British, and was shot soon after she had been captured.

Sergeant Walter Gardiner Gibson, a soldier from the Argyll and Sutherland, appears to be the only survivor who can be located. The sergeant later wrote a book, *The Boat*, in which he described the events that took place during a 26-day drift on the sea.

The other ships in our story, the KPM *Plancius* and the KPM *Ophir*, made it through the war, and were eventually broken up for scrap at Hong Kong in 1959.

Note

1. The remains of the Asiatic Fleet joined with the British, Dutch and Australians to form the ABDA Command (American-British-Dutch-Australian), under the command of Vice Admiral Conrad Helfrich, to fight the delaying Battle of Java Sea.

Further Reading

Gibson, Walter. *The Boat*. Singapore: Monsoon Books, 2007.
Radike, Floyd. *Across the Dark Islands: The War in the Pacific*. Novato, CA: Presidio Press, 2004.
mercantilemarien.org/War-time-stories/kpm.
Smith, Colin. *Singapore Burning*. London: Penguin, 2005.

12. Preempting the Flying Tigers

The twenty-eight-year-old American should have known better. He had been flying in China for several years and had already seen many chances to test his skills, as well as those of his airplane. Perhaps he was just a little overconfident. A month earlier he had attacked three Japanese fighters near the city of Nanxiangzhen and shot down one piloted by Lieutenant Kidokoro of the Imperial Naval Attaché Air Unit. The other two had turned away from the fight. So when he found himself facing a formation of six planes — three bombers escorted by three Mitsubishi B1M two-seaters that had flown off the Japanese aircraft carrier IJN *Kaga*— he felt confident he could handle them. The Japanese planes were bombing a refugee train at Suzhou Station, and Robert Short decided to do battle.

Short was flying an American Boeing XP925 (an experimental modified 218) that was well armed for the time, and one with which he was very familiar. Turning toward the formation of Japanese planes and meeting them head-on, he was able to wound the commander of the bomber flight, Lieutenant Kotani, on the first pass. Then, circling back to renew his attack, he found himself the target of the two other escorts. Pulling up, he was hit by fire from the plane of Lieutenant Yoshir Sakemago, who was closing up from behind. The shots were accurate and the American's plane caught fire immediately. Short was unable to control the damaged ship and it went down in a blaze within seconds. The battle that took place over the village of Soochow, China, on 22 February 1932 had lasted for two minutes, about average for aerial combat at the time. As a result, Robert Short, a first lieutenant in the United States Army Reserves, had the questionable honor of being the first American man to be shot down in aerial combat by the Japanese in what would eventually become World War II.

The death of Robert Short, who was much loved by the Chinese people, was much more of a shock to them than to his companions who had already been fighting the Japanese for some time. This was not the first encounter, and there had been many near misses, but this was the first confirmed casualty. Short was buried in a steel coffin in a pleasant spot near Hongjiao Airport in Shanghai. There half a million people showed up for what was the "biggest funeral ever given to a white man in China." A memorial was established and a small statue located near the airport. Yet, while the Chinese grieved this American airman who fought in their name, the people in the United States were not even aware he and others like him were in China, much less that they were on the front line against Japanese pilots. Who was he and what was he doing there?

To answer the question we need to look at what was happening in China in the early 1930s. There, more than ten years before Claire Chennault's famous Flying Tigers appeared on the scene in China, both American pilots and American airplanes were involved in the Chinese air war. These adventurers first came in support of the Nationalist government in their effort against rebellious warlords, then flew in the conflict with the expanding Communist forces, and then fought in the mid-1930s against the Japanese in the Sino-Japanese War. Their presence finally lasted into the opening days of World War II.

In the beginning these aerial adventurers were primarily salesmen. By 1930 China was breaking into its own air age, both in the realization of how much the airplane could contribute to the ability to govern such a large nation, and in the awareness that the Japanese were presenting an ever-enlarging threat. There were no doubts about the Japanese air intentions. Because the market was there, and the money to purchase planes was available, China became an area of fierce competition for those in the business of selling airplanes. Salesmen came from just about every country that manufactured a plane. Among those early salespersons was a restless young man named Jimmy Doolittle, who went to China to sell fighters. He had resigned from the Army Air Corps in early 1930 and earned the reputation as a top acrobatic pilot and aeronautical engineer. His demonstrations of the Curtiss Hawk fighter, including the supposedly impossible outside loop, quickly made him a top salesman. At the time the most popular fighter in use by the Chinese was the Italian Fiat C-R-32, a fast and sturdy ship, but one that was quickly becoming obsolete. Through the efforts of Doolittle and others from Curtis Hawk, this particular American plane, which was particularly well constructed and daringly demonstrated, provided serious competition and their number grew. Shortly it became the primary fighter available.

The Chinese had a small and widely varied group of planes including a Junkers K-47, a two-seater monoplane fighter made by Germany with a BMW engine and a speed of 300 kmh; a Blackburn F.2 Lincock monoplane flying boat made by Great Britain; and the Waco 240A powered by Wright Whirlwind, made in the United States. But these were hardly sufficient, and the Chinese were seeking uniformity of service. As many as twenty separate air forces operated in China in the period from 1920 to 1937, most of which did not survive.

But the Chinese problem was not limited to the purchase of airplanes, no matter how good they were. As the war clouds gathered, the Nationalist government had to face the hard fact that, in 1931, there were only five Chinese pilots competent to fly most types of aircraft. In addition they had another twenty who were still in training, but this was not nearly enough. What they needed was pilots and they needed them at once. They also needed men who could train the Chinese for the future. To solve the first problem they entertained the idea of mercenaries, and many men would respond to the opportunity. For the second aspect of their plan they needed advisors and instructors.

The mercenaries came. It is difficult to document just who they were and how many were involved. After all, this was a totally clandestine affair and few or no records were kept — but there is considerable second-hand evidence that as early as 1931, pilots from the United States, Great Britain, France, Italy, Russia, and even some from Germany, were flying combat missions for the Chinese government. Those from Russia and Italy were officially sanctioned by their governments, but most of the pilots "worked" for Chinese companies. The majority were volunteers and among them were a good many of those men who had come to China earlier to demonstrate, and hopefully sell, their own brand of fighters.

Robert Short was one of the latter. Born in 1904 in Tacoma, Washington, he had been approached by an agent to travel to China in order to train pilots. He had been the manager of a local airport but had quickly learned he was not well suited for administrative work. Short had received his flight training from the Army and graduated from March Field in the class of 1928 as a second lieutenant in the Army Reserves. He worked for a while flying the mail. Broke and with little opportunity on the horizon, he accepted the offer and went to China presumably with an airline job. He was hired by L.E. Gal and Company to demonstrate the Boeing 218 fighter to the Chinese government. While it was a civilian contract, it is hard to believe that this was done without the full knowledge of Boeing Aircraft, and most likely even the American War Department.

There were American pilots flying in 1931 when two Boeing bombers were used against rebellious warlords who were challenging any effort at the creation of a unified government. In January 1932 American pilots took part in what history has chosen to call the Shanghai incident. In reaction to a Chinese boycott of Japanese goods, the Japanese attacked Shanghai. It was an "incident" that led to two months of hot combat. During this time the Chinese Air Force fared badly despite the fact that they had on hand nearly 200 American, British, French, Russian and Italian planes and dozens of highly qualified foreign pilots. The organization and execution of the air raid on Shanghai was so slack that they even mistakenly hit an American warship, the USS *Augusta*, that was in the harbor.

The second phase of the Chinese plan was to begin the serious training of its own pilots. To do this the Nationalists turned to the United States. On 8 July 1932, Major John H. Jouett of the United States Army Air Corps arrived in China as the head of an American training mission. Other sources list him as Colonel, and as a retired army officer. His cover story was that he had been released from the Air Corps because of budget cuts and had taken a job in China. Accompanying him were a group of handpicked instructors and mechanics who arrived in Shanghai on the *President Hoover* along with 15 Fleet Trainers.

By the end of that month what was known as the Jouett Mission had built and was running the Central Aviation School at Chiao Airfield at Hangchow, about 100 miles down the coast from Shanghai. The Americans who came with the mission were allowed to keep their reserve status and rank. There is even evidence that they were allowed to keep their place on promotion lists. But they were most definitely told to keep quite about their association with the Chinese. At the height of the mission there were about thirty American pilots on call, along with mechanics, riggers, and engineers. The instruction at the school was in English and provided the students nearly 100 hours a month of flight training. The plan was to be able to provide a hundred qualified graduates and instructors a year. Despite the constant difficulties of poor equipment, untrained handlers, and the bad physical conditions, the mission proved to be highly successful.

The Chinese government felt the school had fulfilled its mission by 1935, and so the contract was not renewed. They had turned out numerous pilots who could handle most of the planes that were available, and some were even involved in instructing other pilots. There were political as well as economic reasons behind the non-renewal, however; and the underlying reason, generally considered to be decisive, was that the United States had refused to participate in the attack on the dissident 19th private army during the Fujian Rebellion in late 1933.

This may have been the official position of the United States but it hardly expressed the view of those more immediately involved. During this early period some of the pilots at the school, as well as many of the covey of flying salesmen, were called upon to do "confidential assignments," both for the Chinese military and for some of the leaders of the Nationalist movement. The pilots did so at some risk. The isolationist sentiment in the United States was so high at this point that if any of the pilots had been caught engaged in acts of war, it was understood that they would lose their American citizenship. Later, as the conflict continued, the Neutrality Act was less stringently enforced, and finally, in April 1941, President Franklin D. Roosevelt issued an executive order permitting military pilots to fly and fight abroad for up to one year.

Most of these pilots and mechanics worked for a Chinese company of sorts. Funds for the payment of pilots and ground crews obviously could not come from the United States government, or politically from Chinese funds, so instead they were paid by the Central Aircraft Manufacturing Corporation (CAMCO), formed for that purpose. The funds used for payment and the purchase of needed equipment came from the CAMCO by way of grants from the Chinese and the Soviet governments.

As the Japanese became increasingly aggressive, the Nationalist government started to purchase more planes. In 1932 alone they bought 72 of the Douglas O-2MC, 20 Vought V92C Corsairs, and 24 Heinkel HE 66Ch biplane dive bombers. Perhaps more aware of their immediate concerns than the long-range needs, they had not purchased as well as they might. What they bought were excellent planes suited for close support of infantry and punitive raids on the underdefended villages held by warlords, but the quality that made them so useful in ground operations left the two-seaters poorly able to defend themselves against other fighters. Nevertheless, by late 1934 the Chinese had nearly 200 warplanes.

After the school closed, the Nationalists, still aware that they were not competitive against the Japanese, held a fund drive to celebrate the birthday of Chiang Kai-shek. They raised a million dollars that was to be used to purchase additional planes. Late in that year the Chinese bought ten Boeing P25A fighters, known as pea shooters, that were finally based in Nanking. At the time they were flown by a mixture of Chinese pilots and American mercenaries. The plan for their use was not comprehensive, and though they were originally successful, the lack of parts and proper maintenance soon put them out of action.

On 7 July 1937 the Sino-Japanese war began in earnest, and in the following month a small group of American P-26s shot down six Japanese bombers that were attacking Nanking. But this was no longer a series of raids, and in immediate retaliation, mercenaries, mostly from the United States, but also one or two from France and Australia, conducted air attacks. The Japanese aggression also led several Soviet airmen to come into China, equipped with their 1-15 fighter biplanes and Polikarpov 1-16 monoplanes. The long-range bombers available to the Chinese were 3e Tupolev SB-2as flown by Russians. Among the Americans were a variety of veterans flying a vast array of planes. They tended to be led by World War I veteran Vincent Schmidt, and they flew Vultee V-11s, Northrop 2E light bombers, a couple of Martin 139 medium bombers, an armed Bellanea 29-90 racing plane, and a pair of Dewoitine D-510 fighters.

It was into this world of confusion that Claire L. Chennault appeared. Chennault was released from the United States Army Air Corps on 30 April 1937. A brilliant air combat tactician, he had been grounded because of damaged hearing, as well as a long list of grievances enumerated by his superiors. Despite his reputation as an outstanding acrobatic pilot, he had ruffled so many feathers that he ended up assigned to the command of the Air Corps exhibition team. Admittedly he was not an easy man to get along with, but there was no doubt he was a man of considerable ability. Through friends — very probably General Douglas MacArthur — he received an invitation to become the aviation advisor to the Kuomintang (Nationalists). Madame Chiang took an immediate liking to him, and asked him to go to Kunming, the capital of Yunnan Province in western China, where he could develop a modern and competitive Chinese Air Force, which was to be modeled on the American plan. This was to be the beginning of the Flying Tigers, but it would be some time before they came into play.

Like so much of what was going on in China at the time, the status of the man and his mission is not really clear even today. He was a retired army captain, a civilian by all accounts, with no legal status as a belligerent. His job was listed as the civilian advisor (and in this role the *de facto* Air Chief of Staff) to the Chinese Secretary of the Commission for Aeronautical Affairs, who, in this case, turned out to be Madame Chiang. He was, however, listed as an employee of, and paid by, the Central Bank of China. His passport listed his occupation as a farmer.

Whatever his status, he got started immediately. He was behind the organization of the 14th Volunteer Bombardment Group, called by some the International Air Squadron. There were never, at one time, more than a dozen pilots involved, even considering a Frenchman who showed up once in awhile. The hard core men in the outfit, all handpicked by Chennault, were James W.M. Allison, a veteran of the Spanish Civil War who, after a stint with the American volunteers, became the chief pilot and operating manager for the Chinese National Air Corporation; William C. "Billy" Mac-Donald, a chubby but totally likeable young flyer; John "Luke" Williamson, redheaded and freckle-faced, one of the more effective pilots, who had been a sergeant in the regular army but was granted temporary rank as a lieutenant in the Army Air Corps Reserves. When his request for a permanent commission was denied, the redheaded man quit and joined the Jouett mission in China. Also present were George Weigle, and World War I veteran Vincent Schmidt, who rather naturally took on the role of leader. These men were all connected, in some way, to the aircraft industry.

There were as well other successful pilots who served at one time or another. Among these was Allen "Pat" Patterson, a Canadian-born adventurer who fit the stereotype of the dashing young pilot: tall, ash blond, blue-eyed and slender. He was a World War I aviator who had returned to become a barnstormer, to operate an airfield in Gardena, California, and to be a flyer in Howard Hughes's *Hell's Angels*. He became the VP of the General Airplane Company in New York, but when wiped out by the depression, took a job from Carl Knamacher, a Hudson car dealer in Shanghai, to sell American airplanes. He eventually sold more than 200 Fleet Trainers. A bold and active flyer, he held Chinese Flying License #2. He was in Nanking with the American group when, in December 1937, the Japanese attacked. Fleeing to the relative safety of the American gunboat *Panay*, he was on the fantail when she was struck by Japanese bombs. He was knocked into the water but managed to climb onto a sampan still tethered to the *Panay*. He was reported dead but got away unhurt.

Others who made their mark were Christopher Mathewson, Jr., who was the son of the National Hall of Fame baseball player of the same name. He lost his leg in a crash, and then his life when he continued flying with an artificial leg. Another was Harry T. Rowland, who had served with the 9th Bomb Squadron in World War I, and later would serve as Air Advisor to Madame Chiang. He would be killed in Hangzhou.

Equally involved in both sanctioned and clandestine raids were Thomas Taylor and Cornelius Burmood, who fell under the influence of Madame Chiang, and became embroiled in the fighting despite some effort to avoid it.

Others who flew at one time or another would include Art Chen, E.D. Dorsey, Cecil Folmar, Franklyn Gay, Harvey Greenlaw, L. Roy Holbrook,

W.C. Kent, M.R. Knight, John May, George Reinburg, Ronald Sansbury, John Schweitzer, Ellis Shannon, Sterling Tatum, and Lyman Woelpel.

The Japanese were well aware of the role being played by American pilots, and while there was not a lot they could do about it, they managed to let their feelings be known. One such case was Elwyn Herbert Gibbon, a 27-year-old from Everett, Washington, who had served with the air forces between 1937 and 1938. At the end of his service he decided to return to the United States and booked passage on the *Empress of Asia*, heading for Vancouver. When the ship reached Yokohama on 22 April 1938 he was removed from the ship by Japanese authorities. The ship, with his wife aboard, sailed without him. He was eventually let go after intense questioning, and returned home on the *President Taft* a month later. He was killed 19 August 1942 while test flying a Vultee Banguar P-66 to be used by the Chinese Air Force.

When the 14th Volunteer Group was organized it was stationed at Hankow and shared the area with two Soviet contingents. The Soviets flew twin-engine Tupolev SB-2 bombers and Polikarpov 1-15 biplanes as well as some 1-16 monoplanes. The group's first experience did not go well. Shells from the Japanese warships on the Whangpoo River began to rain down on Shanghai, killing hundreds, possibly thousands, of civilians. The barrage was prior to landing troops and designed to punish the inhabitants. At Madame Chiang's request, Chennault organized a bomber strike against the naval vessels, but it turned out to be a complete failure. Disorganized volunteers, poorly trained Chinese pilots, and varied equipment meant that many of the bombs fell off target and killed additional civilians.

What happened after a pilot was shot down was often as dangerous as air combat, so every effort was made to be sure the Chinese knew what the foreigners were up to, and to take care of them if they were shot down. The written promise to help downed airmen was provided on a piece of cloth, called *hu chau* (later called Blood Chits), sewn onto the leather jackets the airmen wore, which came to be identified by others as the Flying Tiger's jacket.

The life of the 14th Volunteer Group was a hectic one, with long hours, many missions, and little or no relief. On 27 February 1938, Vultee and Northrop bombers attacked the Japanese troops in the vicinity of Loyang on the Yellow River, but this was to be one of the last of the official missions. For, despite its success, the 14th was only in formal existence for a little over five months. It was disbanded 22 March 1938. The reason was harsh indeed. Through the efforts of William Pawley, the 14th received thirty single-engine Vultee bombers. Carrying a three-man crew, and with a range of 2,000 miles, the Vultee could deliver a heavy bomb load. Early in March, however, in preparation for a mission scheduled late in the day, the planes had been lined up on the airfield. In the mid-afternoon, Japanese bombers, somehow forewarned, unloaded on the planes, destroying them all.

The disbanding, however, did not mean the end of American pilots serving in China. On 29 April 1938, they participated with Soviet pilots who drew the Japanese into a trap where, during a tremendous battle later called the "fur ball," sixty Chinese fighters took on 12 Japanese bombers and 25 fighters. In the end eight enemy bombers and thirteen fighters had been destroyed with a loss of only of their own planes.

Despite the early Chinese success, the Japanese were not going away. In 1939 they changed tactics somewhat and decided to break Chinese resistance by bombing every population center in Free China. During this time the Chinese Air Force was at its lowest rate and the Japanese, flying Mitsubishi B2Ms off their carriers *Kaga* and *Ryuujo*, appeared to be unopposed. What the Chinese needed was a more formal structure, more and better equipment, and more pilots. In the fall of 1940 Generalissimo Chiang Kai-shek requested that Chennault go to the United States for the sole purpose of soliciting American planes and American pilots to provide some defense.

The story from this point on is well known. The first contingent of pilots for the new volunteer group left San Francisco on 10 July 1941 aboard the Dutch ship *Jaetensfontain* and the group was formally established in September. The Flying Tigers, as they are better known, operated until the 4th of July, 1942, when they were officially disbanded. Each of the flyers was offered a commission in the U.S. Army Air Corps. Some accepted the offer. Others returned to the ranks of the service to fight in other theaters. Eighteen accepted offers to fly for the China National Aviation Corporation. The aircraft remained in China with the new China Air Task Force. In March of 1943 the Chinese Air Force became the 14th U.S. Air Force, which it remained throughout the rest of World War II. The controversial General Claire Chennault finished his tour in China as the commanding general of the unit.

Even before the Flying Tigers played their significant role, other Americans as far back as 1930 were helping the Kuomintang maintain control of much of its contested countryside. These areas were later to provide the bases needed for major Allied campaigns against the Japanese. Without those early and often obscure men using their skills flying a series of planes, some good and some bad, and willing to sacrifice for the job they had taken on, the chances are good that there would have been no heroic story of the airborne supply line over the hump, and the history of the 14th Air Force would have been much less exciting and successful.

Further Reading

Ford, Daniel. *Flying Tigers: Claire Chennault and His American Volunteers, 1941–1942.* New York: HarperCollins, 2007.

Klinkowitz, Jerome. *With the Tigers Over China 1941–1942.* Lexington: University Press of Kentucky, 1999.

Schultz, Duane. *The Maverick of War: Chennault and the Flying Tigers.* New York: St. Martin's Press, 1987.

Van Patten, Robert E. "Before the Flying Tigers." *Air Force Magazine*, June 1999.

13. Winston's Special

Ensign Franklin Roosevelt, Jr., was the officer of the deck (OOD) standing the forenoon watch on the USS *Maryant* on 7 December 1941, when word came to the Convoy William Sail that the Imperial Japanese had bombed American naval forces at Pearl Harbor. It was shocking news, but surely it was not all that unexpected. Besides, contrary to American law, Ensign Franklin D. Roosevelt, Jr., the convoy, and the destroyer *Maryant* (DD 402), under the command of Lieutenant Commander E.A. Taylor, were already involved in an act of war. What was going on?

The year 1941 was one of the most dangerous years in history. The world seemed to be coming apart. War had broken out in China in 1937 and in Europe in 1939, and now the scope of the wars was threatening to go worldwide. The United States, still deeply imbedded in the isolationism that emerged from World War I, was holding on to the unrealistic dream that they could stay out of the war. Many believed, at times way beyond reason, that by some miracle, the vast oceans that separated them from Europe and Japan would keep them safe. Among those who knew better was the America's president, Franklin D. Roosevelt, who knew that war was coming, but who also knew that his political options were severely limited.

Great Britain, already deeply involved in the war with Germany, was just barely hanging on. The loss of men, supplies, and equipment was becoming harder to sustain. The extent of her empire made Great Britain vulnerable just about everywhere and the military needs of men and equipment were quickly surpassing her ability to provide them. Japan stood on the brink of their Far East holdings, rattling her saber and predicting the future of her sphere of influence. Since she was stretched as thin as she was, the demands of yet another front for Great Britain loomed like a disaster on her horizon. She could not survive without help.

Meeting on board the HMS *Prince of Wales* at Placement Bay, Newfoundland, in August 1941, British Prime Minister Winston Churchill and Franklin D. Roosevelt had come together to discuss the disintegrating situation. In that brief time they found that they could be friends and colleagues. Both agreed on the need for cooperation between the two countries, and that eventually the American people would support their British cousins. It was also very clear that the American president's hands were tied, and that the British were running out of time.

The outcome of these meetings — pledges from the two nations to defend freedom and establish an international organization to promote peace — was not enough for the prime minister. He needed more. Apparently he got it, for he would tell the Parliament that America was behind them. At first it appeared to be political posturing, but then all of it became real, for on 1 September 1941, Winston Churchill sent a desperate and most secret message to President Roosevelt asking for immediate assistance. In this message he requested that United States Navy troopships, manned by U.S. naval personnel and escorted by U.S. fighting ships, be made available to transport British troops in an effort to reinforce the Empire's troops in the Middle East. Both Churchill and Roosevelt knew what this unprecedented request, if acted upon, would mean.

Yet within five days, and despite the limitations of the American Neutrality Act, President Roosevelt sent a response to the British wartime leader that assured him of a willingness to provide him what was needed. Six vessels capable of carrying 20,000 troops and their equipment, and escorted by ships of the U.S. Navy, would be made available. This involvement was scheduled to take place three months before the American entry into World War II, and within the period in which the Neutrality Act was still in force. It was not made clear just what would happen if one of the American ships were sunk while on this mission.

On 26 September 1941 the Chief of Naval Operations issued a top-secret document identified as Operation Plan 14.3-A, which ordered Troopship Divisions 17 and 19 to prepare for a six-month operation. They were told to load to capacity with food, ammunition, medical supplies, fuel and water and to prepare for a contingent of 20,000 men. The anticipated duration of the trip was 90 days. Once prepared, the divisions were to arrive at Halifax, Nova Scotia, on or about 6 November 1941. Halifax, it was determined, had the harbor necessary for such an event and, perhaps far more important at the time, was outside the view of most inquisitive Americans.

Then, on 20 October 1941, the captains of eighteen United States Naval warships and military transports received a six-page, single-spaced message stamped Secret. The message, from Admiral H.R. Stark, Chief of Naval Operations, read as follows:

> Pursuant to a revised agreement with the British government, Task Force 14 will proceed on or about 3 November 1941 from the United States for the Middle East via Halifax, Trinidad, and Capetown, South Africa and return to the United States. From Halifax to the Middle East, Task Force 14, will transport one division of British troops consisting of approximately 20,000 men.[1]

The role of the ships was to deliver men and equipment of the British 18th Division from Halifax to Capetown and Bombay. The trip was later extended, with the final destination as Singapore. This assignment for Task Force 14, the least known of the U.S. activities, was anything but a minor movement. Even on the eve of war a revision to the Neutrality Act, allowing the arming of U.S. merchant ships, barely passed Congress, but it has to be understood that neither the original act nor the revision allowed the peacetime transport of troops of a belligerent nation in U.S. ships. Why did the U.S. send her three most important passenger ships into harm's way a month before the entry into World War II?

The highly secret message from the Chief of Naval Operations had to be kept among those with a "need to know." Any discussion of the event, even afterwards, was limited. This would not be the last time that Roosevelt would circumvent the Neutrality Act, but it was certainly the most blatant.

In accordance with their orders the assigned ships of Task Force 14 began to arrive at Halifax on the afternoon of 5 November, and were anchored far out in the harbor. Several of the arrivals had been delayed by fog, and in one case there had been a near collision. Fresh water and fuel were provided and a segment of the crews were allowed liberty. The ships that made up the convoy had been designated as William Sail 12X and were under the command of the highly experienced Captain Donald B. Beary, the captain of the troopship *Mount Vernon* sailing out of Boston.

Captain Beary was chosen particularly for this assignment. An Academy graduate, he held the Navy Cross for service during World War I, and had become an expert in the formation and escorting of convoys. Rising to the rank of vice admiral, he would later devise the system which enabled fast carrier task forces to remain on station while refueling and replenishing.

Also on the *Mount Vernon* was Henry Manning, who had been the ship's captain when she was the SS *Washington*, and who was serving as the ship's navigator. Manning was a world-renowned mariner and navigator and had been Amelia Earhart's navigator prior to her final flight.

The other transport ships that made up the convoy were the *Wakefield* from New York; the *West Point, Orizaba* and *Joseph T. Dickman* from Norfolk, Virginia; and the *Leonard Wood* from Newport, Rhode Island.

The cost of the venture became a key for defending it. Who was to pay for the effort? As it turned out, the funds for water and meals would come from the money assigned to the lend-lease program which Congress had authorized, though not with this in mind. The cost of the transit was covered by listing the troops as "supernumeraries," suggesting it was but one more of the joint exercises run by the British and Americans. The ships were all ex-passenger ships that had earlier been requisitioned by the military in anticipation of their need sooner or later. The ships were as follows:

The *Mount Vernon* (AP 22), formerly the SS *Washington*, still wore some of the red, white, and blue livery of the United States Line. She was commanded by Captain D.B. Beary, who would serve as the convoy commander.

The USS *Wakefield* (AP 21), which was a twin to the *Mount Vernon*, was launched 5 December 1931 as the SS *Manhattan*, a passenger liner that had been sponsored by Edith Kermit Roosevelt, widow of the former president Theodore Roosevelt. It had made the New York to Hamburg run as "the fastest cabin ship in the world," until the outbreak of World War II. Requisitioned by the military, she was converted to a troop transport and, on 15 June 1941, was under the command of Commander W.K. Seammel (USCG).

The *West Point* (AP 23) was launched with great fanfare on 31 August 1939, a crowd of 30,000 in attendance, and was commissioned by Eleanor Roosevelt as the SS *America*. She was built with what was called "defense factor," which meant that she could easily be converted for military use. She was intended for the Atlantic trade and had just retuned from a pleasure cruise when, in June 1941, she was requisitioned by the Navy and converted to a troopship. Commander F.H. Kelley was in command. Somewhere along the line the *West Point* adopted the nickname "the Grey Ghost." Interestingly, for some time before she was converted, the *America* housed two German spies, Franz Joseph Stigler and Edwin Wilhelm Siegler, in her crew. They were reporting on ship movement and on details of the Panama Canal.

Acquired by the military on 11 April 1918, the year-old *Orizaba* (AP 24) had been commissioned 27 May 1918. She was decommissioned in 1919 and returned to the Ward Line, chartered to address the slow rate of returning American citizens trying to flee Europe. Finally purchased by the Army on 27 February 1941, she was then transferred to the Navy on 4 June. She was finally commissioned the *Orizaba* on 15 June 1941. While assigned to the convoy she was commanded by Captain C. Gulbranson.

The *Joseph T. Dickman* was built in 1921 for the transatlantic trade. She had been named *President Pierce* and in August 1922 renamed *President Roosevelt*. Taken over by the War Department in October 1940, she was renamed *Joseph T. Dickman* and converted to a troopship under Commander C.W. Harwood (USCG). She was manned by the Coast Guard.

The sixth troop ship was the *Leonard Wood* (AP 25), the former *Nutmeg State* and *Western World*. She had been built in 1922 by Bethlehem Shipbuilding. She was purchased by the War Department in 1939 and renamed for the World War I general. Acquired by the Coast Guard, she was under the command of Commander H.G. Bradbury.

Most of the British troops had arrived at Halifax by 5 November, and on 8 November the advanced party of the British began to board the American ships. There had been several close calls coming into the fog-shrouded channel, but they were all accounted for by 0739 hours on 8 November. Most of the men were Territorial troops, much like the American National Guard, and they had only arrived at Halifax a few days earlier. The troops had sailed on six ships, including the liner *Orcades*, which were escorted by HMS *Exeter* and HMS *Dorsetshire*. American involvement in the process came early, for at about halfway across the Atlantic the escorts were relieved by American warships that took the troops into Halifax. Having just completed a ten-day passage, the troops welcomed the short time it took to move from one ship to the other; they were in for a much longer cruise this time.

At this point the American rules took over and the British troops were to conform to the U.S. Navy ship regulations, which meant that there would be no liquor provided or permitted. The loading took the better part of the day and the next. Then on 10 November tugs began to move the loaded transports away from the pier and within half an hour they were in formation. The convoy was escorted out of the harbor by the HMS *Annapolis*. A little after noon the U.S. escorts arrived and the *Annapolis* was detached.

As the dawn broke on the following day, the USS *Winslow*, an American destroyer, joined the group. She had been scheduled but held up by some damage sustained in an earlier storm. As the convoy headed out the lead was taken by the USS *Ranger*, the aircraft carrier that was to perform this task during much of the trip. Her job was twofold: to serve as the eyes and ears of the convoy, and to be sure that it maneuvered in such a way as to avoid approaching ships of other nations. They did not wish to be seen. In fulfillment of these tasks she launched aircraft during the daylight. On some days other seaplanes would be provided to help with the task. The naval escort was available if needed, and the transports themselves were equipped with old World War I surface guns, three- and five-inch, as well as some twenty-three dual purpose weapons. These were single-action weapons, however, manually loaded and adjusted.

They sailed down the east coast of the United States and on the 12th entered the Gulf Stream. Each day got warmer and it was increasingly uncomfortable in the spaces where the troops were packed in with their equipment. The ships had been built originally for the Atlantic trade and were not as well ventilated as was necessary for warmer regions. The trip started out on an even keel with little happening to break the monotony of the sailing day. On the 12th, however, the cruiser USS *Vincennes* pulled out of the convoy and headed further out to sea in search of calmer water in order for her surgeons to perform an appendectomy.

The following day was clear and quiet and troops were allowed on deck, 3200 at a time, for much-needed exercise. In the morning there was usually fog, and it was generally greeted with appreciation since it hid their movements. However, early on, the *Orizaba* and the *Dickman* nearly collided in the fog and at 0505 on the 14th the destroyers *Maryant* and *Rowan* collided harshly enough that the *Maryant* began taking on water. Both vessels were told to head for San Juan for repairs. It was not a good start.

For part of the next few days patrol planes from Patrol Squadron 31 at Bortinquen Field, Puerto Rico, provided anti-submarine surveillance, and were then replaced by the cruiser's seaplanes. As the convoy approached Trinidad, land-based planes were able to provide coverage. On the 17th the coast of Venezuela was sighted and the ships entered harbor and anchored. Once the convoy was docked, the British and American authorities quickly provided fuel and water and whatever else was needed. Some liberty was granted to a few of the naval ratings and even a few of the troops were allowed ashore. While the ships were supplying, the USS *Cimarron*, a fleet oiler, joined the group, and the destroyers *Maryant* and *Rowan* returned after quick repairs.

The stop was brief and by 1400 hours on the 19th they were at sea again. It was becoming obvious that the *Leonard Wood* was having trouble keeping up the necessary fifteen knots, due to a lack of draft needed to supply her boilers. Because of this her speed was limited to 12–14 knots, and with the zigzag patterns required during the day, that speed was not enough to keep up. Rather than hold up the rest of the convoy she was dispatched to go on alone, accompanied by the destroyer USS *Moffett*, commanded by P.R. Heinean.

Three of the transports had been given surface guns but they were old, manually loaded and never combat tested. While their crews were well trained it remained the case that evasive action was their best defense. The *Ranger* launched aircraft to provide continuous cover for ASW during the daylight hours, launching fresh aircraft on two-hour intervals. The cruisers also put their seaplanes into the air at the hint of any approaching danger. The bombers, which were with the carriers, were loaded with a new depth charge bomb for use against submarines.

Once again the convoy fell into the routine. On the 19th, scout planes reported an unidentified warship some 45 miles distant, and they watched it for awhile but it showed no interest in the convoy. Float mines were discovered the same day, requiring some alteration of course, and the USS *Dickman* suffered a brief problem with its steering. On the *Dickman*, as well, the captain reported the death of a young seaman who had hanged himself for undisclosed reasons. The following day the American commander proclaimed Thanksgiving and all aboard were served turkey and trimmings, much to the delight of the British on board. With the calm seas available the *Cimarron* began fueling the first of the five destroyers. The following day the *Maryant* picked up underwater contacts and the formation took evasive action, but nothing more came of it. On the 24th, most of the ships took the time to provide the traditional "crossing the line" ceremonies, and by the end of the day most were granted the rank of "Trusty Shellbacks." During the initiation ceremony, which often was quite an ordeal, there were a few minor injuries. Later that day the *Maryant* picked up an underwater contact and the convoy was sent into evasive action. The escorts watched for some time but could not discover the source of the ping that had been recorded.

The *Leonard Wood* returned to the fold on the 27th, along with her escort *Moffet*, after they had rigged a bigger blower. Just before noon on that day a seaman on the *Mount Vernon* jumped overboard and was not found. Edward Hemley had been in trouble over a breach of naval regulations. Around supper that evening the *Wainwright* reported a submarine contact but after a careful search nothing was found. The following day the *Ranger* reported the loss of an aircraft that had not returned to the ship and the *Vincennes* reported sighting a periscope, but no contact. Later on that day, Chief Water Tender Anthony F. Rudolph died of heatstroke, and the *Wakefield* reported the death of J.J. Wood, who died for unreported reasons while in sickbay.

December came quietly with the ships reporting an occasional danger requiring brief course changes, but no attacks or damage resulted. On the

3rd two planes from the escort *Quincy* went down in the fog, but the pilots were recovered. The calm seas were not to last, however, and on the 5th visibility begin to diminish. During the night the winds rose and the convoy was hit with the first effects of a southeastern gale. On 6–7 December they suffered the ravages of another of nature's outbursts. All the ships lost life rafts and sustained damage to their superstructures. There were some injuries among sailors on the destroyers, which were the most susceptible to the storm. The sea logged at 28 to 33 knots and two destroyers reported they had experienced a most dangerous roll of 63 degrees. The *Mount Vernon* temporarily lost steering and was out of formation for twenty minutes, but soon caught up.

Shortly before their arrival at Capetown the convoy received the news of the Japanese attack on Pearl Harbor. America was now in the war. The convoy arrived at Capetown without further incident, but only stayed briefly and was away again on 11 December. But everything had changed. In effect, Convoy William Sail ceased to exist, but the troops on board were more badly needed than ever before. Now they were needed in Singapore, and it was the responsibility of the convoy leaders to get them there. As a result of this new development what had been a single convoy, primarily under British control, now became two. One segment was to continue to Bombay and the other to head for Singapore.

The vessels that were to continue on to Bombay were identified as Task Force 14.2. They were escorted by the cruiser HMS *Dorsetshire* and headed at normal speeds toward that destination. The *Dorsetshire* was already famous for having delivered the final blow to the German super-battleship *Bismarck*. At 0700 hours on the 27th, orders arrived that the *West Point* and *Wakefield* were to increase speed to 20 knots and to arrive at Bombay at 1600. Later in the day the *Wakefield* moored at Ballard Pier and started discharging troops and equipment. The *West Point*, *Leonard Wood* and *Dickman* anchored in the harbor and were unloaded. By the 29th all the troops and equipment were ashore and they were ready to leave when they received orders from the British Admiralty to delay. On 6 January the *Orizaba* joined the Navy troopships in Bombay and unloaded the troops aboard. Word was that the three smaller transports would be returned to the U.S. via Capetown. They were provided with no escorts. But this was not to be the case.

When the word was received of the desperate conditions in Malaya, plans were changed. The *West Point* and *Wakefield* were loaded with the available troops and on the 29th these ships set sail for Singapore with Captain Kelley as commodore. Besides the two American transports, three other troopships, the *Duchess of Bedford*, *Empress of India*, and *Empire State*, joined the armada. The HMS *Caledon* and *Glasgow* were assigned as escorts.

The second half of Convoy William Sail joined with a group identified as DM1. The *Mount Vernon* and *Emerald* met up with Convoy DM1 on 30 December. At this point the convoy consisted of the merchant ships *Aurangi*, *Narkunda*, *Sussex* (carrying 51 fighter planes dismantled) and the *Abbekirk*. At 1000 hours on 4 January the *Mount Vernon* along with DM1 left for Sundra Straits, escorted by the HMS *Emerald*, *Exeter,* and *Juma*. On the 9th, as they neared the shoal waters of the Sundra Straits, they were joined by the HMS *Durban* and the Dutch battle cruiser *DeRuyter*.

On the following day, with Captain Beary now in command of DM1, mine sweeping was ordered and the course altered and speed adjusted several times to avoid being sighted. At 1156, as the convoy reached deep water, it was joined by HMS *Jupiter*, the *Encounter*, the Australian destroyer *Vampire*, and the HMS *H-10*, *G-85*, and *I-68*. The convoy was further reinforced on the 11th by the arrival of the HNMS *Van Tromp* and three other unnamed Dutch destroyers. As a body they negotiated the Karimata Straits and passed into the South China Sea. As they moved steadily toward their destination, events on land were worsening, as more than 85,000 British, Australian, and Indian troops were being driven down the last narrow causeway leading to Singapore.

As the convoy moved forward it came under the command of the ABDA. At 0404 they were ordered into single file and their air defenses set at the highest priority as Japanese planes were flying over Singapore at the time. Avoiding attack from the air, they maneuvered through the night, and on Tuesday the 13th, Dutch minesweepers cleared the way, allowing them to enter the harbor. They arrived through the front door, under the silent and useless 15-inch and 9.2-inch naval guns of Fort Connaught.

The *Mount Vernon* moored at 1315 and the 53rd were sent ashore. The troops had been at sea a long time, none had combat experience, few had been trained in jungle fighting, and they arrived without the land transport or artillery that was still on vessels coming from Bombay. When unloading was complete, the *Mount Vernon* took on 363,970 gallons of bunker oil and 350 tons of fresh water and made preparations to leave. She was delayed, however, by yet another high-flying Japanese bomber attack. Surviving the attack, she boarded a few lucky refugees and officials, and by 1511 hours cleared the Changi buoy and set out at high speed for a run for the Sundra Strait. The HMS *Juma* and *Jupiter* followed as escorts. She was in the Indian Ocean by 0800 hours on 17 January 1942. John H. Horrigan, who was a sailor on board the *Mount Vernon*, recalled leaving Singapore, knowing that they left behind desperate men and women facing certain defeat.

To make matters worse, the aged *Empress of Asia*, the ship that carried most of the 18th Division's artillery, ammunition, trucks, automatic weapons, and rations, went down in the channel, caught by Japanese dive bombers. It was the only ship lost on the trip.

A few days behind them and zigzagging toward the Straits were the *West Point* and *Wakefield*, still making their way toward Singapore. On the 29th the escort commander ordered the two ships, along with the *Empress of India*, to make a run for it. They increased their speed and headed toward Singapore, via the Berthala Straits. Late in the day the *Wakefield*, having made it without incident, began disembarking 6,000 British troops, most of whom were on line within three days.

The *Wakefield* was refueling on the morning of the 30th when Japanese planes returned and bombs fell close, one hitting the midsection and killing five men. The air raids continued as she managed to get evacuees, women and children, wounded British servicemen, and merchant mariners on board and out to sea. At sea they would hold services for the five dead and witness the birth of a baby boy.

The *West Point* arrived on the 29th as well, with officers and men of the 55th Brigade Hertfordshire. She managed to unload during the bombings and then took on evacuees, including several naval officers and their families, and was able to get back to sea without further incident.

The trip undertaken by the men and ships of William Sail 12X was the longest of the war. It was both dangerous and illegal. All in all it covered nearly 18,090 miles and managed to cross a good portion of the world, taking almost three months to complete. It delivered troops to Singapore, where they made a heroic stand, but most were soon dead or prisoners of war. For those who made the run and then got away, there was further service and recognition. For his services, Captain Beary was awarded the Bronze Star with Combat V for meritorious achievement. For their service with Convoy William Sail, officers and men were awarded the American Defense medal with Bronze A, and the American Theater Medal. The various ships went on to serve the nation in a variety of capacities. The *Cimarron* continued in service throughout World War II, then in Korea and later in Vietnam. She was decommissioned in September 1968 as the oldest U.S. Navy ship in continuous service.

The *Mount Vernon* continued its service, and neither she nor any member of her crew ever received a scratch. On her way back from her convoy duties she picked up the survivors from the USS *Langley*, lost to enemy fire. During the war she made 18 unescorted voyages to the South Pacific and 17 to Europe, traveling more than 419,000 nautical miles.

The USS *Wakefield* caught fire in September of 1942 and burned for 8 days until it was finally taken under control. Pulled out of service for repairs, she did not sail again until April 1944, but still managed to contribute to the war, having carried more than 217,000 troops.

The *Leonard Wood* was converted to an attack transport (APA) on 1 February 1943. During the war she was involved in the invasion of Sicily, North Africa, the Gilbert and Marshall Islands, Saipan and the Philippines. She was decommissioned after the war and sold to Consolidated Building and broken up for scrap. She earned eight battle stars for her service in the Pacific.

The *West Point*, now renamed the *America*, was sold and again renamed, this time as the RHMS *Australis*. Then, in 1978, she became the *American Star* for an Italian group transporting emigrants. She was run aground by a storm at Fuerteventura Island and sank.

The *Joseph T. Dickman* served with the Western Naval Task Force and took part in every amphibious operation in the European-African theatre. After the war she was decommissioned and scrapped in March 1948. She received six battle stars for her participation.

William Sail was the longest convoy both in terms of distance and time. She began in peacetime America and ended up in the heat of the British defeat at Malaya. It was a gamble, perhaps a necessary gamble, but it came too late; for it can not be suggested as a reason for the Japanese attack, neither did it prevent the Japanese victory at Singapore. Of all the convoys of that long and desperate war, who can judge the significance of one over the others? Perhaps it was her illegitimacy that made William Sail unique.

Note

There were several convoys named William Sail, only one with the nickname "Winston's Special." This was not the first or last time Roosevelt's somewhat unorthodox reading of the Neutrality Act led to militant behavior. In the late 1930s he authorized the Navy, in violation of this act, to place armed Americans on merchant ships on the Yangtze River. Later, in December 1941, he sent out a "provocative patrol" in hopes it would lure the Japanese into firing the first shot. See Chapter 1, "The Sitting Duck."

Further Reading

Barber, Noel. *Sinister Twilight*. London: Collins, 1968.
"Convoy William Sail 12X: Task Force 14." www.cofepow.org.uk/pages/ships_convoy_william_sail.htm.

Prange, Gordon. *At Dawn We Slept*. New York: Penguin, 1981.
Winslow, W.G. *The Fleet the Gods Forgot: The U.S. Asiatic Fleet in World War II*. Annapolis: Naval Institute Press, 1982.
Zacharias, Ellis M. *Secret Missions*. Annapolis: Naval Institute Press, 1942.

14. The Paukenschlag of April 1942

It was in the early morning hours of 8 April 1942. Silently, almost without causing a ripple, the conning tower of submarine U-123 broke the surface of the still waters. After a long night lying in wait for its prey, the boat rose for a kill. Carefully stalking his target under the aid of a quarter moon, the commander lined up his shot. In the distance he could see the glow from the lights of the city. Moving cautiously, the German officer was able to get to within 500 yards before he ordered the attack. With the order to fire, a torpedo leaped from the tube and, moving with alarming speed, struck the tanker in the engine room. The fate of the ship was quickly determined as the damage was overwhelming. This unescorted and unarmed vessel that moments before had been boldly sailing, now began to sink. With her went nearly four and a half million gallons of much-needed Allied oil. It was an often repeated story during World War II, when hundreds of merchant ships went to the deep in the Atlantic. It was the high cost of trying to maintain a war.

But this was not an ordinary sinking, and it was not conducted in the mid–Atlantic where merchant ships traveled in the expectation of such events. This sinking happened within shouting distance of St. Simons Island, Georgia, and it was executed just ten miles from the lights of the holiday beach that lit up the sky for miles around. It was within sight of carefree Americans who were enjoying themselves in the imagined peace of their powerful nation. It was a period in which America's failure to accept the reality of war was costing them dearly in terms of materiel and lives.

The commander of this submarine was Kapitanleutnant Reinhard Hardegan, and he was on a mission called Paukenschlag. The mission, personally approved by German Chancellor Adolf Hitler, was designed to bring the cost of the war to the United States. The U-boats were there to prevent the shipping of war materials that were arriving in the United States for transshipment to Great Britain. The early phase, conducted during April 1942, resulted in the destruction of a significant amount of cargo and the loss of many lives.

The attacks on the American shoreline were made possible by the existence of twelve Type IX boats, the only ones in the German fleet that were capable of traveling long distances. Of the twelve constructed, only six were identified for this particular mission, and one of the remaining was unable to complete the assignment. The five that finally traveled to their assignment in the New World included the U-123, which left Germany on 23 December 1941, the others following soon after. For U-123 and Kapitanleutnant Reinhard Hardegan, it was the ninth tour.

The plan was also pushed forward by German Admiral Karl Doenitz's near-total disregard for the American defense. Sure that the Americans were not really ready for war, he determined that Navy and Coast Guard crews were "undistinguished, inexperienced, and not very tenacious in pursuit" of their targets. He had reasons for his belief, as America had not done very well in the defense of its west coast.[1]

Once the German submarines arrived in the area, they would lie low in order to remain undetected, resting on the shallow continental shelf in what was often less than 100 feet of water. In most cases they would have been visible from the air. Left undetected, however, they waited for the shipping — their target — to come to them.

The initial attack of Paukenschlag (the Americans called it Operation Drumbeat) occurred on 8 April 1942. It began with the striking of the SS *Oklahoma*. The rest of the month would see the sinking of the SS *Esso Baton Rouge*, also on 8 April; the SS *Esparta*, sunk the following day; the SS *Gulf-America*, torpedoed on 11 April; and the *Leslie* and the *Korsholm* on the 13th. The submarines were not particularly choosy, but preferred the oil-rich tankers that headed toward them alone and usually unarmed.

The SS *Oklahoma* was such a tanker. She was carrying 38 men when sighted and torpedoed by the German U-boat 123. Her location when she was struck was just off the resort island of St. Simons, Georgia. Nineteen of the men aboard were killed in the explosion. The ship quickly began to sink into the forty feet of water. The blast of the torpedo and the explosion that followed was said to have shattered glass in Brunswick, some miles inland, and the resulting fire lit up the whole area. When the *Oklahoma* finally settled, her bow still remained above the water. Quickly, as the blast was heard and the situation was understood, several Coast Guard vessels and a boat owned by Charles Candler, Coca-Cola magnate, arrived on the scene and began to rescue any survivor they could locate, bringing the men out of the water and the saturating oil.

In reporting on the action and the successful sinking, the commander of the German U-boat said that his shot was made much easier both because of the moonlight, and by the considerable light that was coming from the shore. Before launching the attack, he reported that he could see a good many people, a roller coaster and streams of car lights heading toward the beach. No one seemed the slightest bit concerned that there was a war on, or that German submarines might be in the area.

The second ship to be attacked that day was the *Esso Baton Rouge*, carrying 3.8 million gallons of oil. The *Baton Rouge*'s crew of forty-one took to the lifeboats as quickly as they were struck, but three of their number were already dead. In one area the Coast Guard, fearing that Germans were landing, set up a horse patrol to look for saboteurs who might be coming ashore. But that was not the mission of these men and their boats.

About twelve miles southeast of the St. Simons Sound light buoy, the SS *Esparta* was discovered, and she was to be the third victim. The *Esparta* was a fast cold storage ship of 3365 tons, which belonged to the United Fruit Company. It had been built in 1904 as the first banana reefer. The German sub U-123 set her up, and then launched a single torpedo which hit cleanly. A column of dirty water rose up near the mast. It was a mortal wound. The time was 0716 hours on 9 April, and Alfred L. Case was in command. The explosion struck rear of the midsection, causing a massive rupture, and the ship began to sink by the stern. Several men jumped overboard to avoid escaping ammonia gas, while the rest took off in two lifeboats. The *Esparta* was just 14 miles south of Brunswick, Georgia. Fortunately, decisive action by the crew, and a quick arrival by the Navy crash boat USS *Tyrer*, kept the loss at two men.

Two days later the submarine was able to strike again. This time it was the *GulfAmerica* that was struck by a torpedo. The attack came at 0422 hours on 11 April. The unescorted oiler was under the command of Captain Oscar Anderson, and was on her maiden voyage. The captain, unaccountably deciding that his ship was no longer in danger, had just stopped zigzagging. The torpedo fired from the half-hidden U-123 struck her as she neared the beach of Jacksonville, Florida. The ship had been illuminated by the lights of Jacksonville Beach, and made an easy target. During the attack nineteen men were killed: two officers, two men who had been placed there as armed guards, and fifteen of the crew. Five more men died a little later when the lifeboat they were in capsized.

14. The Paukenschlag of April 1942   135

In this case the *GulfAmerica* was unique. In an effort to respond to the increasing loss of merchant ships, the Navy had finally presented her with one four-inch 50 SP Mark IX Model gun and two .50 caliber Browning Mark II machine guns. Seven Naval crewmen and an ensign had been placed aboard to man the weapons. In the report on the loss, no explanation was provided as to why the guns had not been fired. We do know that the submarine was on the surface some of the time during the attack.

After firing the torpedo the U-123 came in closer and the commander decided to put the *GulfAmerica* down with shell fire. Acknowledging that the ship was between the submarine and the beaches of Jacksonville, and outlined by the lights, he realized that any shells that missed the mark might well drop into the populated area. So, recognizing the danger into which he was placing his ship, he nevertheless took the time to maneuver around so that he was facing the open sea before he began to fire. Twelve shells hit the wounded tanker, and she began to drop deeper into the water.

Rescued by the Coast Guard, the *GulfAmerica* did not actually sink for five days, during which time the transport discharged more than 90,000 barrels of fuel oil. The *GulfAmerica* was the first American merchant ship to be fitted with weapons, but this did not seem to make any difference. She had been sailing from Port Arthur, Texas, to New York for the transshipment of fuel oil. At the scene, and even with the sinking taking place in full view of the people on the beach that night, the lights of the city were not blacked out for another forty minutes. By then it was far too late.

The SS *Leslie* was a small 2,609-ton freighter, American-owned and en route, unarmed, from Antilla, Cuba, with 3,300 tons of pure raw sugar. She was hit on 13 April. Built in 1919 as the *Lake Flagstaff*, she was sailing under the command of Albert Eriksson. The ship was traveling at six knots, zigzagging, the radio silent, with no lights burning. She was just three miles south of Hetzel Shoals when Hardegen's torpedo caught her number three hold, blasting open the bulkhead and flooding the ship with a mixture of sea water and sugar. There was nothing that could be done, so Captain Eriksson ordered his crew to abandon ship. The ship immediately caught fire and sank within fifteen minutes. The ship's radio had been destroyed in the first blast, so there was no opportunity to even release a distress call. One lifeboat that had broken away was retrieved, and in it some managed to reach land just north of the lighthouse. Another survivor was rescued by the SS *Esso Bayonne* and put ashore. Three of the crew of 68 were killed in the attack.

The German U-boat captain did not stay around to watch the destruction he had caused, but rather turned his attention to what he thought was an oil tanker coming into view. In fact it was not a tanker but the *Korsholm*, a 2,647-ton freighter, en route from Port Tampa, Florida, to Liverpool, England, by way of Halifax with a load of nearly 5,000 tons of phosphate. This ship was the second victory for the day, 13 April, and was accomplished not by torpedoes but by accurate shell bombardment. During the bombardment the *Korsholm* was able to get off several of its lifeboats, but fire broke out amidships and quickly spread through the ship. In time the Dutch ship SS *Bacchus* and the American SS *Esso Bayonne* were able to pick up a good number of the survivors. Nine, however, including the master of the ship, were never found. The ship, some seventy miles from Cape Canaveral, still lies there in the deep water.

April's total is only illustrative of the U-boat campaign that lasted for several months. Each of these sinkings came in locations well under the control of the American military. They occurred in areas in which full alert warnings had been given. But, as it was, the submarine operators, who might legitimately have been working under highly difficult conditions, moved about fairly easily. The government, for whatever reason, did not establish the safeguards that one might expect, and the civilians, for their own reasons, failed to acknowledge that their failure to blackout was giving the submariners a highly significant advantage.

What is most difficult to understand is the reaction, or rather the lack of reaction, of the American people living in the area. The merchant ships were easily silhouetted against the light of American cities along the coast, cities that were reluctant to dim their lights. Submarines off the coast of New York reported that they could see the lights from the city for 25 miles out to sea. In fact, America provided so little response to the danger that Admiral Doenitz felt secure in sending additional waves of submarines into the area, and would do so in the future at great cost to the Allied war effort.

The sinking set off a wave of hysteria along the east coast, and to some degree along the gulf coast as well, but the fear did not generate the sort of action that might have been expected. While dead bodies, debris, and oil washed up on the shores after a long night of killings, men and women still frolicked on the beaches, lit up their towns and cities, and took months in many of the areas involved to impose a blackout.

Lack of authority was not the culprit. On 19 February 1942, President Roosevelt had provided Executive Order 9066, which gave the military services the authority so assume control over beach lighting to avoid silhouetting ships. But the military was reluctant to take action, because of pressure from business owners who did not want to "inconvenience tourists."

14. The Paukenschlag of April 1942

The success of the venture, as far as Germany is concerned, can be measured in the fact that between January and June of 1942, four hundred ships carrying three million tons of war materials were sunk along the Atlantic and in the Gulf of Mexico. The effort, according to Chief of Staff General George C. Marshall, "threatened our entire war effort." But again, delayed by indecision, it was not until May of 1942 that a Convoy and Routing Section was established under the Chief of Naval Operations.

It is generally believed that the American government was so concerned with covering up the event in order to avoid panic along the coasts that they failed to fully recognize the danger or to take care of those involved. It is equally true that neither the government nor the American people provided much recognition for those men and women involved in the transportation of the goods of war. Unfortunately this has been true all over the world, as few nations have acknowledged the service provided or the dangers involved for the men and women who sailed on the merchant ships. It was not until 1988, more than forty years after the conclusion of the war, that Congress granted merchant marines the status of veterans.

On the German side of the story, there were great rewards for those who successfully conducted these raids. Equally impressive, for them, is the fact that during the height of the period of activity, between January and May of 1942, only a few German submarines were sighted in the area and only three were reported as being sunk.

So what is the rest of the story? There is a certain amount of irony arising from all this. Captain Reinhard Hardegan, who received the Knight's Cross from the Fuehrer for his sinking of the American oilers, including the SS *Oklahoma*, later worked for Texaco, the company that owned the ill-fated ship. He was acknowledged by the city of Jacksonville, Florida, in 1990, because when setting up for the attack on 11 April he noticed the beach was flooded with tourists and maneuvered so as not to harm them. In doing so he placed his boat in danger of attack. Hardegan was received by the mayor of Jacksonville and the town expressed its thanks.

The submarine U-123 and its commander Reinhard Hardegen provide an excellent example of the underwater war Hitler launched against the Allies. It "mirrored at once both the great strategy of war and its everyday horror," as German naval historian Michael Salewski suggested. Certainly there is no romance in what was done, but it must be stated that Hardegen made a significant contribution to his service. In five war patrols during which he commanded the U-123, he sank twenty-five ships, a figure in keeping with the best records of U.S. Navy skipper Richard H. O'Kane in five patrols on the

USS *Tang*. On the other side it is perhaps only fair to remember of the 863 U-boats that sailed for Germany, 754 did not return.²

As a result of the devastation, and the awareness that the attacks were greatly harming the war effort, the Navy, under Admiral Ernest J. King, set up what was known, if known at all, as 10th Fleet. Having no ships, its fifty sailors traveled no further than a building in the Navy Department complex in Washington, D.C. From here, in the secret room, high-frequency radio messages were monitored which allowed the Navy to pinpoint the presence of German submarines. When one was located, a recommendation was sent to the Allied ships in the Atlantic to intercept. The system was amazingly successful.

The *Oklahoma* was raised and, on 20 April 1942, taken to an area near the King and Princess Hotel, where bodies were removed from the wreck. Four of those killed on board the *Oklahoma* were burned beyond recognition and buried in Brunswick's Palmetto Cemetery in graves marked as "Unknown Seaman, 1942." The *Oklahoma* was salvaged and repaired, and went on to carry oil throughout most of the war. On 23 March 1945 she left St. Nicholas harbor, Aruba, carrying over 100,000 barrels of high octane gasoline. At approximately 0135 hours she was struck by a torpedo from the German submarine U-532, and sank.

Work on salvaging the SS *Esso Baton Rouge* began almost immediately. For seven days crews worked to bring her up, all the time keeping a wide submarine watch. They were finally able to tow her back to St. Simons Sound. There the 25-foot hole that had been blown in her side was repaired, and she was able to return to her work in later May 1942. However, on 23 February 1943 she was torpedoed for the second time and this time was unsalvageable.

Despite being in shallow water, the SS *Leslie* was not raised from her grave of 85 feet of water until August of 1954. She was discovered to be in such bad shape she was broken up and sold.

The *GulfAmerica* was destroyed on its maiden voyage, and now lies in sixty feet of water. The U-123, having used considerable time in positioning herself so as not to hit the beaches, was slow getting away and was tracked for some distance by the destroyer USS *Dahlgren* (DD 187). The Clemson-class destroyer located what they thought was the submarine and dropped six depth charges. The U-123 suffered some damage, but not enough to prevent her heading home to her port in France. There is a historical marker depicting the events at the entrance to Jackson Beach.

The *Esparta* lies in 56 feet of water about 35 miles east of Jacksonville.

It was not located for awhile as the position sent in her last SOS was incorrect. There was no effort to raise her.

Perhaps the most incredible response was from author Ernest Hemingway, who managed to talk the American embassy in Havana, Cuba, into giving him some .50 caliber machine guns and a bazooka with which he armed his private yacht, the *Pilar*. Turing the boat into what he envisioned as an American Q-boat, he and a small crew sailed the northern waters of Cuba in hopes of locating a sub on the surface. They did see one but it was too far away for them to take any action.

From Operation Drumbeat and other such efforts have come some incredible myths, most if not all of which have no factual base at all. Some have said that German submarines sunk along the U.S. Gulf Coast had on board packages of U.S.–made bread and bakery items it is claimed were purchased by German sailors landing and going ashore to shop. Others claim that the bodies of German sailors washed up on shore had American movie ticket stubs in their pockets. The more realistic truth is that the few Germans who did land on American soil were not shopping, but hoping to conduct espionage, and all were captured.

Notes

1. Allen Cronenberg, "U-Boats in the Gulf: The Underwater War in 1942," *Gulf Coast Historical Review* 5, no. 2 (Fall 1990).
2. Michael Gannon, *Operation Drumbeat: The Dramatic True Story of Germany's First U-Boat Attacks Along the American Coast in World War II*. Annapolis: Naval Institute Press, 1990.

Further Reading

Baker, Carlos. *Ernest Hemingway: A Life's Story*. New York: Scribner's, 1989.
Cronenberg, Allen. "U-Boats in the Gulf." *Gulf Coast Historical Review* 5, no. 2, Fall 1990.
Hendricks, William. "Close to Home." *Atlanta Journal-Constitution*, 14 February 1999.
Hickam, Homer H. *Torpedo Junction: The U-Boat War off American's East Coast*. Annapolis: Naval Institute Press, 1989.
Hoyt, Edwin. *Death of the U-Boat*. London: Graffton, 1988.
Ships of the Esso Fleet in World War II. Standard Oil Company of New Jersey, 1946.

Part III

Events Worth Remembering

How does history select what will be remembered? Many events are remembered because of some personal attachment to them, such as a father or grandfather who tells and retells the story as a part of his life cycle. Some events and the expanded stories that surround them are remembered because of the magnitude of the event; "Remember Pearl Harbor" recalls an event so astounding in world history it will never be forgotten. But there are hundreds of other stories which display much of the courage as well as the desperation of World War II, and they deserve to be remembered in their own right. These are stories of unusual events, of personal sacrifice, of history-changing confrontations, or sometimes just stories of people and places of significance. Certainly among these would fall the highly significant Battle for Buna in New Guinea, where Americans and Australians fought one of the first offensive battles and slowed the Japanese advance.

There has been too much forgetting in some cases, as for example the memory of the American prisoners of war at the island camp at Palawan. This is a story that America needs to remember, as it does some of the great stories of heroic action. Also worth remembering is the voyage of the little passenger ship turned giant killer, the *Li Wo*, or the terrible events that were taking place during the long desperate battle for Okinawa, at the underground field hospital where hundreds of Japanese schoolchildren died in their beliefs. Personal stories like the journey of Annie Clark, who represents the thousands who sought, on old and beat-up ships, to escape from the Japanese advance on Singapore, should never be forgotten. Likewise the story of John Lang, the epitome of the American serviceman, who seemed to show up in the heart of battle.

Perhaps no story better epitomizes the conflict created by war than that of the children of England who set sail for the new world, perhaps in the hope that luck and innocence would see them safely home.

15. The *City of Benares*

The children were in their pajamas and asleep when the torpedo hit. They had spent the day in a variety of activities designed to keep them occupied, and had gone to bed tired after a brief evening program. It had been a cheerful but exhausting day for most of them. The vast majority were in their quarters below deck and toward the stern. It was here that the explosion struck the 11,000-ton passenger liner *City of Benares*, en route from Liverpool, England, sailing at sixteen knots heading for Halifax, Nova Scotia. On board were 100 British evacuee children who ranged in age from four to fifteen.

During the afternoon the winds had picked up and overnight the sea had become choppy with winds reaching a gale force. *City of Benares* was the largest of the ships in the nineteen-vessel convoy identified as OB-213, under the command of Admiral Mackinnon. The ship, a passenger liner built for the Ellerman Lines in 1936, had two centrally mounted tunnels painted yellow and did not look much like a freighter. But that did not seem to matter. It was September 17, 1940, and the world was at war.

The strike occurred at about 2230 hours. There was first an enormous explosion that shook the ship. The impact came near the stern and caused an immediate rupture of the hull. *City of Benares* began to slow, immediately taking on water and dragging to one side. At this point in her journey the ship was more than six hundred miles out to sea. The ship was badly damaged and the crew turned to making every effort to save her, but they quickly became aware that they could not prevent the sea from rushing in, so they turned their attention to freeing the lifeboats. Working in gale-force winds and against the increasing list of the ship, they managed to launch a few. However, in the rolling seas, many of them immediately swamped upon reaching the water, sending the passengers and children into the ocean. Within twenty minutes of the moment when the torpedo struck, *City of Benares*, once a proud passenger ship, sank beneath the waves of Atlantic. She took with her a good many of the lost 256 passengers, a number that included 77 of the 100 children who had been traveling to Canada.

On orders from the convoy commander, and to the disbelief of many of the passengers expecting immediate pickup, the other ships in the convoy quickly dispersed. It was a sign of the times and the necessities of survival learned by the hard experiences of the past, as each of the convoy ships took off, trying to save itself. Moving away, they left the survivors of *City of Benares* alone.

What were these children doing there?

Since the beginning of World War II, the English government had been considering ways to get people out of the high-risk urban bombing areas and into rural environments where they might be far safer. Beginning in early September 1939, Operation Pied Piper was put in place. This effort would eventually move more than one and a half million persons from the cities into the countryside, where strangers took them in for the duration. A large percentage of the number had been children. But even this did not seem to be enough.

As the bombing increased and with them the number of deaths, the government began looking for a more pragmatic solution. For help they turned to the Commonwealth, and out of this came the creation of the Child Overseas Reception Board (CORB). This group, which operated from July to September 1940, planned trips, and made arrangements for the relocation of youngsters to British Dominion countries, primarily Canada, South Africa, Australia and New Zealand. Some few, it was determined, could also go to America.

Looking back, it seems a highly questionable risk to be run, but out of the fears and concerns of the parents, more than 210,000 applications were made. They came from concerned parents anxious to get their children out of the cities, out from under the bombs, and away from the possibility of invasion.

And so, in early September 1942, parents and children gathered at the docks at Liverpool to begin such a journey. The young boys and girls that had been collected to sail gathered on the *City of Benares*, scheduled for the trip to Canada. They had come from all over England and represented just about every class and culture on the Island. Some have suggested that those selected may have been from more wealthy parents, but this does not appear to be true at all. What they shared in common was their parents' belief that each child was better off taking the risk of the trip, than remaining under these conditions they were facing. These were parents who no longer believed that an evacuation to the interior or the South of England would be sufficient to guarantee their safety. They wanted the children out of England.

Looking at it all from the disadvantage of seventy years, it may be a little hard to explain why parents would be willing to separate from their children for such a long time. Even more difficult to understand, perhaps, is why they would subject them to the danger of a long ship voyage passing through enemy waters. There were several reasons for both these decisions. Certainly one must believe they were frightened for their children. Not only were the bombings continuing they were spreading out and taking many more lives. But more than that, there was a growing fear that Germany was about the invade England. Every evidence was that Hitler's strategy included the invasion. And preparations were being made. The more realistic of the English knew that there was little available to stop Hitler if and when he decided to move. If that was going to happen, they wanted their children as far away from harm as they could get them.

Another reason for running the risk, perhaps, was that most of the British population was not fully aware of the dangers at sea. This was still early and while they had certainly heard about the sinking of ships, such events were played down when they could be. It was a risk, but the danger may well have been understated, or at least made a feasible alternative for the children, so that it appeared less a risk than having their children caught up in a German occupation.

Some parents were also aware that if the children were gone and taken care of, that they would be able to present themselves more fully for the war effort, freed of both the responsibility of the children and their fear for them. The demand for labor was drawing most of the parents away from the home, and the absence of the children was sometimes seen as a significant advantage.

For some families the desire to get their children out of the area led them to send several children. Many sent two, and one family sent two children who had only recently been rescued from the sinking of the *Volendam*, the first liner carrying children that was torpedoed.[1]

But it was still an awful risk and the authorities were well aware of the danger faced by those sailing in an Atlantic convoy. Not only were the Atlantic merchant fleets suffering huge losses but the children's evacuation process had already faced one crisis. Just two weeks before, the passenger ship *Volendam*, outward bound from England under Captain Weaster, with 320 children on board, had been torpedoed without warning on the 31 August 1940. She was hit in the number one hold while sailing about 300 miles from the Irish coast and west of the Bloody Foreland. The attack was launched by the German U-60. Because of the immediate response of three other ships in the convoy, all were saved except for one member of the crew. Later, after the *Volendam* had been towed back to England, a second, unexploded torpedo was discovered embedded in the bow of the ship. The fact that all the children had been saved would turn out to be a mixed blessing: certainly it was wonderful for the parents and children involved, but it sent a false message of safety that was not warranted.

City of Benares sailed on Friday the 13th of September 1940. It was attacked by the German U-boat U-48 four days later. The U-48 was one of the more successful German submarines during the war. Under the command of Korvettenkapitan Heinrich Bleichrodt, it was on the last leg of its seventh patrol, and had already made several kills. On board was a nineteen-year-old radio operator named Rolf Hilse, who will show up later in this story, but who remembered that his sub had sunk sixty Allied ships during the first two years of the war.

With either advanced information, or an early sighting report, the U-48 had been watching the convoy for some time and waiting for just the right moment. The experienced submarine captain had deliberately selected the largest ship in the convoy to attack. This ship happened to be the *City of Benares*. No one on board the submarine had any idea of its cargo or the nature of its passengers, nor were there any strong reasons for them to have suspected anything. Some critics will later assume that the U-boat should have recognized the *Benares* as a passenger ship. But it did not.

Once the excitement of the initial separation had passed for the children, the days at sea had been pretty much routine. For many of the children the unlimited food, served by trained waiters on cloth covered tables, was more than they could have imagined. After the rationing at home it seemed like a dream come true, and the government and the ship company had gone out of their way to make it comfortable for the travelers.

When the children awoke on the morning of the fourth day, they noted that the escorts had left the convoy. Those who bothered to ask were told, as had been the sponsors sailing with them, that they had sailed far enough to be out of the anticipated war zone and that the escort, no longer needed, had sailed off to meet the eastbound Convoy HY71, which was arriving. Earlier in the voyage they had all rehearsed the lifeboat drill, but other than that there had been no special preparation in case of attack.

When it came, there was no time to take anything and only a few tried, quickly abandoning the effort in the rush toward the decks. As soon as the ship was hit, the children, often aided by the other passengers, began to move toward the deck. The sponsors assigned to the children ushered them quickly through the maze of corridors. The noise of straining and twisting steel hastened then on. The lights flickered and then went off, as interior pipes broke, adding to the cascading water they had to fight along the companionways.

Now moving with surprisingly little panic, the crew worked the lifeboats, and the children's sponsors guided their young charges toward the deck to their assignments. The ship was sinking rapidly so there was little time. The rolling of the sea and the Force 5 wind made it increasingly difficult just to get off, and then once in the water, to stay afloat hoping to be picked up.

When the ship finally slipped beneath the waters it left a stream of bobbing survivors fighting the waves and seeking something to hang onto. There was not very much. Those that found something survived, but only a few of those with nothing but lifebelts made it through the night. From the moment of the attack the radio operators had sent the call for help, and it was to be assumed that rescue was on the way. But they were pretty far away from any intended help.

The call was heard by the destroyer HMS *Hurricane.* Moving out quickly and with great dispatch, it arrived at 1415 hours, a day and a half after the sinking of the *Benares.* Once the spot was located they managed to pick up all the survivors that could be found. After a prolonged search, and when no more were to be found, the *Hurricane* reluctantly headed home. The rescuers had not pulled many from the water, and the word was going out ahead of them that since no more could be located, the children had to be presumed dead.

However, this fortunately was not the case. They had missed a boatload of survivors who were clinging in lifeboat #12, under the able control of 4th Officer Ronnie Cooper. On board, as well, was the young Ken Sparks, just thirteen.

In the confusion Ken Sparks missed his assigned lifeboat, but was given a seat on one just pulling down. It was, for him, a fortunate circumstance, since lifeboat #5, the boat to which he had been assigned, was tipped and had foundered in the choppy sea. Lifeboat #12 was terribly full and difficult to control as the sea was still howling and huge swells pushed the smaller boats about. There were 43 souls aboard the boat as it began to drift away from the location of the sinking.

Fortunately for all, Mary Cornish, a 41-year-old music teacher, and the only one of the adult escorts to survive the sinking, was also on board. With her were 30 Indian seamen; 6 young male evacuees, including Paul Shearing and Fred Steel, both 12; and a Roman Catholic priest named O'Sullivan.

Life in the boat was difficult. The heavy seas made several of them sick, and sufferings from exhaustion, most tried desperately to sleep. It was nearly impossible in the cramped conditions, the cold and wet, and the constant rocking of the small craft. The shortage of water led to the only casualty suffered, when one crewmember died after drinking some of the sea water. Young Sparks remembered they had some rations, recalling a daily meal of a piece of tinned peach, a ship's biscuit, and a sip of water once a day.

After drifting afloat for more than eight days, the small lifeboat was picked up by the British destroyer HMS *Anthony*. Earlier the boat had been spotted from the air by the crew of a Sunderland flying boat. The survivors were taken to Greenock, Scotland, still too weak to walk, and housed in the Bay Hotel. There they were taken care of by the proprietor, known locally as Two Ton Tessie, before being returned to their homes throughout England.

When the final count was taken, 248 of the 406 passengers and crew on board had died in the attack. Of these seventy-seven of the deaths were among the traveling children. One family lost five children in the sinking, another family lost four.

The sinking of the *City of Benares* brought an abrupt halt of the evacuation program designed to send children overseas. There were later, apparently, some private individuals who sought ways to send their children off the English island, but no more official efforts. The count is generally given as 1,532 going to Canada, 576 to Australia, 353 to South Africa, and 203 to New Zealand. Some 11,000 were sent privately with them, about evenly divided between Canada and the United States.

Among the survivors were many interesting stories. Two young girlfriends, Beth Cummings and Bess Walder, had been found clinging to the keel of lifeboat #14. It was recorded that the two were singing when they were rescued. They had been tossed from a lifeboat that swamped but managed to swim over to the overturned boat, where they hung on for dear life until rescued. They remained friends for the rest of their lives and one later married the brother of the other. Bess's brother Louis also survived.

Beth Cummings, now Williams, later found herself in contact with Rolf, the young radio operator on board the submarine who got in contact after seeing Beth's story in the foreword of a book about the event. The radio operator expressed his sorrow, and that of many of the crew, when they learned that the children had been on board. But he reaffirmed the German position that there was no way the submarine could have known who was on board. All six of the boys who survived the voyage in lifeboat #12 went on to serve in the Navy.

Both the radio operator Rolf Hilse and the U-48 engineering officer Krause Edouard Hansen, showed up at some of the early reunions of the *City of Benares* survivors and got along well with those involved.

Mary Cornish, one of the children's sponsors who had gone back into the lower deck looking for her girls, and then played such an important role in the survival of those in lifeboat #12, was later awarded the Order of the British Empire in 1941. She died of cancer in 1964. Ronnie Cooper also received the Order of the British Empire and was well remembered for his role in the successful journey of lifeboat #12. He died in 1979. Annie Ryan received the King's Commendation for Good Services for her heroic action in lifeboat #10.

Captain of the rescue ship *Hurricane*, Hugh Crofton Simms, was mortally wounded when his new command, the HMS *Snapdragon*, was bombed.

After the war Lieutenant Commander Heinrich Bleichrodt, captain of the U-boat, was tried as a war criminal for the sinking of the *City of Benares*. He claimed that he had no knowledge of what the ship was carrying and refused to apologize for his actions which, he claimed, were strictly within the bounds of military policy. In later life he managed a factory and died in 1977 at the age of 67.

For the children who made it to Canada or Australia, it was a difficult change. Not only had they been uprooted from their families but they had been delivered into a different culture, in many respect a somewhat different language, as well as differences of perspective and of humor. For most, of course, the separation in itself was difficult, as was the fact that while they tended to come into happy, kind, and helpful families, the families could not really understand what they had been through.

Some claim that the risk of sending children overseas was done for an entirely different reason. They suggest that Great Britain, which was in desperate straits facing Germany, knew that there could be no greater incentive for America to enter the war than for the Germans to sink a boat load of children. There is little evidence that this was the case, other perhaps than someone thinking out loud, but in any case, the sinking did have that result. On hearing of the sinking, American Secretary of State Cordell Hull listed it as the "most dastardly act," but that was all he did.

Note

1. Details of this event are available in *Official Report on the Sinking of the S.S.* City of Benares, October 1940, Imperial War Museum, London.

Further Reading

Barker, Ralph. *Children of the Benares: A War Crime and Its Victims.* London: Grafton, 1997.
Bridgland, Tony. *Waves of Hate: Naval Atrocities of the Second World War.* Annapolis: Naval Institute Press, 2002.
Henderson, Michael. "The Evacuation of British Children to North America in World War II." *Children at War—The International Journal of Evacuee and War Child Studies,* December 2005.
Heneghan, James. *Wish Me Luck.* New York: Farrar, Straus and Giroux, 1997.
Menzies, Janet. *Children of the Doomed Voyage.* Chinchester: John Wiley and Sons, 2005.
Nagorski, Tom. *Miracles on the Water: The Heroic Survivors of a World War II U-Boat Attack.* New York: Hyperion, 2006.

16. The Battle of Buna

The Japanese moved south with incredible speed, taking and consuming just about everything they ran up against. There was every reason to believe in November of 1942 that the Japanese, if they were not stopped, would be able to land troops on Australia. And Australia, despite the presence of General Douglas MacArthur and a small contingency of American troops, was not in any position to offer much resistance. In May, fortunately, the Allied success at the Battle of the Coral Sea had slowed the enemy down somewhat.

The Japanese planned a two-pronged attack against Port Moresby. The ambition was to be able to place an airfield there that would give them air access to northeast Australia. With some advanced warning from Ultra and more immediate information provided by coast watchers, it was determined that one prong of this attack needed to be met with an offensive action at sea. In the first major check of the great Japanese offensive, Japanese forward movement was slowed by the arrival of an Allied task force under Admiral Frank Jack Fletcher, and built around the carriers USS *Lexington* and USS *Yorktown*.

The Japanese force built around two carriers met the Allied force built around two carriers in a battle fought mainly with planes, the result of which was significant. While the immediate conflict ended after two days, combat would be continued some time later at Midway. The naval victory could be given to either side, but the strategic victory was definitively American, since it led to the Japanese withdrawal of this aspect of the invasion fleet headed for Port Moresby.

Accompanying the victory at Coral Sea was the decision to meet the remaining Port Moresby invasion with an offensive response that might, if successful, even discourage any ambitions for Australia. The area which was selected for the site of this desperate move was at Papua New Guinea, in an area known as Buna, which ran along the coast for three miles in Papua.

Port Moresby, the largest and capital city of Papua, had been an Australian administrative center for years. It became a prime Japanese goal as the war broke out. After the invasion force headed for Port Moresby was met and turned back at the Battle of the Coral Sea, the Japanese then turned their attention to taking the port city by landing troops along the east coast, and driving them overland along the Kokoda Track.[1] It was a long and treacherous invasion route. While they were moving, life on Moresby grew very difficult under Japanese air bombardment, almost day and night, from 2 February 1942.

At the western tip near the Girau River, the Japanese occupied Buna, a small village with no seeming importance. It was separated from Buna Mission by the small Entrance Creek. East of Buna Mission there was an open area known as the Government Gardens. Beyond that was a swampy area that went inland from Giropa Point. To the east a short distance were two airfields: the Old Strip, south of Strip Point, and then a little further east another small primitive field known as the New Strip. Beyond the airfield lay the final Japanese-occupied obstacle, the Duropa Plantation, that was just south of Buna and on the coast. If the Japanese were to be removed it would require Allied forces taking all these areas from the entrenched enemy.

The Japanese who occupied the area had the strongest defenses at the eastern and western ends of the airfields, where they were in a position to block both of the two potential routes for an attack. The first route was the coastal track that was blocked by the Duropa Plantation south of Cape Endaiadere. The second, a road that ran between the two airfields, was where the Japanese had built their main defense. There they had a clear field of fire again any oncoming units. At this point the Japanese in this area were estimated at 2,500 troops and were commanded on the eastern edge by Colonel Shizuo Yokoyama and at the western edge by Captain Yasuda. Included in these forces were more than a thousand from the 5th Special Naval Landing Force, an elite group.

Since mid–July 1942, the Japanese had been fighting their way toward Port Moresby against units of the Australian militia and a few regulars. The militia had been established originally for home front protection, but as the Japanese progressed, the militia took on more formal organization. It was increased to a force of about 265,000 men divided into two cavalry and five infantry divisions.

So far the Japanese 144th Infantry Regiment had been very successful in driving the Australians back and steadily they were advancing toward the sea and their objective, Port Moresby. When they fought their way to their most advanced position they were within thirty miles of the port. Their forward movement had been desperate, and was greatly hampered by the growing length of their supply line, as well as by the incredibly difficult country over which supplies had to travel to reach them.

Then, without explanation, the 144th Infantry Regiment was suddenly ordered to withdraw to the village of Buna, where they were to consolidate their forces in preparation for an attack. Their instructions were to hold on at Buna while other Japanese units were concentrating their forces on the battle for Guadalcanal. Thus, suddenly, the tables were turned and the now retreating Japanese regiment was being chased by elements of the Australian 7th Infantry Division, assigned to the defense of Port Moresby.

This was the Allies' chance, and it would be General Douglas MacArthur's first offensive campaign against the Japanese during World War II. He planned the offensive in the belief that his soldiers were ready to fight, that they would be able to seize the Japanese forward base at Buna on Papua quickly, and that it could be done with few casualties. He had been informed by his intelligence officer, General Willoughby,[2] that the Japanese gave "little indication of an attempt to make a strong stand against the Allied advance." With the assurances of the intelligence officer for the Southwest Pacific Area (SWPA), General MacArthur, the supreme commander, ordered his troops — both American and Australian — to seize the Japanese forward base at Buna. Willoughby had assured them it was held by a thousand sick and malnourished Japanese soldiers.

General MacArthur, fresh from his retreat from Corregidor, needed a victory. And he wanted it done with few casualties and with as much speed as possible. The American unit to be involved, the 32nd Infantry Division, expected a swift victory because they were inexperienced and did not know what was coming. They had been told that the fight for Buna would be easy because they were fighting an under strength, sick and badly mauled force. The Australians knew better.

The 32nd Infantry Division, known as the "Red Arrow," was made up of men from the Michigan and Wisconsin National Guard units. They had been mobilized on 15 October 1940 and after training had been assigned to Ireland. But they were redirected and sent to Australia instead, where they were to prepare for the threatened Japanese invasion of Australia. They arrived there on May 1942.

Under MacArthur's new plan they were sent on to Port Moresby, New Guinea, in September 1942. The division's 126th Infantry Regiment went by ship, while the 128th Regiment was to be the first mass troop movement by air during the war. They joined the Australians at Port Moresby on 16 November 1942. Their destination was Buna.

16. The Battle of Buna

The Allies were going into battle with three strikes against them. First of all, the intelligence provided by General Willoughby vastly underestimated the number of Japanese who were involved; time would show 6,000, not 1500 to 2000, were involved. Second, there was such little understanding of either the site or the enemy that intelligence was unable to warn the Allies about Japanese defensive positions. True, the swampy ground made it hard to dig trenches and build earthen bunkers. The Japanese, knowing this, and with the help of a Japanese construction battalion, set up hundreds of coconut log bunkers, some with reinforced steel beams, and a few steel and concrete pillboxes constructed of 55-gallon drums filled with sand, located near the abandoned airstrip. The fortifications were excellently and tactically constructed, placed in deep terrains with trees and vegetation surrounding and firing slits placed in such a manner as to make them nearly invisible to the advancing Americans.

Lieutenant General Richard K. Sutherland, MacArthur's chief of staff, was unfamiliar with the situation, as well as the terrain, and had identified these fortifications as "hasty field entrenchments." He had no idea, nor did any of the senior officers, of the type of ground over which the Americans were to cross. But more than that, after failing to understand the conditions under which their men had to battle, they grossly underestimated the Japanese determination to hold Buna regardless of costs. By now surely the Americans should have learned that the Japanese were a powerful and determined people.

The third major flaw was in the estimations of the strength of the American forces. The 32nd Infantry Division simply was not ready for the task and their officers knew it. They warned MacArthur that they were unfit for such an extended operation but he insisted that they move ahead. Almost immediately it was made evident that the Americans were not prepared for forced marches through the jungle.

So as November ended, the Australians, assured that the Japanese defense force had been whittled down by casualties and disease, and convinced that those still alive were no more inclined to fight than the American officers believed, began to push them away from Port Moresby. They reported that the Japanese were starving and, having nothing else to eat, had taken to eating the bodies of the dead Australians. The truth of this claim is still hazy, but the barbarism of the Japanese in the Buna campaign was appalling to most of the Allies. At the end it was recognized that not a single Allied soldier taken prisoner in the six months of the Buna campaign had been allowed to live.

The key to the battle and its significance lay with the Kokoda Trail. It is a single-file footpath that runs for 95 kilometers (60 miles trail, 37 miles straight) through the Owen Stanley Range in Papua, New Guinea. The range, which runs some 300 miles southeast to northeast, peaks at Mount Victoria, and is made up of ridges, like razorbacks, which make it difficult to climb. Often climbers have had to resort to going on hands and knees and cutting toeholds as they climb. It is hot and humid during the day and intensely cold at night. Today a popular hiking trail, there is even an annual challenge race there, but at the time it was the center of most of the fighting. As they retreated, the Japanese fought hard, slowly withdrawing along the Kokoda Trail, followed by the Americans of the 32nd Division.

The American unit, known as Warren Force, consisting of the 1st and 3rd Battalions of the 128th Infantry Regiment, along with Brigadier Wooten's Australians, was to attack along the coast. The force suffered a serious setback even before they arrived when four ships carrying much of the food, ammunition, and equipment were sunk by Japanese Zeros that attacked them in the harbor. A day later, two of the remaining coastal ships were lost. Short on supplies, untested, and unprepared for the heat and humidity of the jungle, they made little progress, and by the end of November were still short of the strip. As the Americans fought to move forward the lack of decent supply lines began to take its toll on the Americans troops. Most were hungry, quite a few were sick from the swampy conditions and high temperature, and all were harassed by insects of all kinds.

They began to close in on the Buna area around the first of November 1942. The American attack was to come with one unit attacking from the south toward the village, and a second on the airstrip that lay to the east.

The first few days of the battle did not go well. The Japanese, well dug in and rested, were faced by troops that had been advancing though the jungle. Within the first three days the Australian 7th Infantry Division had lost 204 men, and within the first two weeks, the casualties for the 32nd Infantry were 392. Having been told by General MacArthur to "attack at all costs," the Allied forces ran into heavy machine gun fire from guns concealed in bunkers, and well-directed sniper fire from in among the trees.

On the 29th the Japanese were reinforced by sea by about 500 men from the 41st Infantry Regiment and the Allied assault was stymied. General MacArthur had become frustrated at this point, primarily with the 32nd Infantry and its officers. They were not taking the initiative. He relieved General Harding and replaced him with Major General Robert L. Eichelberger with orders to remove any officer that would not fight. It was done, taking out most regimental and battalion commanders. Eichelberger took a breather in order to reorganize and to allow his food and medical supplies to catch up. Then, on 5 December, he ordered an attack. The 32nd was finally able to push a wedge into the Japanese lines. During the day Staff Sergeant Herman Bottcher and a platoon of 31 men were able to push forward enough to separate Buna Mission and Buna Village. The next day the Australians captured Buna Village and Americans took on Buna Mission.

The Japanese had not given up. They landed an additional 1,300 reinforcements and took up the remaining positions. On 18 December the Allies were reinforced by the Australian 7th Division's 18th Brigade. The 18th, commanded by Brigadier General George Wootten, was accompanied by a squad of tanks from the 2/6 Australian Armored Regiment. It moved in from Mine Bay to reinforce the Americans. The brigade's first attack was launched in the airfield area as the 2/9 and 2/10 battalions hit on the morning of 18 December. In the next ten days of fighting the Allies were able to advance along the coast. By 20 December the combined Australian and American forces reached the western end of the New Strip and were threatening Old Strip from the north. By the 23rd they had cleared the area between the airfield and the coast, leaving only the resistance around the western end of the Old Strip. Four tanks that went in to support the Allied push were destroyed, but the fighting continued, and by the last day of the year, the Old Strip finally fell.

After pausing to allow for more proper planning and the replacement of the tanks, as well as replacing the depleted 2/10 with the 2/12, the Allies attacked on the morning of 1 January with tanks and infantry, and destroyed the final Japanese positions by nightfall. The American troops attacking east from Buna Village had secured Buna Government Station, and joined with forces from strips. There the final attack on Buna Mission came on 1–2 January 1943. Japanese soldiers had been attempting to escape by sea. The two senior Japanese officers, Colonel Tamamoto and Captain Tasueda, had already taken their own lives.

On the second day of January 1943, the Buna area fell to the Allied forces. The last of the surviving Japanese defensive fortifications were cleared up and the few remaining Japanese soldiers taken prisoner. The cost of the defense had been high for the Japanese, and more than 1,400 were buried by the Allies. More important, perhaps, it was the first defeat for the Japanese Army in the field in modern history.

The cost for the Allies was no less awful: 620 dead, 2,065 wounded, 2,952 hospitalized for disease, and 132 missing in action. Nearly 70 percent of the casualties were in the three core 32nd Division regiments, the rest in the 18th Brigade.

The tactical importance of the Battle of Buna is far more significant than the two small settlements involved. Both Buna Mission and Buna Village were minute, consisting of only a few huts and a building or two. They were located on the far side of the island from the only significant town in New Guinea, Port Moresby. They had little significance in their own right, but the defeat of the Imperial Japanese Army at this point was highly important. The Japanese failure at the Battle of the Coral Sea, and then this significant ground action loss, were the first two of many victories for the Allied troops in the Pacific. They were testing grounds for both Americans and Australians, and many a hard lesson was learned. It was a testimony to the fact, however, that the Allied soldiers had the determination to fight this war, even in the most desperate of situations.

In terms of cost, the Papuan campaign resulted in more deaths, and wounded more men, than the fighting on Guadalcanal. Perhaps it is worth remembering. Two sergeants from the 32nd Division who were killed in action near Buna — Elmer J. Burr and Kenneth E. Gruenert — were awarded the Medal of Honor.

Notes

1. There is some historic disagreement about the name, the belief being that the Americans identified it as a train when it was originally, and should be remembered as, a track. The American Army officially defined it as a trail in October 1942.
2. General Willoughby would make this same basic claim about the Chinese during the early days of the Korean War (1950–1953), just before a hundred thousand-plus Chinese volunteers attacked the United Nations forces at the Chosin Reservoir.

Further Reading

Brune, Peter. *A Bastard of a Place: The Australians in Papua.* New York: Allen and Unwin, 2005.
Fuller, Richard. *Shokan: Hirohito's Samurai.* London: Arms and Armor, 1992.
Mayo, Lida. *Bloody Buna: The Campaign That Halted the Japanese Invasion of Australia.* New York: Doubleday, 1974.
Papuan Campaign, 16 November 1942 – 23 January 1943. Washington, DC: Center of Military History, United States Army, 1945.

17. The Massacre at Palawan

He escaped by breaking through the strands of barbed wire fence, pulling them aside with his bare hands, and then leaping off the cliffs that rose next to the bay. He had already evaded the fire in the tunnels where they were held, but had managed to break through the timbers being used as a roof, and got to the cliffs. In the process he had been shot in the leg and, after a struggle, was able to turn their own weapons on the guards and kill three of those who got in his way. Pulling himself into the water, he moved along the shore until he found a location hidden by some rocks where he believed he could hide from the Japanese troops searching the area. He remained there, hidden from view, wounded, and hearing the voices of the guards looking for him. Whenever the Japanese found a prisoner hiding among the rocks they dragged him out onto the beach and beat him to death. After what seemed to be an eternity, it grew dark and the soldiers' voices faded further into the distance. He decided that his only hope of escape lay in the water. Moving into the shark-infested waters of the bay, the young Marine slowly swam the nearly five miles, his wound and lack of a decent diet sapping his strength. Once ashore, however, he was discovered by men who were tuberculosis patients at the Palawan Penal Colony, and they agreed to help him. The Marine, Sergeant Douglas Bogue, was finally brought to the guerilla headquarters, where there was contact with the Allies. In time they were able to help him get back to the 7th Fleet headquarters at Leyte. There he provided information for the forthcoming attack on Palawan.

But from whom and what was Marine Sergeant Bogue escaping and why?

Eight hours after the attack on Pearl Harbor, the Japanese launched their invasion of the Philippines, and with determination marched across the islands until, on 9 April 1942, Luzon fell. As the battle raged and the poorly equipped and supplied Philippine Scouts and U.S. military fought back, the Japanese began to collect vast numbers of prisoners. These ranks were swelled with the eventual fall of Corregidor, at which time an estimated

72,000 POWs came under the control of the Japanese. The stronger among these, as well as some of the civilians with useful skills, were stuffed into the suffocating holds of cargo ships and sent back to Japan to work as slave labor in the mines and manufacturing plants.

A significant number remained in the Philippines, where they performed a variety of construction tasks. However, when the Allied successes began to multiply and the Japanese found themselves anticipating an invasion designed to retake the Philippines, Japanese military authorities took the drastic step of ordering the deaths of those prisoners who were in a position to be rescued. Apparently fearing that the American prisoners of war being held on the Philippine island of Palawan would be liberated by the quickly approaching Allied forces, the Japanese ordered the deaths of the remaining 150 prisoners. The instructions, sent to all the Japanese POW camp commanders, left little to be questioned, for the directions concluded with this statement: "The aim [is] not to allow the escape of a single one, to annihilate them all, and not leave any traces."[1]

To accomplish this mission the prisoners were ordered into three covered trenches that had been built under the guise of air raid shelters. As they were being forced into the trenches some noticed that there were additional machine-gun posts set up, and groups of riflemen posted along their route. Once the prisoners had been forced inside the trenches, and the opening closed, the guards began to bring buckets of gasoline in what one described as a bucket brigade. As each soldier rushed forward he would douse the men and the trench with the fluid until the stink of it was making the men sick. Then the fuel was lighted.

As the fire started the prisoners began to panic. They had no weapons or means to protect themselves from the danger, and the area in which they were held was crowded with few exits. As they tried to escape the fire, pushing their way out of the trenches, the men were shot by the waiting guards. This was 15 December 1944.

Some few were able to get out of the trench and headed toward the cliffs, the only reasonable direction for escape. A few managed to get over these bluffs that ran along one side of the camp and not far from the trenches. They rose to about 50 feet above the shore but were climbable. A few, like Sergeant Bogue, made it down to the water, but most of those who made it that far were hunted down and killed. Several were killed in the effort to climb down. It is believed that between 133 and 141 of the men who had been prisoners of war were killed either in the fire or in the effort to escape. Only 11 survived.

The camp at Palawan was not atypical. During the early days of World War II, as the Japanese military advanced, tens of thousands of American military and civilian prisoners were captured. Many were in terrible shape when captured, and were sent into filthy, overcrowded POW camps. A good many of these camps were located in the Philippines in abandoned military and civilian buildings. One of these was set up on the offshore island of Palawan, which stretched from Mindoro in the northeast to Borneo in the southwest.

The indigenous people of the islands consisted of three tribes, the Tagbanua, Tau't Batu, and Batak, who lived in remote inland villages. In most incidences the Filipino natives stayed away from either of the warring parties, but there were several among them who were hostile to the Japanese and who took pity on the Americans and helped them in their return to Allied lines. Most of those who escaped from Palawan were helped in some fashion by the natives living on the island.

Most of what is known of the POW camp at Palawan is from the men who had been there but who, for medical reasons, had been taken off before the massacre. These include Dan Crowley of Simsbury, Connecticut, whose arm was broken so badly that it was basically useless; and Joseph DuPont, who had managed to get off Palawan by faking a bad case of malaria. But few men, once assigned, got off.

Those who made up the main body of prisoners included 346 men who were sent from the Cabanatuan POW camp north of Manila to Puerto Princesa on the island of Palawan, located on the western perimeter of the Sulu Sea. Officially it was the Palawan Military POW Camp #10A, Princesa, Palawan Province. The prisoners had been collected from numerous holding areas and included men from all the service branches as well as a few civilians. The prisoners were housed in dilapidated Filipino constabulary buildings. They were dirty and hot, and the "housing" consisted of little more than a place to lie down, with little or no protection from the weather. What outbuildings were there either housed the Japanese guards or were used for the storage of equipment. The prisoners usually ate their noon meal in the field, leaving early after a breakfast of rice and weak tea, and returned late. A vast majority of the meals consisted of what the prisoners called *Lugao*, which was rice soaked in water and enriched by worms, bits of dogs, or an occasional vegetable. When eaten, it was briefly filling, but lacked most of the nourishment they needed.

The prisoners worked long hard days in the sun, expending their remaining energy trying to survive under these conditions without proper food or medical supplies. The prisoners suffered from a wide variety of diseases: dengue fever, malaria, rickets, dysentery, scurvy, pellagra, beriberi and tropical ulcers. They had none of the necessities most had come to expect, such as toothpaste, fresh water, and soap. Nor were the prisoners, working all day in the sun, allowed any salt. They suffered unrestrained physical abuse, for the guards dealt with them as if they were little other than work animals best controlled by violence. The men suffered severe beatings, broken bones, and one more than one occasion, being burned alive.

Obviously the Japanese view of prisoners was different from that of the Western nations. The idea of an honorable surrender was foreign to them, since they felt instead that the only honor lay in fighting to the death. Japan had not signed the Geneva Convention, not because they were an evil people but primarily because it was meaningless to them; becoming a prisoner of war brought disgrace on the individual and on his family, and the situation was not expected to arise. For them, since being a prisoner was the moral equivalent of death, there was nothing worse.

The prisoners were sent to Palawan to construct an airfield needed for the longer-range planes. It was necessary to hack the airstrip from the jungle, beating the ground to make a hard surface, and then smashing the stones and mixing concrete to make a runway. Most of the prisoners' clothes had fallen into rags, and the prisoners covered themselves with G-strings provided by the Japanese. But they did little to protect the prisoners' bodies from the sun. A few were able to find or construct a hat of some sort. Few, if any, had shoes. While the number of prisoners varied at any particular time, the number involved remained about the same; new prisoners were brought in to replace those who died off. The men worked hard, side by side with Japanese construction soldiers that ran the machinery and took charge. Work halted only occasionally and days of rest were few and far between.

Responsibility for the camp and for the construction of the airfield went to Captain Nagayoshi Kojima and the 131st Airfield Battalion. The prisoners called Kojima "the weasel." The unit had been sent from Formosa on 10 July 1942 for the construction, and was under considerable pressure to get their work done, and to keep the airfield open and workable despite the continued bombing by American planes.

Even though the construction was still unfinished, 159 of the POWs from Palawan were sent back to Manila in September 1944 to take on other construction assignments. This left the remaining 150 men to complete the airfield. This number was far too few, so the guards lengthened the work day and pushed the prisoners even harder. Soon they were crushing coral gravel by hand and pouring and smoothing concrete six and seven days a week.

On 19 October 1944, an American Consolidated B-24 Liberator bomber hit the area and damaged two ships resting in the small harbor, as well as several planes at Palawan. More American planes returned on the 28th, destroying nearly 60 Japanese aircraft that were still on the ground. The morale in camp increased immediately on seeing the return of the Americans, but it was a mixed emotion, since the raid angered the Japanese guards and the treatment grew increasingly harsher. As one concession to the bombings, and after several requests, the POWs were finally given permission to paint a sign on the roofs of their building that identified them as a POW camp. Once the sign was painted, and notice was taken that the buildings were spared, the Japanese began to use the marked buildings to store their supplies. The raids were a forewarning, however, for the American forces had landed at Leyte on the 19th.

The fear of continued and increasingly heavy raids led the Japanese to have the prisoners construct three shelters, each of which was 150 feet long and 4 feet high. The Japanese ordered the entrances at each end of the trench to be large enough to admit only one man at a time. Over the top they created a roof with large logs, dirt and grass. The trenches were located along the beach at the side of the camp just about where the cliffs dropped to the sea.

On 14 December an Allied convoy that was headed for Mindoro was mistakenly reported to be heading for Palawan. The Japanese authorities on the island reacted accordingly to this latest communication. The Japanese were growing fearful, having been aware of the American State Department communication concerning Japanese treatment of prisoners and possibly of trying them for war crimes. Rather than ease up on their treatment of the prisoners, as might have been expected, the Japanese response was the creation of a "kill-all policy" directed to camp commanders. This came as a written order from the supreme commander, General Hideki Tojo, to the Japanese commander in the Philippines, General Tomyuki Yamashita, the "Tiger of Malaya." He was ordered to kill the American prisoners of war to prevent them from being liberated.

When two American Lockheed P-38 Lighting fighter planes were sighted overhead, the prisoners were ordered into the covered trenches. The number of American planes flying overhead had increased daily, and this seemed like just one more occasion. But when the planes passed over without causing any damage to the field or the camp, the prisoners were not returned to work but rather were ordered to remain inside the trenches. One or two men tried to avoid going in, perhaps sensing what was coming, and were killed on the spot. Then, as if some sort of signal had been passed, more than fifty Japanese soldiers orchestrated under Lieutenant Yoshikaza Sato began to move toward the shelters. It was just 1300 hours. The guards carried with them buckets of aviation gasoline with which, as they drew closer, they doused the shelters. Coming behind them were men with torches and hand grenades that were used to light the fires. The trenches went up in a whoosh, fire quickly engulfing the area, and setting the men inside on fire.

Caught in what was little more than a crawl space and with the flames quickly filling the area, the prisoners inside tied to get out any way they could. Some were able to scramble out at the ends of the trenches, but as they came out they were immediately caught in streams of machine gun fire, or individually bayoneted or clubbed to death with the butts of the soldiers' rifles. A few broke through the roof of the trench and were able to get as far as the first line of guards. There they attacked the Japanese and, perhaps thinking that they would at least take some of the enemy with them, managed to kill a few of the guards. But there were too many, and the Japanese overpowered and killed them.

A few that made it outside the trench chose to run for it, hoping to make it away from the expanding fire and the bark of the guns. Somewhere between thirty and forty Americans managed to get to, and then through or under, the barbed wire fence that surrounded the camp. In one spot along the fenced area natural erosion had created a shallow ledge. Previous ventures outside the wire had set up potential escape routes that had been created for just such an emergency. Now the frightened men were taking full advantage of them. Once through the wire, some too exhausted to climb fell down the cliffs to the beach below. Others were able to climb down and made it to the rocks, hoping to be able to hide there. A few immediately tried to swim the distance across Puerto Princesa Bay while it was still daylight, but it was too difficult and the Japanese soldiers picked them off one by one with rifle shots from the cliffs.

On the beach the Japanese soldiers were stationed and were making a systematic search of the caves, rocks, and crevices seeking anyone who might have escaped. When a prisoner was discovered he was dragged out onto the beach and killed on the spot, either by gun or bayonet. Occasionally the Japanese would take the time to torture the one caught, setting him on fire and watching him burn. The soldiers continued to search until, finally, a call for dinner sent most of them scurrying back to the camp. One or two of the prisoners, separating themselves from the others, were able to hide out in a sewer pipe that had been cut into the cliffs. There they waited for night to come, then moved out into the bay hoping to be able to swim the five miles. Some of the stories of the survivors are known, though not all of them.

Joseph Fern Barta, a radioman first class, was able to make it across the bay, swimming nearly nine hours, and then set out looking for help. He wandered the dense jungle for more than ten days, barely able to survive on what he could find to eat and drink, when he finally ran across some natives willing to help. They eventually got him in touch with the Allied military and he was evacuated from Brooke Point.

Dan Crowley, a marine from Simsbury, Connecticut, had lost his arm in the escape effort, but managed to get away despite the wound. He was finally rescued by some Philippine fishermen who found him hiding in one of their traps. Within a few days they had managed to transport him to Allied lines.

Glen McDole of M Company, 1st Battalion, 4th Marine Regiment, from Ankeny, Iowa, managed to escape through a hatch the prisoners had created in the trench. He had been at the Cavite Naval Yard when the war broke out and had been finally captured on 6 May 1942. After getting out of the burning trench, stark naked, he was able to make it to a pile of trash from the camp. He took refuge there among the filth and the bugs and insects drawn to it. When the confusion cleared he was able to climb through the fence and down the cliff to a coral reef. He was later found clinging to a fish trap far out in the bay. Local fishermen rescued him. His story is the best account we have of what life was like at the camp, as well as the details of his escape effort.

Army Private First Class Donald Joseph Martyn from New York City apparently managed to make the five-mile swim across the bay, but after that there is no record of where he tried to go, or what eventually happened to him. He was never seen again.

Army Private Eugene Nielsen, of B Battery, 59th Coast Artillery Regiment, had been one of the first to note that the Japanese were acting somewhat differently, and was on the lookout for something unexpected to happen. During the fighting that followed the fire he was wounded three different times as he tried to get away. Despite a loss of blood, however, he managed to climb down the cliff bluffs and made it to the shore. He located a spot and hid for several hours before making an escape attempt. Fighting increasing weakness, he managed to swim to the far shore of Puerto Princesa Bay. After a quick rest he moved into the swamp, where he traveled for some time before running across a friendly Filipino. The native led him to three other survivors and he was evacuated.

Albert D. Pacheco, Headquarters Battery, 200th Coast Artillery Regiment (AA), escaped by swimming across Puerto Princesa Bay. He and Edwin Petry had hidden in a coral cave for most of the rest of the day and part of the night before making the swim. They were eventually found by natives, joined up with Nielsen, and they were helped until reaching Allied forces.

Edwin A. Petry, 7th Materials Squadron, 19th Bomber Group, had hidden in a coral cave with Pacheco as long as they could until being driven out by high tide and crabs. They made the swim across and were finally helped by natives who took Nielsen, Pacheco, and Petry to authorities who moved them out. Petry died in California on 7 May 1987.

Rufus "Smitty" Smith, L Company, 3rd Battalion, 4th Marine Regiment, was badly bitten by a shark on his left arm as he tried to make the swim to relative safety. Nevertheless, he was able to make it to the opposite shore, where he hid out in a sewer pipe. After a few days in hiding he was discovered by friendly forces and helped in the location of Allied troops.

We are aware that William J. Balchus of I Battery, 60th Coast Artillery Regiment (AA), escaped, but the details are not yet known. U.S. Air Corps enlisted man Tommy "Pops" Daniels also made it out eventually. Also escaping were Elmo V. Deal, A Battery, 59th Coast Artillery Regiment, and Earnest J. Koblos of C Battery, 59th Coast Artillery Regiment, but just how that was done is not recorded. There is little information about Joseph Dupont as well, but we know he made it out because he was the one who would later spearhead the efforts to place a memorial marker at the cemetery.

Major Bogue, who had received a battlefield commission in Korea in 1951, died in March of 2004 in Lompoc, California.

The battle for Palawan Island began on 28 February 1945 and lasted until 22 April. In what were identified as Operations Victor I and Victor II, Lieutenant General Robert Eichelberger were instructed to take the island. A combination of American and Filipino forces managed to complete the assignment by the last of April, but the U.S. was able to use the captured airfield by mid–March. There was little left of the prisoner of war camp when the troops arrived.

There were no civilian witnesses to what was already being called the Palawan massacre. When the camp area was liberated by the 186th Infantry Regiment of the 41st Division, all civilians from the area were excavated in order to locate and properly bury the dead. The atrocities were well documented, however, mostly through the memories of those involved. In 1952 the remains of 123 of the 139 victims of the massacre at Palawan were transferred to the Jefferson Barracks National Cemetery, located at 2900 Sheridan Road in South St. Louis, Missouri. There they lie in a mass grave marked with the names, ranks, and branches of service of those buried there. The remaining sixteen were interred in private cemeteries by their next of kin.

As for the Japanese, there was little justice done. Lieutenant Yoshiwara and Captain Kojima, the camp commander, could not be found at the end of the war. The same was true for a good many of the officers and men involved. The battle for the island was intense and costly, and chances are most of them died in battle. Not all, however. Six men who were camp guards and charged with abuse were acquitted for lack of evidence; ten were found guilty and given sentences of from two years to death for one of them. Sattaichi Deguchi, "the meanest man in the camp," was given a death sentence, but this was commuted to life by General Douglas MacArthur. Toru Ogawa, the commander of 131st Airfield Battalion, who directed the labor, and who was accused of the abuse of more than 300 prisoners, was given two years of hard labor which was then reduced for time served. The same fate was true of Tomisabura Sawa.

For those interested, the site of the massacre can still be visited. Little has been done there to acknowledge what happened, but the location has not changed much. On site it is possible to follow the story, as it is partially told by Glenn McDole in his book *Last Man Out*. The site itself can be seen in the opening scenes of the 2005 Miramax movie *The Great Raid*.

Note

1. *Journal Taiwan POW Camp Headquarters in Taihoku,* 1 August 1944, translated by Steven H. Green, American cryptographer.

Further Reading

Kerr, E. Bartlett. *Surrender and Survivor: The Experience of the American POW in the Pacific, 1941–1945.* New York: William Morrow, 1985.

McDole, Glenn. *Last Man Out.* Jefferson, NC: McFarland, 2004.

Sides, Hampton. *Ghost Soldiers: The Forgotten Epic Story of World War II's Most Dramatic Mission.* New York: Doubleday, 2007.

Wrynn, V. Dennis. "American Prisoners of War: Massacre at Palawan." *World War II Magazine,* November 1997.

18. The Voyage of the *Li Wo*

The Japanese attack had been without warning and the Imperial Japanese Army and Navy were moving ahead with a timetable that left the Allies little if any time to prepare. Almost before they knew it, Malaya and the Philippines were under heavy attack, and while the Allies had few men to bring into the fight, the Japanese were pouring in men and equipment by the shipload, watched over by powerful escorts. The only way to slow down the Japanese was to do something about the transports. There were, however, few ships indeed that had any chance of stopping them. The remains of the Asiatic Fleet, joined by Dutch vessels and some British and Australian ships, simply did not have enough firepower.

Most of the sea power that was available was either in the defense of Java and Australia, or involved in trying to deal with the immediate problems of resupplying those fighting at Singapore. Then, in late January and early February, the priority changed to the evacuation of the island fortress. The Japanese were doing the impossible and no one seemed able to stop them. It was time to get out, and just about every vessel capable of moving was trying to accomplish that. Most of the ships had left or were in preparation for leaving when, late on Thursday evening of 12 February 1942, the converted passenger ship *Li Wo* slipped out of the embattled harbor of Singapore. Singapore was under siege: Japanese troops, having crossed the causeway, were so close small arms fire could be heard. The intention of the crew and passengers of the small boat was to run the gauntlet of the Japanese navy and make it to the relative safety of Java.

The *Li Wo* was an excellent little ship when allowed to do what she had been created to do, but she was not much when compared to the warships that she would eventually sail among. Despite her size, however, she was to make her mark on history. The *Li Wo*, a vessel of 1,000 tons, had been built in 1938 as a shallow-draft boat that was specifically designed to carry passengers up and down the rapids of the upper Yangtze River. She was designed with tall sides, a fairly flat bottom, and a powerful engine to fight the current of the Yangtze. The boat had been originally built in Hong Kong by Jardine Matheson & Company for the China Navigation Company. During the 1930s, passenger traffic and cargo shipments on the Yangtze were increasingly profitable and the new ship was doing well. But the *Li Wo* had enjoyed only a short career in the passenger business when, in June of 1940, she was requisitioned by the British Royal Navy as an auxiliary.

Despite the seeming friendliness of the Japanese at Shanghai, and the fact that the Japanese tried to separate their fight with the Chinese from any fight with the Western nations, the Japanese intentions were fairly clear, and affected governments were doing what they could to prepare. The British Navy, suddenly in need of vessels of all kinds, commissioned the *Li Wo* as an auxiliary patrol craft. As the war clouds filled with thunder, the Royal Navy was trying to get its services in order and had moved a good many of the requisitioned vessels out. Unfortunately most of them had been sent to Singapore.

As was the case for a good many other eligible civilian seamen at the time, Thomas Wilkinson, who was the captain of the passenger steamer *Li Wo*, was also inducted into the service. Wilkinson was commissioned as a Temporary Lieutenant of the Royal Navy Reserves. He was 43 at the time. He had been born 1 August 1898 to a seafaring family, and lived in West Derby, Lancashire. He had served for the Blue Funnel Line, and then for awhile on the SS *Alicinious*, a converted troopship, during World War I. After that he joined the Indo-China Steam Navigation Company and by 1936 had become one of their ship masters. While a qualified merchant captain, his experience was primarily on the Yangtze River.

At first the navy put the small boat to use patrolling the inland harbor, and then as an escort for the few remaining gunboats. Finally, the converted passenger steamer was ordered out along with the other military units as the Japanese invasion moved aggressively toward them. The *Li Wo* and her catch-all crew were sent to Singapore, the last British stronghold in the area. It was still believed that they could hold out a while longer. The British had greatly underestimated the Japanese, and the capability of their army, and were now paying the price.

During her drive toward Singapore the *Li Wo* was able to come to the rescue of some of the survivors of the HMS *Lipes*, under Captain Steel, which had been sunk by three Japanese planes near Sultan Shoal. In doing so she returned many to Singapore who felt they had finally gotten away. Once she arrived in Singapore the *Li Wo* received her final crew aboard. There is no record of just how they were selected, for they represented the wide variety of individuals who were in Singapore at the time. The ship's complement consisted of 84 officers and men. Most of the original crew had been replaced, as many of the Chinese who had once manned her preferred to remain in their own country, even with the threat of the Japanese. To fill the gaps left in her crew, unattached and unassigned men were assembled from those who had been survivors of other ships and units. On board she carried 19 navy ratings, five army ranks, and two Royal Air Force sergeants, 34 Europeans (mostly civilians), ten Malaysians and six Chinese. Most of the naval ratings were survivors from the HMS *Repulse* or the HMS *Prince of Wales*, which had been sunk east of Malaya by Japanese land-based bombers in the South China Sea on 10 December 1941. Many of the army personnel had been with the Plymouth Argyles. A good many assigned to the crew had been in Malaya, and had gathered together in Singapore and assigned to the *Li Wo* for a last-minute dash for freedom. The names of the Europeans on board, other than the names of the one or two who survived as prisoners, are not recorded.

When she was confiscated by the Navy, very little was done to improve the *Li Wo* as a fighting warship. The only significant additions had been four ancient four-inch guns and two Vickers machine guns, which could have provided some firepower, but it was later discovered that she had almost no ammunition. Army and Navy personnel, either picked up off the docks or following orders to escape, had been assigned as gunners. There was nothing they could do under the circumstances to improve the speed of the little ship, or give her any greater stability considering her flat bottom. No one was under any illusions about the little ship's ability to deal with the ocean dash. But, according to her captain, when she left Singapore she was sailing out as a warship under her own orders.

Captain G.F.A. Mulock of the Extended Defense Office had collected sixteen highly diverse vessels to evacuate as many refugees as they could. Mulock and his motley armada were trying to leave at the same time as the *Li Wo*, as a result of which the *Li Wo* is sometimes included in that group. But she was not an official part of that effort. The evacuation fleet was scheduled to leave Singapore on the same date, but running into their own difficulties, only a few of those ships made it to safety.

Twenty-four hours after receiving orders to move, and just at the last minute, the *Li Wo* sailed from her harbor at Singapore in hope of getting to Batavia before the Japanese took control of the whole area. The Japanese were advancing at an incredible rate and, while the army was doing what it could, there was no doubt on anyone's part that the battle for Singapore was about over. What was left for the British at this point was to save as many of the ships, as much of the equipment, and all the men possible that might be used to fight another day. The escape route planned was a long and dangerous one, especially for a shallow-draft craft that was not designed for the open sea. And they would be sailing through seas that were now almost completely controlled by the Imperial Japanese Navy and under constant sight of the air force. Three days later, on the 15th of February, the advance forces of the Japanese Imperial Army occupied the key city of Singapore, and with it took control of the Netherlands East Indies.

Most of the men aboard the *Li Wo* had been assigned, that is, sent their by their commands in order for them to get away. Few had any experience fighting the Japanese, and any who might possess skills or information that would help the Allied cause were being returned to safety in the hope of training more troops in the tactics of the new enemy. This included several men who were survivors from the sinking of the British capital ships, the HMS *Repulse* and the *Prince of Wales*, who had been ordered aboard the *Li Wo* at the last minute.

When the *Li Wo* pulled out she was accompanied by her sister ship *Fu Wo* (*Fhu Woo*), which planned to make the same journey. She had aboard just about the same complement. While the *Li Wo* managed to make some distance out of port, the *Fu Wo*, under Lieutenant N. Cooke, was damaged shortly after starting out and found it necessary to return to Singapore. Her captain was hoping that she might be repaired and he could get her underway again, but that was not to be. She was later destroyed in the harbor to avoid capture by the Japanese. But things were not going well for the *Li Wo* either.

Moving as quickly as she could, and running away when spotted, she was still attacked from the air four separate times by land-based planes during the first 12-hour period. The planes swooped down on the struggling ship, firing their machine guns and causing considerable damage. But each time the little ship survived. The worst news perhaps was that the damage had made the radio useless. It had not been much help anyway, since they were traveling under radio silence, but now they had no way to communicate with other naval vessels. They were definitely on their own.

On the 14th, just two days out, the ship dropped anchor close to shore at one of the islands, where Captain Wilkinson intended to wait it out until dark. The hope was that if they could make it through the day, then under cover of night they would make a dash through the 80 miles of the Banka Straits. It was a good plan, but it was not to be. Before long they were spotted and the captain decided to make a run for it. About 1100 hours the boat was attacked by a Japanese seaplane. With unbelievable determination the small crew of the *Li Wo* was able to fight off enemy action for nearly three hours. But, during the conflict, the hull and deck of the *Li Wo* were badly damaged.

Once more sailing without harassment, Captain Wilkinson began to think the ship might just get away with it and that they might make it to Java. The *Li Wo* moved ahead as quickly as it could, considering its damaged hull. Within an hour, however, those on the bridge spotted smoke on the horizon. It was somewhere between 1630 and 1700 hours but still light enough to see. Lieutenant Wilkinson was not sure if he would recognize the nationality of the ships, so he called for a crew member who had served on the HMS *Prince of Wales*. The seaman had no trouble identifying one of the spotted ships as a Japanese light cruiser. While the captain was still trying to think what his next move should be, the lookouts called out. They had spotted more ships, this time off the starboard bow. It did not take long for Captain Wilkinson to realize that the *Li Wo* was caught between the converging Japanese forces. They were surrounded.

The *Li Wo*'s situation could not have been worse, for what they had sighted was a significant part of the massive Japanese invasion fleet heading toward Java under the command of Vice Admiral Ozawa Jisaburo. It was less than ten miles away from them at this point. Several efforts had been made by Admiral Doorman's hodgepodge command of American, British, Dutch and Australian ships to stop, or at least to slow, the steady advance. But the odds against them were overwhelming, and in a series of hit-and-run attacks, the Allies had accomplished little other than to damage a few of the enemy ship, and lose many of their own few remaining vessels. The escorts for the Japanese fleet Wilkinson was facing consisted of the carrier IJN *Ryujo*, four heavy cruisers, one light cruiser and three destroyers. There did not seem to be any way for the little *Li Wo* to avoid them. But at that moment it no longer mattered, for Captain Wilkinson had other plans in mind.

Perhaps believing that the best (maybe, in this case, the only) defense was a good offense, the newly commissioned captain called on his gun crews for an ammunition check. They had left Singapore in such a hurry they had not had time or opportunity to pick up supplies. Checking with leading seaman Thomas Henry Parsons, the gunner, Wilkinson soon discovered that they had only six semi-armor-piercing shells on board. The rest of the ammunition consisted of four graze-fuse shells, three AA shells and three practice shells. They had more, but not enough, cartridges for the machine guns. It was hardly enough to even sight the guns, let alone take on a major warship.

In addition, the boat had no range finder and no inclinometer to help in aiming the ancient guns.

These disadvantages did not, however, change the captain's opinion that they were a warship and that they should indeed act like one. As he saw it, their duty was to engage the enemy when and where the enemy was found. Talking with the crew, he told them of his intentions, and from all available evidence they wholeheartedly joined in with him. Acknowledging that it would be best for them to try to get the greatest bang for the buck, he determined that they should make the effort to sink one or more of the transports. These were the targets with the most appeal and in the long run would do the most damage to the Japanese cause.

Captain Wilkinson selected as his first target one of the smaller transports that he estimated was between four and five thousand tons and sailing a little off to one side of the formation. Checking to see that everyone was in his place, he called down for the straining boilers to give him all they had, and turned his bow toward the enemy. At first the Japanese escorts either did not see the *Li Wo* or perhaps had mistaken her for one of their own, because they paid the steaming vessel no mind. The helmsman was able seaman William Thomas Snow. The *Li Wo* was able to close on the transport they had targeted with little opposition but the churning sea. At four thousand yards the converted passenger ship opened fire.

The ship's executive officer and two other officers joined with Petty Officer Arthur Thompson, an Australian stoker, and two able seamen, to man the exposed 4-inch gun on the foredeck. The first shell was fired to determine the range and landed well over target. The sight was quickly adjusted and the gunners ordered to fire again. One by one they pumped the five remaining armor-piercing shells into the target, hitting the superstructure and quickly setting the ship on fire. Their skill had been graced with luck as well, and within minutes the transport was sinking. The crew of the *Li Wo* could already see men were beginning to jump over the sides in an effort to avoid the flames. As they watched, the transport began to list, and Wilkinson was fairly sure that it would not be afloat for long. The only problem was that the short attack had taken all of the ammunition. The ship had nothing left to throw at the enemy other than some shells from the Vickers machine gun.

This deficiency, however, did not seem to deter Captain Wilkinson or his determined crew. Calling again for all the steam he could get, he selected his second target. Lying nearest to him was an 800-ton transport crowded with soldiers on their way to Java. The coxswain at the helm of the *Li Wo* was Able Seaman William Thomas Snow, 19, of Sussex. Moving at her best possible speed, and heading directly toward their new target, the *Li Wo* moved swiftly to close the gap. As they did so the RAF sergeant who was manning the Vickers gun concentrated his fire on the transport's gun crew, who were trying to get their one weapon into play. He managed to keep them from firing on the highly vulnerable auxiliary ship as it closed the distance between them. Chugging with all she was worth and unsteady in the choppy seas, the *Li Wo* moved like an arrow to the target. Then, with a tremendous crash, a shattering of wood and screeching of twisting metal, the *Li Wo* struck the transport with all the power left in its aged engines. The Japanese transport was badly hurt and immediately began to take on water. It soon began to list.

The *Li Wo* was able to pull back a bit and stood by watching as the transport began to sink beneath the waters. The sea was soon covered with the bobbing heads of the soldiers who had been on board. There was nothing much else the *Li Wo* could do. There is some doubt as to whether the *Li Wo* at this point was under control.

By this time the Japanese escorts had awakened to the fact the convoy was being attacked. Smaller ships turned into the scene, seeking to join in. The larger ships opened up in an effort to judge the range. At first the aim from the massive battle wagons was not good, and shells flew over the ship, doing no damage. Then the Japanese gunners corrected and the fire quickly became more accurate. Several of the enemy ships were now firing. Within a few minutes the little *Li Wo* had received several immediate hits both to her superstructure and hull. Suffering major damage and having lost way, she began to list to the starboard. Fire was breaking out at several locations, too many to handle. There were not enough men to fight them all.

At first Wilkinson may have thought there was a chance to keep her afloat long enough for an attack on another transport, but that was not going to happen. The little ship was sinking fast by the stern, its hull raked and the superstructure almost down. The *Li Wo* was settling to the bottom of the ocean. It was time to get away. Lieutenant Wilkinson called for his crew to abandon ship, and those of the men still able to do so took to the troubled waters. There had been no time to set out what few lifeboats they had. The captain, only in command for a few months and in the Royal Navy even less time, chose to remain on the bridge of his ship as it went down. Lieutenant James Gall, the chief engineer for the *Li Wo*, was also killed in the action.

Within moments the Japanese destroyers came into the area to begin picking up their own survivors. The sea was filled with wounded and drowning soldiers who had been previously crammed into the transports. Many had been hurt and all were gasping for air in the oil-filled water. Whatever expectations the *Li Wo*'s sailors might have had about rescue were soon dashed. The Japanese, terribly upset with the arrogant little ship and its crew, were firing into the water with their machine guns, dropping grenades, and speeding through the area, where their churning screws killed more than a few.

Chief Petty Officer Charles Roberts, along with one other seaman and a Malaysian man, found a raft that had once belonged to the *Li Wo* and managed to hold on. Within a few hours they had the good fortune to drift into a small boat which, while damaged, still had its oars and sail. It proved to be seaworthy. They managed to get the sail up and shortly found two other rafts onto which men were clinging. One of these was James Bruce Douglas Hadley, who was already a survivor of the HMS *Repulse*. He would later die of unknown causes while a POW.

Lieutenant Derbridge managed to escape by hanging onto a small raft. He and the small crew with him eventually reached Banka Island. Dragging themselves ashore they soon discovered that the Japanese invasion had already taken place and the area was covered with Japanese. A few of the exhausted men were determined to get away and tried to move inland, but they were given up to the Japanese by unfriendly natives. They were all taken prisoner. Derbridge died somewhat later as the prisoners were being taken to Muntok.

At one point Lieutenant Stanton, though wounded, was attempting to get those who survived into shelter when they were attacked by Chinese refugees. After several days of trying to survive without help, it became necessary to surrender to the Japanese in order for the wounded to receive medical treatment. Most of the surviving men were held in a temporary POW camp at Muntok on Banka Island until transferred to a more permanent camp where they were held to the end of the war. Of the original *Li Wo* complement of 84 men who had sailed out of Singapore, only nine men remained alive at the end of the war.[1]

Some time later, in recognition of his bravery, the captain of the *Li Wo*, Temporary Lieutenant Thomas Wilkinson, was awarded a posthumous Victoria Cross. Others were also decorated. Sub-lieutenant Ronald George Gladstone Stanton was awarded the Distinguished Service Order. Stanton was the first lieutenant of the *Li Wo* and the only surviving officer, and he had served as a voluntary member of the 4-inch gun crew which continued to fire as long as the ammunition lasted. Acting Petty Officer Arthur William Thompson was to receive the Conspicuous Gallantry Medal for his involvement and particularly for his service on the gun.

Leading Seaman Victor Spencer and Able Seaman Albert Spendlove both received the Distinguished Service Medal. Six others of the crew, Lieutenant Edgar Neil Derbridge, Sub Lieutenant (Jg.) Petherbridge, Able Seaman Desmond Palmer, Chief Petty Officer Charles Halme Rogers, Leading Seaman William Dick Wilding, and Able Seaman John Smith were mentioned in dispatches.

Seaman Thomas Henry Parsons was belatedly acknowledged by the Secretary of State for Defense, on 20 February 1986.

Two deaths are confused. Richard Clarence Farley was killed aboard the *Li Wo* (as listed by Sellwood), but is also listed by the British as having been killed aboard the HMS *Kung Wo*. And Edward Hanan, formerly of the HMS *Stronghold*, is listed as a casualty on the *Li Wo*. There is also some confusion about 19-year-old Coxswain William Thomas Snow, who was reported killed during the attack, but whose name shows up later.

The *Li Wo* itself was one of the most decorated ships of World War II. Today, in remembrance of what she did, and of the men who sailed her into harm's way, a small scale model of the *Li Wo* stands in the Imperial War Museum in London. She is fitted as she was when she left Singapore, and at her bow is the Union Jack and the white ensign at her masthead. It is located there along with Lieutenant Wilkinson's Victoria Cross.

The crew and passenger total is assumed at 84, but the record of survivors is mixed, running from seven to thirteen. There is no account for the differences other than the fact that different individuals and agencies were making the reports.

The loss of life included five — Charles Rogers, Cecil Huntley, John Bennett, Cyril John Cartwright, and James Hadley — who had been rescued from the HMS *Repulse*; two from the *Prince of Wales*, Leading Seaman Countant and Thomas Henry Parsons; and Richard Farley from the HMS *Stronghold*.

The *Li Wo* left late during the closing hours of Singapore's defense, and is generally considered to be the last ship out of Singapore. Perhaps because of its late departure date, or the fact that most of those aboard were military rather than civilian evacuees, the *Li Wo* is generally not listed among ships that evacuated passengers from Singapore.

Note

1. The most complete story of the *Li Wo* discovered is the display caption at the Imperial War Museum, London.

Further Reading

Illustrated London News. 28 December 1948, p. 75.
http://singaporeevacuation1942.kedah.html.
Sellwood, A.V. *Stand by to Die.* London: New English Library, 1961.
Smith, Colin. *Singapore Burning: Heroism and Surrender in World War II.* New York: Penguin, 2005.
Smyth, John George. *Percival and the Tragedy of Singapore.* London: MacDonald, 1971.

19. The Saga of Annie Clark

The final straw was the decision, on 5 February 1941, to close the ANZAC Club. As far as she was concerned things were getting bad fast and she had finally given up any hope that they were going to get any better. The club, a refuge built and manned especially for Australian and New Zealand servicemen stationed in Singapore, was the last vestige of normalcy, as far as she was concerned. After putting it off for as long as she could, Annie Clark determined it was time to get out.

But the decision meant little by itself. Just about anyone who could do so had already left, and those just now deciding to leave were finding it difficult. With the confusion, as well as the lack of coordination between ships and the shipping officers, it was getting even more difficult. The military had its hands full; besides, the rumor going around about the *Empress of Asia* turned out to be true. A commercial liner that took passengers from British Columbia to the Orient, she had been converted to an auxiliary cruiser during World War I, and at the beginning of World War II to a troop transport ship. She was on her way to Singapore bringing troops in, and hopefully prepared to take persons out, when she was sunk on 5 February 1942 in the Sultan Shoal. Outgoing ships, it was being said, were not making it beyond the line of Japanese ships waiting for them.

Annie Clark was a kind and gentle New Zealander who was well traveled in the Far East, and had been at numerous stations working with her husband, an engineer. His assignments had taken them to Siam, Borneo, Shanghai, and by 1940 to Malaya. In 1941 they moved to Singapore where Norman "Nobby" Clark, also a New Zealander, worked as an engineer at the Government Rice Mills. Norman Clark was no stranger to the military, having served as an artilleryman during the Gallipoli campaign. Their daughter, Kathleen, was also in Singapore. She was married to Harold Pether, an Englishman who was a manager with C.C. Wakefield and Company (later identified as Castor Oil). They had a daughter, Maureen. In December 1941, when the Japanese first invaded Malaya, Harold had been uncomfortable with the way things were going, and so put his wife and daughter on a ship to New Zealand. Annie Clark, however, opted to stay with her husband. She had a son, recently returned from schooling, who was now working in Singapore.

But now they had all agreed it was time for Annie to leave. Seeking a way out, Annie, along with several others who had come to the same conclusion, made the trip to Cluny Road where the P & O offices were located, to see if they could get a permit to leave. Once there they were informed that there were no ships leaving. This was not exactly true, however, and most of them knew it, but there appeared little they could do.

With no other real options in mind, a number of the would-be evacuees retired to the lounge of the Adelphi Hotel on Coleman Road, where they were still able to locate what food and liquor they wanted. The next day they relocated at the Masonic Club. The club had built an air-raid shelter as quickly as possible when the Japanese attacks increased. There a good number of them waited while every effort was being made to contact any ship that might be leaving with room to take them aboard.

By morning on the 9th, as Japanese shells heading for the north side of the island were passing overhead, news came to them that the Japanese troops had crossed over the Johor Straits that separated the Malaysian state of Johor from Singapore, and had taken the village of Tengah. There, the Japanese had found some of the American Hurricane fighters, sent to aid in the defense, still in their packing cases.

Officially they were still getting the same answers. The agents for the Peninsular and Oriental Steam Navigation Company kept telling them there were no permits, and there were no ships. Their delegates got the same answer on the 10th, thought most knew that the SS *Lee Sang* was gearing up to make an attempt to sail for India later in the afternoon. Still they were told there were no ships leaving Singapore.

Suddenly things changed. Norman Clark knew one of the agents for the *Lee Sang* (some accounts list the ship as the *Li Sang*), and through the kindness of a Mr. P.C. managed to get passage on the ship for Annie if she would hurry. If she was going to make it she needed to be at the Clifford Pier by 1500 hours. The pier was beside Collyer Quay at Mariana Bay. Quickly scrambling to locate what official documents she could, and what little she thought she might be able to carry, Annie arrived at the dock. There she discovered there was a party of about 14 others who were also waiting to go aboard. As they waited, the Japanese bombed the docks once again, but all managed to avoid injury.

However, the launch that was supposed to appear from the *Lee Sang* to pick them up never appeared. Then a young RNVR lieutenant, whose name they never knew, and who was commanding a tender, heard their story. He agreed to try to get them to the ship in time. The small launch was so crowed, however, that they were forced to leave their suitcases, and all their clothes, behind. Goodbyes were said quickly. As the women in the group left, they did so with the knowledge of what might be facing the men they were leaving behind. In Annie's case they were her husband, son-in-law and son.

The launch moved out into the harbor only to discover, after just a few minutes, that the *Lee Sang* had already sailed. The reserve lieutenant, however, was not giving up. They spent the rest of the daylight hours going from ship to ship trying to find one that would take the women on board. None had the room, for most were already crowded far beyond their normal capacity. Then about midnight he approached a little auxiliary minesweeper. The captain listened to their story and then agreed to take them on board. He warned them, however, that he had little food or water for the trip. Seeing no other alternative, however, the exhausted women went aboard. The captain's crew and passenger list now totaled 174 women and ten men.

The ship they had located was the *Scott Harley*. The little ship had been requisitioned by the Royal Navy and put into service as an auxiliary minesweeper, but so far had seen little activity. She was 620 tons and had been built in 1913. She was ripe with age, slow, and coal-burning. There was concern because the smoke from her stacks could most likely be seen for miles.

Almost from the beginning the shortage of drinking water became apparent. The heat made it even harder, but those on board shared what water they had. Several of those who had been taken aboard were sailors who had survived the sinking of the *Prince of Wales* and *Repulse*. They made the best of what they could find, even draining off a bit of hot water from the condenser in the engine room to make some stew and cocoa. The other accommodations were not a lot better. Annie Clark shared her mess dish, a dirty cigarette tin she had scrounged up, with two other women.

Several of the passengers were known to Annie but in the main they represented a cross-section of Singapore's population. Most of the passengers were women, but there were also some men and one or two families. Dr. J.W. Scarff was on board with his wife, their daughters Elizabeth and Jopin, as well as their two sons. There was a Russian mother with her daughter. The mother had been a hairdresser at the Raffles Hotel in Singapore. There was a woman referred to only as the Secretary to the Governor of Singapore and described as 35 years old and 16 stone; Mrs. Ray and one child from the municipality; and Joyce Fitzpatrick, whose husband was with Singapore Cold Storage.

The delay of the *Scott Harley* meant that she did not leave until the 13th, and thus was a part of what history has identified as Black Friday, the 13th of February 1942. This was the day when a significant effort was made to get key officials, military leaders, specialists, and many other evacuees out. Sixteen vessels, known in history as the Empire Star Convoy, sailed at dawn from the British colony of Singapore.

There was little time left. An earlier request that they surrender had been refused by the British, and now twenty-seven thousand Japanese troops on 18,000 bicycles, under the command of General Yamashita Tornoyuri, rushed down the peninsula. Now they had taken Johore Baharu.

The convoy, though it was not a convoy in the strictest sense of the word, was the work of Captain George F.A. Mulock, DSO, who served as the Extended Defenses Officer Singapore from August 1939 until the city fell. The exact number of the ships that left is not known. Those for which we have records include the Blue Star cargo ship SS *Empire Star*.

Sailing in an attempt to reach safety, the SS *Vyner Brooke* made her escape from Singapore on the same day, but was hounded by the Japanese from the beginning. She was finally caught by fighters and sunk in the Danka Strait on 14 February. Those on board included several Australian nurses who were taken captive and then later murdered by the Japanese. One of the few survivors, Agnes Betty Jeffrey, later recounted her experience in the book *White Coolie*.

The convoy also included the HMS *Malacca*, identified as a minesweeper, which left on the 13th. Setting sail as the Japanese bombed the pier, she was ordered to move along the wharf and pick up anyone who needed to get out. Within an hour there were 62 on board, both women and children and some military. On the way out, she led five ships seeking a path through the minefield, but they soon passed her up as the *Malacca* was only capable of doing 6 knots. Holding up on the 14th the crew counted 187 Japanese planes passing overhead, but not of them spotted the *Malacca*. Running slowly and off course, they finally arrived at Kuala Lajau Delts, making their way a little bit at a time. The damaged ship was finally scuttled.

Other ships included the old Blue Funnel Line's coastal ship the *Gorgon*. John and Katherine Caseley reported finding deck room as she headed out. They had been refused space on the *Empire Star*, as all space was reserved for RAF personnel. Also on board were two American liaison officers, Colonels Tormey and Craig. Katherine was an MD and was quickly accepted as the ship's doctor. The captain of the *Gorgon* decided to bypass Batavia and head straight for Java. The ship, however, had engine trouble on its approach to Java and was for a time a sitting duck for any Japanese in the area. The engineer managed to get it fixed, however, and they made it safely to Fremantle. Katherine Caseley, who lost everything as they scurried to get aboard the *Gorgon*, remembered her cat sitting in the window washing its face as the saddest thing of all.

Also sailing was the SS *Dalamore*, which left on the 11th with SS *Jalibar*, *Jalikrishna*, and *Lin Sang*. Of this group the *Jalikrishna* was hit by an air attack and the bow of the ship badly damaged. She finally made it to Tandjong, but she was carrying no passengers.

In the group, but sailing pretty much on its own, was the *Scott Harley*. She awakened to a day bright after a heavy tropical downpour during the night. Soot and ashes from the struggling funnel had covered many on deck with dark grime. There were no signs of any of the other ships that had left Singapore. Later in the afternoon a shower eased things a bit but it provided very little drinking water. The single toilet on board was overwhelmed.

On the morning of 14 February the Japanese found them. Around 0830 three planes were spotted and proclaimed to be British, but they were soon reevaluated as they lined up, dived, and unloaded their bombs. Not one of the bombs actually hit the ship, though some damage was sustained. Three hours later the planes came again, and while the ship escaped, considerable damage was done and sections of the deck destroyed. Later in the afternoon they passed a tug that was stranded. It was full of British and American soldiers but there was no room on the *Scott*, and so they sailed on. Another raid later in the afternoon split some of the planking and set a fire in the engine room. The crew then decided it was important to dump the depth charges they had been carrying, and the loss of weight helped some, but they were still listing badly.

The situation became more difficult as the damage was effecting the safe operation of the ship. Besides that, the water supply was very low. At this point the captain gave some thought to beaching the ship on the coast of Sumatra, but realized that this left them in considerable danger, and worried about the women on board, he decided to try to make it to Batavia.

They spent another long night. With dawn on 15 February came some good news for those who had just weathered another night without adequate food or water. One of the officers, a Lieutenant H., was able to inform the anxious passengers that with luck they would be in Batavia about noontime. It raised all spirits but, still, there were many who could not come to believe it. This time the prediction was accurate, but once they had arrived and were safe, they were not able to get off the *Scott Harley*. They were dirty, exhausted, and needing toilet facilities, but the Dutch were trying to deal with the hundreds of refugees appearing on their shores, and they were not happy with the fact that all these people had arrived without the proper papers. It took some effort by both Lieutenant H. and a Mr. W. of Singapore, who managed to get them clearance and they were able to come ashore.

With little or no time to get rested or cleaned up, the survivors were then put aboard buses and taken further down the wharf. Most of the European passengers were assigned to be shipped out of Batavia and would be heading for Bombay on the *Plancius*. The Dutch ship *Plancius* had previously accompanied the *Empress of Asia* in the delivery of troops to Singapore. After a short drive they arrived and went aboard, where some 850 of them joined those already on board. It was while they were boarding that they heard that Singapore had fallen.

The accounts of the other ships making the dash out of Singapore are varied. The HMS *Kedah* was a small coastal ship that had belonged to the Straits Shipping Company. She waited as long as possible leaving on the 14th, at which time she was shelled by both air and sea forces. On board they had managed to load close to 750 passengers. Captain J.L. Sinclair (DSO) managed to get her out of the harbor and headed for Batavia. After being repeatedly bombed and escaping, the little ship zigzagged and dodged its way to Batavia, where it finally arrived safely. Included among her passengers was Mrs. Muriel Reilly, a cipher officer to the governor. The brave little ship was ordered back to Singapore to rescue General Wavell and others heading for Colombo, but suffered an engineering failure and had to be towed by the HMS *Dragon*. The *Kedah* survived the war and was one of the first ships to return to Singapore in 1945.

The SS *Redang*, a 531-ton ship owned by the Thai Navigation Company, pulled out of Singapore on 12 February. She was carrying a full crew and approximately 89 passengers, mostly women and children. The ship made it as bar as the Banka Straits where it was located, shelled, and eventually sunk. About thirty of the passengers were able to get into a small boat, but they were captured and made prisoners.

The *Lee Sang* (or *Li Sang*), whose early sailing had disappointed so many, managed to get away from Singapore on 11 February at 1730 hours.

On the 13th the SS *Blumut*, a small ship with the Johore Marine Department, set sail carrying 29 passengers. She was captured by the Japanese off Banka on the 16th.

On 13 February, the SS *Releau*, a palm oil tanker of the Straits Shipping Company, with 66 passengers, sailed without a crew. In command of the ship was the assistant marine superintendent, but there were no seamen on board. During the next two days the ship stopped to pick up survivors. Fortunately 13 of them were ratings from the HMS *Scorpion*, and were able to help in manning the ship. It was as they passed Pom Pong and were approaching the gap between Banka and South Sumatra that they ran into the Japanese. They were taken prisoner and located at Muntok. There they discovered the SS *Rantau*, which had come in believing the area was still in Allied hands.

The SS *Rantau*'s story was nearly the same. Having no crew, S. Baddeley, the marine superintendent, took command with the engineering superintendent, a Mr. Froggatt, as chief engineer. They made the run and successfully arrived at Muntok, only to discover that the area had already been taken by the Japanese, and the crew and passengers were taken prisoner.

The SS *Sing Kheng Seng*, owned by the Straits Shipping Company, left Singapore on the 12th of February with 45 members of the crew from the destroyed *Empress of Asia*.

The HMS *Chang Teh* managed to get out of Singapore on 13 February, but was sunk in the Durian Straits.

The *Sing Wo* left Singapore on 12 February with nearly 200 passengers on board. Most were women and children. The 2500-ton Yangtze river boat was bombed by Japanese planes and forced aground at Muntok. There she and her passengers were taken prisoner. Among those who survived was Roha River, the author of the book *Behind Bamboo*.

The SS *Kuala* left with 500 people on board, including a large detachment of nurses escaping from Singapore. She left on 13 February and was sunk on the 14th near Pom Pong Island.

The *Mata Hari* set out on 12 February with 320 passengers that included several nurses. The ship was bombed and then captured in the Banka Straits and taken to Muntok Harbor, where the passengers and crew were imprisoned.

The HMS *Durban*, commissioned in 1928 and on duty in the Far East, was hoping to act as an escort but was damaged by bombs on 12 February and needed to retreat to Colombo for immediate repairs.

The HMS *Stronghold* had also been sent to help protect and escort evacuee ships along with the *Jupiter* and *Durban*. On 13 February she was attacked by a Japanese submarine but escaped. However, in early March, engaged in battle with the Japanese *Maya, Arashi,* and *Nowaki,* she was sunk after a fierce surface battle.

19. The Saga of Annie Clark

The *Fanling*, a motor launch, was carrying 47 passengers when she was attacked in the Banka Straits and sunk. There were only four survivors. Also making the trip, the *Kwang*, *Kung Wo*, and *Chang Teh* were all sunk.

Most of the European passengers, as they arrived at Batavia on 21 February, were immediately transshipped on to Bombay. In this case Annie, and those traveling with her, were placed on the SS *Plancius*. The *Plancius* took aboard 850, the largest number of them women and children who had come in from Singapore, with plans to deliver them either to South Africa or Bombay. From these destinations the majority went on via Ceylon to Australia, and then in June 1942 she arrived in New Zealand.

During the remainder of the war Annie Clark lived in Dunedin, New Zealand, where she, her daughter Kathleen Pether, and granddaughter Maureen waited to hear the fate of their husbands and father. They were finally informed through the Red Cross that both men were alive and interned. After the war the Clarks spend a good deal of time seeking some word about their son Jack, and while we now know of his death, little is still known about the circumstanced under which he died.

Singapore fell to the Japanese Army on 15 February 1942. It was one of the greatest defeats in the history of the British Army. Singapore, an island at the southern end of the Malaya Peninsula, was considered to be a vital part of the British Empire. At the time, the island fortress was considered impregnable. It was the Gibraltar of the East. The British had already suffered great damage both to the military and to their pride when, on 10 December 1941, both the battleship *Prince of Wales* and the battle cruiser *Repulse* were sunk after repeated attacks from Japanese torpedo bombers. On 31 January 1942, British and Australian forces withdrew across the causeway that tied Singapore to Malaya and a month later the Japanese took complete control. When the fighting stopped, the Japanese had taken more than 100,000 military prisoners and untold numbers of civilians. Among those taken were Annie's husband Norman Clark and her son-in-law Harold Pether, both of whom were interned in the Sime Road Camp #1. The Adelphi Hotel was taken over by the Japanese, who renamed it the Nanto. The building, originally set up in 1830 as the Royals Hotel, was destroyed and an office building, bearing the Adelphi name, stands in the spot today. The Masonic Club in Singapore held its last meeting on 12 February and would soon be taken over as the Japanese Officers' Club.

Annie Clark remembered that on leaving Batavia she discovered that the HMS *Scott Harley* had been sunk in the harbor as she was trying to leave, her proud white ensign still flying. While it is easy to understand her confusion on this point, it does not seem to be the case. Naval records show that the determined little ship was sunk during a naval engagement, probably fought on 3 March 1942 (some reports say 26 February) somewhere southeast of Tijlatap. It was here that she ran into a small Imperial Japanese fleet consisting of the carrier *Nowaki* and the destroyers *Takao* and *Arashi*. It is most likely that it was the destroyer *Arashi* which was responsible for her sinking.

There remains a great deal of confusion about Annie's missing son. Young John "Jack" Clark was seventeen when the Japanese attacked. He had been left behind in Kuala Lumpur, the capital city. Having recently completed his schooling in New Zealand, he had returned to Singapore and was just getting started in his first job as an assistant with ICI, Malaya Ltd. In 1941, as storm clouds gathered, Jack, like many young men in the area, joined the Federated Malaya States Volunteer Force. The Volunteers, know locally as the "Vultures," was a force of about 5,200 young men from varied backgrounds. Clark served as a private in the 2nd Selangor Battalion. It appears that he was captured by the Japanese and sent to the POW camp at Blakang Mati (which translates as "Island on which there is death"). Apparently he escaped from there and may have actually reached Padang in Sumatra along the official escape route. He was recaptured there and taken down to the water's edge and shot. Annie was never given this information. His name is listed among the others on the Singapore War Memorial in Kranji.

Still today, decades after the fact, there remain some vast gaps in our understanding of what happened. Some historians have estimated that more than forty ships left Singapore in the evacuation, a figure that does not include literally hundreds of smaller vessels from junks to rafts, between 11 and 14 February. The best evidence is that only two or three of these reached safety. One in four of the evacuees that left Singapore reached sanctuary.

Note

Most of what is known about the escape from Singapore, especially when one is looking for information about individuals, is known because of the excellent work of Michael Pether, who is responsible for and manages the civilian evacuee list from that incident. His work is thankfully acknowledged.

Further Reading

Farrell, Brian P. *Defense and Fall of Singapore 1940–1942*. London: Tempus, 2006.
George, F.J. *The Singapore Saga*. Singapore: Fernandez Joseph George, 1985.

Hall, Timothy. *The Fall of Singapore*. Methuen, Australia: North Ryde, 1983.
Pether, Michael. "A Little Known Ship of Evacuees from Singapore, HMS *Scott Harley*." www.cofepow.org.uk/pages/civilian_hms_scott_harley.htm.
Warren, Alan. *Singapore 1942: Britain's Greatest Defeat*. London: Hambledon & London, 2003.

20. The Incredible John H. Lang

The planes appeared over the river dropping, down from the clear sky, quickly reducing their altitude, the sun reflecting off the bright red spot on each of their wings. It was a Sunday and the American gunboat USS *Panay* and its crew were at rest. Suddenly it became obvious to even the most relaxed member of the crew that the planes were diving right at them. The first warning came from Quartermaster John H. Lang, who shouted to anyone who could hear: "They're letting go bombs! Get under cover." Having just completed Sunday dinner, Lieutenant Commander James Hughes, the captain, had been informed that the planes were in the area, but that was not unusual as the Japanese were already at war with the Chinese and fighting was continuing on both sides of the river. Hughes responded quickly to the quartermaster's call and turned toward the pilothouse. There were six planes strung out in a line, rapidly losing altitude. Then, just as he reached the limited shelter of the pilothouse, the first of the bombs hit, smashing onto the USS *Panay* just in front of the shelter. The explosion smashed the glass and damaged the house.

Both Commander Hughes and Quartermaster John Lang were wounded by the attack. Within minutes the *Panay*, an American warship on a humanitarian mission and under conditions of peace, sank into the dirty waters of the Yangtze River, many of her crew and passengers dead or badly wounded. The time was 1338 hours on 12 December 1937, and America was not at war.

Despite his wound, Lang, working with the executive officer Lieutenant Arthur Anders, helped organize the survivors. A longtime Yangtze river rat, Lang knew what was expected and worked to get his men into action. Lieutenant Anders, who had been badly cut by glass driven into his throat, could not talk. He used a chalkboard in the pilothouse to issue instruction. When it became evident that the boat could not stay afloat, Quartermaster Lang

20. The Incredible John H. Lang

supervised the loading of one of the smaller lifeboats, and directed it to take the wounded passengers and sailors and help them get to shore. Once he got most of his men ashore he moved inland a way to avoid being seen by the Japanese planes that continued to fly over the area as if in search of the survivors. Then, when a Japanese patrol boat appeared along the shore line as if joining in the search, Lang kept his troops down and out of sight.

This was not the first time that John Henry Lang was involved in military action or, for that matter, the first time he was wounded. The story of John Lang is one of those that crops up from the military and is carried along by soldiers and sailors who tell and retell the story, and in doing so both forget some parts and exaggerate others. In this case the John Lang story is shadowed in some mystery, and suffers from the limited paper trail left by many of his exploits. But his name is remembered and sometimes turns up in other wartime narratives. Who is he, and why of all the individuals involved in the extended period of World War II, does John Lang keep drawing our attention?

According to the best accounts, he was born in 1899, in a place about as far away from the sea as was possible. His birthplace was Casselton, North Dakota, a very small town located in Cass County about twenty miles from Fargo. Originally calling their town The Nursery, then Goose Creek and finally Sean Creek, the settlers finally agreed in 1876 to name the settlement Casselton after George Cass, a wealthy railroad figure who was primarily responsible for its continued existence. Not content to remain in Casselton, Lang traveled to Milwaukee, Wisconsin, where in 1916, at the age of seventeen, he enlisted in the Canadian Army. He was assigned to the Engineers. He soon found a way to get transferred to the more aggressive Canadian Black Watch Infantry. The Black Watch was originally the 5th Battalion of the Royal Light Infantry that had been established in 1862 and was the oldest Highland regiment in Canada. He later transferred, or was temporarily assigned, to the Royal Highland Regiment (the British Black Watch), for he fought with the Highlanders at the Third Battle of Ypres in April 1917. One of the more desperate battles of World War I, it cost a quarter of a million casualties on both sides.

Third Ypres, or, as it was sometimes called, the Battle of Passchendaele, was highly significant historically. Not only was it the first recorded instance of the widespread use of mustard gas during the European war, but it was a point of historical change in world politics, marking the first time that a colonial power (Canada) had pushed back a major European force in battle. And it was at the Third Battle of Ypres that the young John H. Lang received his first major distinction, the British Distinguished Service Medal, awarded him for conspicuous gallantry.

On returning from the war in Europe, Lang decided to remain in the military but did so by changing both countries and services. He enlisted in the United States Navy. At that time most of the action for Americans was to be found in the Far East, and Lang managed to get assigned to the Asiatic Squadron for operations with the then China Fleet on the Yangtze River. He served there in a variety of assignments, rising in rank and experience as he moved around on several gunboats. While tension on the Yangtze increased through the years, most of Lang's activities were limited to fighting off warlords who occasionally got too close to the river, or dodging potshots from sportsmen who liked to fire at the American gunboats as they went by.

Then, in the 1920s, Lang was one of many U.S. servicemen who were assigned to a combined Japanese-American operation that was conducted from the Yangtze against a Chinese warlord. Feeling the pressure from the efforts of an increasingly nationalized government, the warlord had made the mistake of besieging one of the foreign legations located along the river. The offended governments were quick to respond. Such events were not all that unusual, as life at one of the American embassies was always full of risk, but it was unusual for the Japanese and Americans to join in such an endeavor.

While the fighting was not prolonged, it was fierce; the warlord resisted as much as possible until he was defeated and the legions rescued. During the fighting, John Lang once again distinguished himself by his heroism, in acts of courage so noticeable that the Japanese government felt the need to decorate him. They honored Lang with the Japanese Order of the Chrysanthemum (2nd class) for heroism. During this action Lang was wounded, but little other than that is known. His exploits, however, were so outstanding that they not only provided him with recognition from the Japanese government, but the United States awarded him his first Navy Cross as well. It was a somewhat unusual occasion for a man to be awarded medals for the same action from two major powers, especially two powers that would soon be at war.

After recovering from his wounds, Lang returned to the Yangtze Patrol and continued to serve as quartermaster on several of the boats that regularly moved up and down the Yangtze. Eventually, he was assigned as chief quartermaster on board the American gunboat, the USS *Panay*. As quartermaster he was in charge of the watch and responsible for maintaining navigation.

It was on the *Panay*, on 12 December 1937, and for action afterwards, during which he was responsible for the safety of many of the survivors, that Lang was awarded his second Navy Cross.

Following his service with the gunboats, and while war clouds gathered, Lang was reportedly assigned to the commissioning crew of the USS *Massachusetts* (BB 59) a battleship of the South Dakota class, known as "The Big Marnie." Laid down 20 July 1939, she was commissioned 12 May 1942 with Captain Francis E.M. Whiting in command. The battleship took a quick shakedown cruise, then rendezvoused with the Western Task Force and took part, as the flagship for Admiral H. Kent Hewitt, in the battle for North Africa and Operation Torch.

Following service on the *Massachusetts*, the story suggests, Quartermaster Lang was given command of a landing ship tank (LST) that took part in the invasion of the Admiralty Islands, a series of volcanic islands in the southwest Pacific in the Bismarck (New Guinea) Archipelago. During this action the LST he commanded was badly damaged and sunk.

Lang next turns up in the Pacific with Underwater Demolition Team #2, where he assumed the position as executive. Their job was the removal of Japanese mines that had been laid out on the outer reefs of Saipan. It was while he was involved in the clearing of these mines that he was hurt again. A mine, several yards away, but far too close, detonated and killed several frogmen in the water. Lang was desperately wounded and awarded another Purple Heart. In fact, Lang was reported to have received fourteen Purple Hearts.

This time the wound was too much even for Lang, and after two years recovering from his injuries, Lang retired from the U.S. Navy with the rank of a commissioned warrant officer.

Mr. Lang, who was the uncle of Walter Patrick Lang, Jr., a well-known and highly articulate American intelligence officer and author, died in Long Beach, California, in 1970. At his request his ashes were scattered on the waves of the Pacific Ocean.

That in brief is the story of John Lang, one of those individuals whose life exemplifies one of varied service and honor. The John H. Lang recorded here was a man whose life displayed the best in the military tradition, with long years of service, interspersed with moments of courage and heroics. But while there is no doubt that Lang was awarded the Navy Cross by the U.S. Navy on two occasions, that he was significantly involved in the sinking of the USS *Panay*, and that he was responsible for the subsequent rescue of many of the seamen, there remain some questions.

First of all, the award of the Japanese Order of the Chrysanthemum (2nd Class) is well documented by both American and Japanese authorities. But it is nevertheless somehow unexplained. While the Japanese government lists the award given to Lang, it also states in its description of the award that there is no 2nd class award given. It also points out that the decoration is designed primarily for members of the royal family, or on special occasions is given to the heads of foreign states. No further explanation is given as to the circumstances of Lang's award.

Second, while both the Army and the Navy traditionally have enlisted men and commissioned officers, and even some warrant officers, it would be very rare indeed for there to be a commissioned warrant officer. A search of Navy policies suggest that such a rank might have existed, but those policies are not clear on how it is achieved or what it means. Was the rank an honorary one of some kind meant to reflect Lang's long and valid service? If so, how was it commissioned?

Third, the family source for remembering John Lang lists his being awarded fourteen Purple Hearts for wounds received while in active service. Official military lists suggest that the greatest number of Purple Hearts awarded to any one person was six. However, there is some explanation for this, suggesting that both the number six is too low, and that Lang may indeed have received more. First of all, many believe that receiving a wound automatically generates a Purple Heart. This of course is not true, but whoever was counting may have simply meant Lang was wounded 14 times. Also, a good many Purple Hearts were awarded at the side of a hospital bed, or in a recovery unit, often by the commanding officer personally. But in many of these cases the officer involved did not follow up with the necessary paperwork to be sure it was recorded properly. Many a wounded GI can tell stories about unrecorded Purple Hearts.

Finally, some sources say that John Lang was the executive officer of Underwater Demolition Team #2 and that he was finally wounded while in that service. The UDT was a highly specialized unit requiring considerable training, and those responsible were quite focused on recruiting young personnel. At this time Lang would have been 45, and given his active service would most likely not have had time to undergo this training. This does not mean, of course, that he did not find a way to take part while acting as the administrative officer of the unit. That would have been very much like John Lang.

Despite the lack of final answers, there remains no doubt that John Lang was one of America's many, and unique, heroes.

Note

The most consistent source for information on Lang is to be found in http://en.wikipedia.org/wiki/john_H._Lang, though he appears briefly in numerous other references. Information on Japanese decorations can be found at militarycollectablesinc.com.

Further Reading

Cunningham, Chet. *Frogman of World War II: An Oral History of the U.S. Navy's Underwater Demolition Teams.* New York: Pocket Star, 2004.

Icenhower, Joseph B. *The Panay Incident, December 12, 1937.* Danbury, CT: Scholastic Library, 1971.

Hamilton, Darby Perry. *The Panay Incident: Prelude to Pearl Harbor.* New York: Macmillan, 1969.

21. The Cave of the Virgins

On the side of a windswept hill in the semi-mountainous regions of the island of Okinawa there is a memorial site called the "Cave of the Virgins." It marks the spot where, in the dark and disquieted space beneath, 40 young women, ages 13 to 16, took their own lives in an act of deranged morality. The memorial is an effort to retain the image of the youth and innocence lost, and to acknowledge the human struggle and hopelessness represented there. It is also an effort to counteract the growing tendency among nations to let the horrible memories of World War II go unacknowledged.

This story focuses on a group of young women from Okinawa, known as the Star Lily Corps. It is strange how this small girls' school would figure so directly in the events of World War II. We hear from them first in 1937, when the American gunboat USS *Panay* was accidentally sunk on 12 December by Japanese bombers on the Yangtze River. A delegation of these girls, representing the thousands of students at Star Lily Schools, came forward to express their deep sorrow to the American government, and to provide a generous donation for the families of those who were killed.

The second occasion was on 22 August 1944. Aware of the coming battle, the school authorities arranged to send the youngest of the elementary children from Okinawa to Kagoshima for safety. The children were placed aboard the unmarked cargo ship *Tsushima Maru*, which slipped away quietly away in hope of making a quick trip. But, shortly after leaving port, the ship was spotted and torpedoed by the American submarine USS *Bowfish*. The thirty-year-old ship was hit hard and sank in less than twelve minutes. On board were 1,484 civilians, including 768 from the Star Lily School. Only 59 of the escaping children were saved. For the Americans it was a routine hit on a Japanese cargo ship and the crew of the sub, totally unaware of the cargo, did not know about the high cost of the action for more than twenty years.

The third occasion takes longer to tell.

The islands of Okinawa, part of the Ryukyus group, point like an arrow to the mainland of Japan that lies a scant 350 miles away. The Japanese people have long claimed the island, though it was only in the late 19th century that Japan officially annexed Okinawa. Nevertheless, the imperial government considered the people on the island to be living on Japanese soil and to be citizens of that nation. In an effort to make those expectations a reality, the Japanese took a harsh and formalized position designed to assimilate the islands by teaching imperial matters, controlling education, demanding the use of the Japanese language, and the teaching of national and military policy. Thus, in 1945, while the islanders might not have been as emotionally tied to Japan as the government might have wanted, they were nevertheless well versed in how Japan looked at the war, as well as with imperial beliefs, and the responsibilities those beliefs incurred.

The battle for Okinawa, when it came, can only be described as awesome. Not only was it the last major ground battle of World War II, it was the largest amphibious assault by U.S. forces against Japan. The battle also turned out to be the largest ground action in the Pacific War, and the only ground action during which Japanese civilians were killed. The fighting on Okinawa was some of the most desperate of World War II. It lasted continuously for 83 days and nights. The week-long bombardment by ships and planes was followed up by an invasion force of more than four Army and Marine divisions.

The cost of this successful invasion of Okinawa was nearly a quarter of a million dead. The count includes some 12,000 Americans, 110,000 Japanese soldiers, and more than 150,000 civilian conscripts, many of them little more than children. More than 30,000 Americans were wounded, as were nearly one-half of all the citizens of Okinawa. Of the more than 1,300 U.S. naval ships involved, 36 were sunk and 368 damaged by pilots of the Japanese Kamikaze Squadron. Seven hundred sixty-three American planes were shot down.

The Allies called their invasion "Operation Iceberg," for it was to be cold and ruthless, and designated the day of the invasion "Love Day." In heroic tradition it eventually took the lives of both commanders: General Simon Bolivar Buckner, Jr., the son of the Confederate general of the same name, who was killed on 18 June by artillery; and General Ushijima Mitsura, Commander of the Japanese 32nd Army, who committed hari-kiri along with numerous members of his staff on July 13.

As the bombardment began, the Japanese Army initiated the ultimate steps in the mobilization of its forces. Among those called into immediate service were the hundreds of young elementary and high school students situated in schools located all over the island, as well as those in the specialized schools for the blind and for deaf-mutes. The plan for their use had already been implemented. All told, 1,600 of these young men, ages 9 to 16, were conscripted from nine schools into the Japanese Army in what was identified as the "Iron and Blood Corps." With no training and with little expectation of what they were getting involved in, they were given front-line assignments. During the course of the fighting, nearly all the boys in this unit were killed.

Among those called up were the girls of the Star Lily Corps. These young students were the daughters of the elite of Okinawa, a privileged class who were in training to become teachers at one of the two exclusive and expensive girls' schools. They were young and able, and had passed extremely difficult entrance examinations to enter the academies. Once in school their lives were strictly regimented. The school reflected the island-wide policy of keeping girls away from boys to the extent that even the simplest conversation between the sexes would have resulted in severe consequences. By design they were kept from many of the harsher realities of the world.

Yet, these 13-to-18-year-old girls were, overnight, thrown into the ravages of a desperate military situation. Among them were 222 female high school students and their 18 teachers from the Okinawa Daichi Women's High School and the Okinawa Shinhan Women's School. Without consideration of age, they were assigned to locations where they were to provide medical aid and attention for the rapidly growing number of Japanese wounded.

When called together and first informed of their mobilization, they were told that they would work in an army field hospital. The girls envisioned that they would conduct their medical duties in the safe wards of a massive hospital, flying a Red Cross banner, and providing routine duties. The reality was far different. Their assignment was to work at the Haebaru Field Hospital, about five miles southeast of the village of Nana and primarily underground.

In their preparation for what they now understood to the one last desperate battle, the Japanese had established a series of more than thirty shelters built into the hillsides, in an area called Haebaru. They were located on the southern tip of the island where the rock was stable but not too difficult to work. There vast arrays of tunnels were dug by hand and supported by wooden posts cut from the surrounding forests. Some of the shelters were simply expansions of the many existing caves, called gamas, which honeycombed the area. Others were specifically excavated to meet the needs of the service. Once completed they were about 70 meters long, two to four meters wide, and about four meters high. The insides were dark, humid, and generally unsanitary. In those areas designated as barracks, there were double-bunk beds installed along the walls, but no sanitary provisions were made. They were designed to provide medical treatment for more than 2,000 seriously wounded soldiers.

It was in these caves that the girls of the Star Lily were thrown into the midst of constant bombardment, and where they were assigned as nurses' aids to the surgical teams operating in the caves. The hospital at which they had believed they would serve had long since been destroyed and all medical services had been moved underground. The hospital activities were centered on what was identified as Shelter Twenty. This shelter was housed in an extended tunnel that was, in fact, little more than a gap formed by the convergence of two tunnels. There they had set up the Ibara Surgery Shelter. It was a collecting point for the most badly wounded, and there Japanese army physicians, drafted doctors from Okinawa, some few nurses, and scores of Star Lily girls were to function.

When they first arrived, the girls were allowed to sleep in the open, or in one of the shacks that had been set up just outside the cave entrance in hope of getting fresh air But once the bombardment grew closer, the girls were forbidden to go outside except in their efforts to gather supplies, or forage for necessities. Several of the girls sent out to locate food or water for the patients were killed during the search.

Inside the caves the conditions were nearly unbearable. The medical personnel worked long days with little or no food. Soon every space was filled with dying men, 60 or 70 to a room, and the girls had to learn to sleep standing up, leaning against the damp walls of the caves. The walls and ceilings, covered with tent cloth, oozed with condensation. With no forced cross ventilation of any kind, the air was stale and foul. The smell of wet earth, mingled with that of blood, pus, urine, feces, and rancid sweat, was nauseous. What little light there was came from kerosene lamps with wicks made of twisted rags; they filled the area's air with deep smoke, making breathing even harder. For most of the time the day and the night were indistinguishable. There was very little water available, no hot water at all, and lice infected everything.

One young student, Ruriko Morishita, 17, who had expected to be walking through graduation that week, remembered that Ward Three was the worst. It was a set of half a dozen caves that had been designated for those with infectious disease and mental breakdowns, and those recovering from surgery. The work there was not only grisly but conducted under the screams of men broken in battle.

The girls' assignments were varied but all involved dealing with the wounded. They provided a helping hand in operations, even amputations that eventually were carried on without anesthetic. They wrapped wounds as long as there were bandages, and cleaned up the wounded men fresh from the field. All of the wounded were infested with maggots, especially in their mouths and ears, and one of the jobs given the girls was to remove the maggots from the wounds. Miyagi, one of the youngest girls, too small to do anything else, was given the job of carrying away the limbs from amputations and trying to find a place to bury them.

Somewhere around 19 June 1945, the Japanese high command acknowledged the battle was lost, and moved quickly into its annihilation phase. As a part of this condition, medical services would come to an end. The Star Lily Corps was suddenly demobilized and given orders to disperse. They were ordered out of what limited protection was provided by the caves and forced out into the midst of the continuing onslaught of artillery fire and, as that slowly lifted, the overwhelming array of small-arms fire originating with the approaching Americans. There was total confusion, no place to go, no place to avoid the enemy; as one young lady, Motomura, reported fifty years later, "We hid behind what was left of the trees and the rocks." In the waning hours of the conflict, near panic took over among the people and the military.

For most of the girls the question was not so much about where they should go, but rather what they should do. They had left the shelter with limited options. The options had been clearly spelled out for them by the military: they could die in battle, die through rape and torture at the hands of the Americans, or take their own lives. In anticipation of this choice, as they left the caves, some of the medical men with whom they had been working passed out hand grenades to the young girls and gave them instructions on their use. They were urged to kill themselves and to take as many of the enemy soldiers as they could with them in the process. Others of the girls were given capsules filled with potassium cyanide so they could take their own lives when the time came.

The Japanese Field Service Code, issued in January 1941, openly stated that individual Japanese soldiers are not permitted to surrender. It articulated the concept that the mere act of surrender removes the individual from any expectation of humane acceptance, either physically or mentally. Some idea of the wide acceptance of this belief can be better understood, perhaps, by realizing that in the Japanese military structure of the time, if a man committed suicide to avoid capture, he was ensured that the normal military benefits would be sent to his family. The family of a captured soldier received none.

In the Battle of Okinawa, the unification of the military, government, and civilians living together and dying together was emphasized, and a "sense of solidarity about death was cultivated." In the sense of their commitment they too were soldiers. It was this doctrine, a doctrine of moral necessity, that had been taught to the young men of the Iron and Blood Corps and the young women of the Star Lily Corps.

To add to their state of mind, they had been filled with stories of the atrocities committed by the American soldiers on other islands. The girls were taught that the Americans had no respect for their lives, and would torture and rape and then kill them. It was their moral responsibility to prevent this loss of face to the enemy by the taking of their own lives.

Many tried to put off the deadly decision or, perhaps, even to escape the necessity of making it. One of the young women, identified as Miyago, 17, could not bring herself to take her own life. She and two accompanying friends attempted to escape by hiding in the rocks near the base of the seaside cliffs. Here they discovered new dangers: bombardment from the ships at sea and the bombs of low-flying airplanes. It was at these cliffs that the Americans first began to appear. In an effort to get away, Miyago's group climbed up and down the cliffs, scurrying for a place to hide.

On the cliffs, just a few yards away, nine young girls and one of the teachers ended their lives with grenades as an American soldier approached. One young student in the group, named Shimabukuro, was wounded and asked other members of the groups to kill her, but for some reason they did not. Another of the students managed to hide more carefully and got away. She was able to survive living in a cave the Americans used as a garbage dump. She finally came out and was captured on 22 August. She was amazed when the soldiers sent her home.

Many were caught between the sea and the soldiers on the tops of the cliffs. When the Americans called down to those hiding below to surrender, the girls and other citizens of the island would not. So the Americans began to pour gasoline down on them, threatening it would be set on fire if they did not surrender.

At this point some of the young women, more frightened at the thought of taking their own lives than of the Americans who were quickly surrounding them, began to climb out. One of the young women recalls, "When we got to the top of the hill the Americans were waiting for them. It was the first time I had ever seen blue eyes."

Even then some resisted. Mr. Nakamura, now a guide at the memorial but then a young student, said:
> I heard my sister calling out "Kill me now, hurry." She had been told horrible stories about how women had been treated on other islands, and that men had been bound and thrown in front of tanks that were driven over them. As the American grew closer my mother took a piece of rope that she had found, and strangled the girl, her own daughter. It was then that I tried to kill myself, using the same rope, but I kept breathing and soon an American took me captive. He checked to see if I had any weapons, and then gave me candy. It was my first experience with Americans.

Motomura and a classmate decided to try to find safety in northern Okinawa by trying to escape along the eastern shoreline. There they were suddenly discovered by U.S. servicemen and taken captive. They expected to be killed or at least raped, but instead were taken to a refugee camp where she was given the job of taking care of the orphans. In time she was allowed to return to what was left of her home. "After the capture and the realization I was safe," she recalled years later, "I was not sure if it was right for me to continue to stay alive."

The Rev. Shigeaki Kinjo remembered that he had been led to believe that only torture awaited them, so he and others chose death when a Japanese soldier gave the men two hand grenades with instructions to "hurl one at the Americans, and then kill ourselves with the other." Most of the grenades failed to explode, so one village leader broke off a tree branch and killed his wife and children. My brother and I followed suit, "and we struck to death the mother who had given birth to us." Uezu Sachiko, now 84, remembered that as he was fleeing with his mother and elder brother's wife, a Japanese soldier told them to kill themselves by biting off their tongues if they were found by the Americans. Anything was better than being captured. Yet, when he was, he marveled at the kind treatment he received.

Not just the students, but the wounded were also trying to escape. Jo Oka, a soldier with the Ishi Battalion, was the only one of more than a hundred of the wounded in Shelter Twenty to survive. Conscripted into the army in January 1944, he had been given only two weeks' training, and then was sent into battle. He was wounded on the first day. Then, toward the end of the battle, he lay wounded with more than 2,000 others, alone and unattended in a cave. After four days without food, he reported, "uniformed men brought us milk to drink. It tasted funny, but was wonderful in our parched mouths, but it was heavily laced with cyanide. Most of the men who had been given the milk died that same afternoon." Only Jo Oka survived, for he had been too sick to drink much of the milk.

21. The Cave of the Virgins

The memorial to the battle of Okinawa, built in the style of the Vietnam Memorial in Washington, D.C., was dedicated on 18 May 1995. The Cornerstone of Peace, as it is called, lists nearly 237,000 names and identifies every one of the Japanese, Americans, Okinawans, British, Koreans, and Taiwanese who were killed in the battle for the island.

In the background is to be found the Himeyuri Monument, built and dedicated in April 1946, by those few who had survived. Listed among the dead are the names of the 123 young women who died at that particular spot during the battle, and acknowledged that an additional 87 had been released, of whom all but five took their own lives.

One particular display identifies the Cave of the Virgins. Here, in the dark and stifling confines of the cave more, than forty young "princesses" of the best schools, who had been raised according to the teachings of Confucius, separated by gender from the age of seven, protected from the harsh realities of the world, well trained in the culture of their nation, all died together from self-administered poison in the belief that it was their duty.

Today the caves, and the location of Shelter Twenty, have become a national memorial. The Peace Prayer and Memorial Museum, located on Southern Okinawa today, houses the monument dedicated to the young women of the Star Lily Corps. It was designed not as a tribute to the supposed romance of war, but rather is dedicated to the glory of the human spirit. It is designated as a place where the visitor can relive the battle and think about what occurred there. The museum gives a story of each girl's background, where she worked, what service had been required of her, and the eventual cause of her death. The museum has more than 900,000 visitors a year.

The memory of these events, first kept silent by shame and fear, is now beginning to collide with the growing nationalist effort to airbrush the past. There seems little doubt among the people of the island about what happened, about the terrible events, and about the fact that they had been instructed by the Japanese authorities to take their own lives. Both the reality and the concept are enshrined in the Prefectural Memorial Museum, where a spotlight shines down on the glinting bayonet held by a fierce-looking Japanese soldier, standing over an Okinawan family huddled in the caves, the mother trying to smother her babies' cries. Japanese nationalism does not wish to retain the memory, preferring to allow it to die as quickly as possible by removing it from the educational curriculum. But the people on Okinawa do not want it forgotten.

Masahide Ota, who fought as a member of the Iron and Blood Unit, and was one of the few survivors, reported, "I heard people say that they were told by the military to commit suicide using grenades rather than becoming captives." Ota, who had obviously ignored the instructions he was given, went on to become a leading historian and served as the island's governor from 1990 to 1998. Toshinobu Nakazato, chairman of the Okinawa assembly, broke his 62 years of silence to remember: "Inside a shelter where the family had sought shelter, Japanese soldiers handed his family members two poisoned rice balls and told them to give them to his [Nakazato's] younger sister and cousin."

One of the few survivors of the Star Lily Unit remembers the discipline involved and how it applied to the reactions of the young girls. "We had a strict imperial education, so being taken prisoner was the same as being a traitor. We were taught to prefer suicide to becoming captive. Many of the students died, some even using their last breaths to pledge allegiance to the Emperor of Japan."

There is a documentary film now shown at the site of the hospital cave. It is compiled from still photographs and the creators have attached no musical score, fearing that it was already far too emotional for most persons to endure. But, at the very end, they have included a rendition of "Wakare no Uta," the "Farewell Song." The words and music for this work were composed in the spring of 1945 for the graduation of the students from the Okinawa Teachers' School for Women, and No. 1 Prefectural Senior Girls' High School. The graduation was scheduled for 25 March, just two days after the girls were mobilized.

Further Reading

Appleman, Roy, James M. Burns, Russell A. Gugeler, and John Stevens. *Okinawa: The Last Battle.* Washington, DC: Center for Military History, 2000.

Huber, Thomas M. "Japan's Battle for Okinawa, April to June 1945." *Leavenworth Papers #18.* U.S. Army Command and General Staff College, Leavenworth, Kansas.

Yahara, Hiromichi. *The Battle for Okinawa.* New York: John Wiley & Sons, 1995.

Conclusion

These are only a few of the hundreds of stories coming out of World War II that are worth remembering. As well-known military historian Robert Kaplan has noted, "Military history is important because it offers a realistic assessment of the human condition. The wars of the twentieth century, particularly World War II, provide the historian with an abundance of source materials for how humans reacted in desperate and violent circumstances, in victory and defeat."[1] There is, obviously, far more to history than wars and battles, but it is impossible to comprehend the past, especially when trying to do so in a wide scope, without some individual understanding—actual or virtual—of humanity's military experience.

It is important to remember, for it is essential that Americans be informed about the nature, as well as the costs, of war in order to make informed and wise decisions about participating in them.

As time passes, so much is forgotten. It was such a vast war and there was so much going on, so many units and services, each and all with stories to tell. It was truly a world war, with hardly a spot of land or sea that was not under dispute. And out of each of these many locations there were stories to be told. They can never all be captured, of course, for there are as many stories as there were servicemen and women. For each soldier, sailor, marine, merchant marine, and air force personnel, there is a story. Most of the stories share some things in common, but because there are individuals involved they are also different. Some are unique.

Note

1. Donald A. Yerxa, "The Curious State of Military History," *Recent Themes in Military History* (Columbia: University of South Carolina Press, 2008), p. 3.

Bibliography

There are very few books or articles written explicitly about the twenty-one people and events discussed in this book; obviously, that is why they tend to be less well known. Nevertheless, there are several that mention the person or event, or from which some information can be gleaned. The following have been useful in the preparation of this work, and may interest those who wish to read further.

Abbazia, Patrick. *Mr. Roosevelt's Navy: The Private War of the U.S. Atlantic Fleet 1939–1942*. Annapolis: Naval Institute Press, 1975.
Aczel, Amir. *The Jesuit and the Skull*. New York: Riverhead Books, 2008.
Alford, Lodwich H. *Playing for Time: War on an Asiatic Fleet Destroyer*. Bennington, VT: Merriam Press, 2006.
Appleman, Roy, James M. Burns, Russell A. Gugeler, and John Stevens. *Okinawa: The Last Battle*. Washington, DC: Center for Military History, 2000.
"Army Ships: The Ghost Fleet." http://patriot.net/eastln2/Army.htm.
Baker, Carlos. *Earnest Hemingway: A Life Story*. New York: Scribner's, 1989.
Barber, Noel. *Sinister Twilight: The Fall and Rise Again of Singapore*. London: Collins, 1968.
Barker, Ralph. *Children of the Benares: A War Crime and Its Victims*. London: Grafton, 1997.
Berkeley, H.W. *The 32nd Infantry Division in World War II*. 32nd Division Commission, State of Wisconsin, n.d.
Billings, Richard N. *Battleground Atlantic: How the Sinking of a Single Japanese Submarine Assured the Outcome of World War II*. New York: Penguin, 2006.
Blair, Clay. *Hitler's U-Boat War: The Hunters, 1939–1942*. New York: Random House, 1996.
Boaz, Thomas, and Russell Ciochon. *Dragon Bone Hill: An Ice-Age Saga of Homo Erectus*. New York: Oxford University Press, 2004.
Boyd, Carl. "U.S. Navy Radio Intelligence During the Second World War and the Sinking of the Japanese Submarine I-52." *Journal of Military History* (April 1999): pp. 339–354.
Breuer, William B. *The Great Raid on Cabanatuan*. New York: John Wiley & Sons, 1994.
_____. *Unexplained Mysteries of World War II*. New York: John Wiley & Sons, 1998.
Bridgland, Tony. *Waves of Hate: Naval Atrocities of the Second World War*. Annapolis: Naval Institute Press, 2002.
Brune, Peter. *A Bastard of a Place: The Australians in Papua*. New York: Allen and Unwin, 2005.
Burleigh, M. *Death and Deliverance: Euthanasia in Germany 1900–1945*. Cambridge: Cambridge University Press, 1994.

Campbell, James. *The Ghost Mountain Boys: The Epic March and the Terrifying Battle for New Guinea.* New York: Random House, 2007.

Carpenter, Dorr, and Norman Polmer. *Submarines of the Imperial Japanese Navy, 1904-1945.* London: Conway Maritime Press, 1986.

Clark, George B. *Treading Softly: The U.S. Marines in China from the 1840s to the 1940s.* Pike, NH: Brass Hat, 1996.

Clay, Catrine, and Michael Leapman. *Master Race: The Lebensborn Experiment in Nazi Germany.* London: Hodder and Stoughton, 1995.

Coakley, Robert W., and Richard M. Leighton. *United States Army in World War II: The War Department Global Logistics and Strategy 1940-1943.* Washington, DC: Center of Military History, United States Army, 1955.

"Convoy HI-71: USS *Harder's* Last Battle." www.militaryphotos.net.

Cronberg, Allen. "U-Boats in the Gulf: The Underwater War in 1942." *Gulf Coast Historical Review* 5, no. 2 (Fall 1990).

Cunningham, Chet. *The Frogmen of World War II: An Oral History of the U.S. Navy's Underwater Demolition Team.* New York: Pocket Star, 2004.

Drea, Edward J. *New Guinea: The Army Campaigns of World War II.* Washington, DC: Center for Military History, 1993(?).

Edwards, Paul M. *Small United States and United Nations Warships in the Korean War.* Jefferson, NC: McFarland, 2008.

Farago, Ladislas. *The Tenth Fleet.* New York: Ivan Obolensky, 1962.

Farrell, Brian P. *The Defence and the Fall of Singapore 1940-1942.* London: Tempus, 2006.

Fethey, Michael. *The Absurd and the Brave: The True Account of the British Government's World War II Evacuation of Children Overseas.* Sussex: Book Guild, 2003.

Fleming, Thomas. *The New Dealers' War: Franklin D. Roosevelt and the War Within World War II.* New York: Basic Books, 2001.

Ford, Daniel. *Flying Tiger: Claire Chennault and His American Volunteers.* New York: HarperCollins, 2007.

Fukui, Shizuo. *Japanese Naval Vessels at the End of the War.* Annapolis: Naval Institute Press, 2009.

Fuller, Richard. *Shokan: Hirohito's Samurai.* London: Arms and Armour, 1992.

Gannon, Michael. *Operation Drumbeat: The Dramatic True Story of Germany's First U-Boat Attacks Along the American Coast in World War II.* Annapolis: Naval Institute Press, 1990.

Gardner, W.J.R. *Decoding History: The Battle of the Atlantic and Ultra.* Annapolis: Naval Institute Press, 2000.

Gentile, Gary. *Track of the Gray Wolf: U-Boat Warfare on the U.S. Eastern Seaboard, 1942-1945.* New York: Avon Books, 1989.

George, F.J. *The Singapore Saga.* Singapore: Fernandez Joseph George, 1985.

Gibson, Walter. *The Boat.* London: Monsoon Books, 2007.

Green, Steven H., trans. *Journal Taiwan POW Camp Headquarters in Taihoka.* 1 August 1944, 4.

Grenfell, Russell. *Main Fleet to Singapore.* London: Faber and Faber, 1951.

Grover, David H. *American Merchant Ships on the Yangtze, 1920-1941.* Westport, CT: Praeger, 1992.

_____. *U.S. Army Ships and Watercraft of World War II.* Annapolis: U.S. Naval Institute, 1987.

Hall, Timothy. *The Fall of Singapore.* Methuen, Australia: North Ryde, 1989.

Hamilton, Darby Perry. *The Panay Incident: Prelude to Pearl Harbor.* New York: Macmillan, 1969.

Hamilton-Paterson, James. *Three Miles Down: A Hunt for Sunken Treasure*. New York: Lyons Press, 1999.
Hammer, Joshua. "Hitler's Children." *Newsweek International*, March 20, 2000. www.rickross.com/reference/hate_groups164.html.
Heimannsberg, B., and C.J. Schmidt. *The Collective Silence: German Identity and the Legacy of Shame*. San Francisco: Jossey-Bass, 1993.
Heinrich, Waldo. *Threshold of War: Franklin D. Roosevelt & American Entry into World War II*. New York: Oxford University Press, 1988.
Henderson, James. *Wish Me Luck*. New York: Farrar, Straus and Giroux, 1997.
Hendrick, Bill. "Close to Home." *Atlanta Journal-Constitution*, February 14, 1999. www.usmm.org/closetohome.html.
Heneghan, James. *Wish Me Luck*. New York: Farrar, Straus and Giroux, 1997.
Henshall, Phillip. *Vengeance: Hitler's Nuclear Weapon: Fact or Fiction?* London: Sutton, 1995.
Hickam, Homer H. *Torpedo Junction: U-Boat War Off America's East Coast, 1942*. Annapolis: Naval Institute Press, 1989.
Higa, Tomiko, and Dorothy Britton. *The Girl with the White Flag*. New York: Kodansha America, 2003.
Hillel, Marc, and Clarissa Henry. *Of Pure Blood*. Paris: Fayard, 1976.
Hilton, James. *The Story of Dr. Wassell*. New York: Little, Brown, 1943.
Hilton, Stanley. *Hitler's Secret War in South America, 1939–1945: German Military Espionage and Allied Counterespionage in Brazil*. Baton Rouge: Louisiana State University Press, 1999.
Holland, Elizabeth. "A Salute to Those Who Suffered in POW Massacre." *Post Dispatch*, October 2, 2003, 3.
Hoyt, Edwin P. *Lonely Ships*. New York: David McKay, 1976.
_____. *U-Boats Offshore: When Hitler Struck America*. New York: Stein and Day, 1982.
Icenhower, Joseph B. *The Panay Incident, December 12, 1937*. Danbury, CT: Scholastic Library, 1971.
Illustrated London News, 28 December 1948, p. 75.
Janus, Christopher G. *The Search for the Peking Man*. New York: Macmillan, 1973.
Jellison, Charles A. "A Prelude to War." *American History* 34 (December 1999): 53–55.
Jordan, Roger. *The World's Merchant Fleet 1939: The Particulars and Wartime Fates of 6,000 Ships*. Annapolis: Naval Institute Press, 1988.
Kelley, Howard. *Born in the USA—Raised in New Guinea*. Privately printed, n.d.
Kerr, E. Bartlett. *Surrender and Survivor: The Experience of the American POW in the Pacific, 1941–1945*. New York: William Morrow, 1985.
Kimball, Warren F., ed. *Churchill and Roosevelt: The Complete Correspondence*. Princeton: Princeton University Press, 1984.
Klinkowitz, Jerome. *With the Tigers Over China 1941–1942*. Lexington: University Press of Kentucky, 2007.
Koginos, Manny T. *The Panay Incident: Prelude to War*. Purdue: Purdue University, 1967.
Landis, Kenneth, and Rex Gunn. *Deceit at Pearl Harbor: From Pearl Harbor to Midway*. N.p.: 1st Books Library, 2001.
Leck, Greg. *Captives of Empire: The Japanese Internment of Allied Civilians in China, 1941–1945*. Philadelphia: Shandy Press, 2006.
Li Jing. "Clues Shed Light on Mystery of Missing Peking Man." *China Daily*, November 6, 2005, p. 1.
Lowther, W.W. *Wish You Were Here: An Account of Sunderland's Wartime Evacuation*. Wallsend-on-Tyne: Walton, 1989.
Lunney, Bill, and Frank Finch. *Forgotten Fleet: The Small Ships Section of the U.S. Army*

Transportation Corps, Water Division. Medowie, New South Wales: Forfleet Publications, 2004.

Mahnken, Thomas G. *Uncovering Ways of War: U.S. Intelligence and Foreign Military Innovations, 1918–1941*. Ithaca: Cornell University Press, 2002.

Mayo, Lida. *Bloody Buna: The Campaign That Halted the Japanese Invasion of Australia*. New York: Doubleday, 1974.

McCann, Frank. "Brazil and World War II: The Forgotten Ally. What Did You Do in the War?" www.tau.ac.il/eial.VI_2/mccann.htp.

McKenna, Richard. *The Sand Pebbles*. Annapolis: United States Naval Institute, 2008.

Medal, Doris Ann. "The Smoking Cobras: The Brazilian Expeditionary Force in Italy During World War II." Research project, San Jose State University, 1976, 33.

Menzies, Janet. *Children of the Doomed Voyage*. Chinchester: John Wiley & Sons, 2005.

Michaud, Edward. *Corregidor: The Treasure Island of World War II*. http://corregidor.org/chs_trident/trident_02.htm.

Mooney, James L. *Dictionary of American Naval Fighting Ships*. Washington, DC: Government Printing Office, 1968.

Nagorski, Tom. *Miracles on the Water: The Heroic Survivors of a World War II U-Boat Attack*. New York: Hyperion, 2006.

National Oceanic and Atmospheric Administration. "Surveying German Submarines Sunk Off North Carolina During World War II." *Scientific Daily*, July 9, 2008. www.sciencedaily.com/releases/2008/07/080709110046.html.

Niderost, Eric. "Eleventh Hour Peril." *World War II History*, September 2005, www.historymagazine.com/2005/sep/fea-eleventh.html.

O'Connor, Jerome M. "The Ghost Ships of Task Force 14." www.historyarticles.com/ghost_ships.htm.

O'Hara, Vincent P. "The Battle for Badung Strait, February 18–19, 1942." www.microwories.net/pacific/battles/badung_strait.htm.

Orejas, Tonette. "Wreckage of 'Suicide' U.S. Warship found in Subic." *Philippine Daily Inquirer*, 14 November 2003, 1.

Owen, Frank. *The Fall of Singapore*. London: Michael Joseph, 1960.

Parker, Geoffrey, ed. *The Cambridge Illustrated History of Warfare: The Triumph of the West*. Cambridge: Cambridge University Press, 1995.

Pether, Michael. "A Little Known Ship of Evacuees from Singapore, HMS *Scott Harley*." www.cofepow.org.uk/pages/civilian_hms_scott_harley.htm.

Prange, Gordon. *At Dawn We Slept*. New York: Penguin, 1981.

Radike, Floyd W. *Across the Dark Islands: The War in the Pacific*. Novato, CA: Presidio Press, 2004.

Ready, J. Lee. *Forgotten Allies: The Military Contribution of the Colonies, Exiled Governments and Lesser Powers to the Allied Victory in World War II*. Jefferson, NC: McFarland, 1985.

Roberts, Denis Russell. *Spotlight on Singapore*. London: Anthony Gibbs and Phillips, 1965.

Roscoe, Theodore. *United States Destroyer Operations of World War II*. Annapolis: Naval Institute Press, 1953.

Saqqal, George. "A Short Philatelic History of the Yangtze Patrol." *Log*. March-April-May 2004. http://ahoy.tk-jk.net/macslog/PhilatelicHistoryoftheYan.html.

Sawyer, Frederick Lewis. *Sons of Gunboats*. Annapolis: Naval Institute Press, 1946.

Schultz, Duane P. *The Maverick of War: Chennault and the Flying Tigers*. New York: St. Martin's Press, 1987.

Seagraves, Sterling. *The Marcos Dynasty*. New York: Harper and Row, 1988.

_____, and Peggy Seagraves. *Gold Warriors: America's Secret Recovery of Yamashita's Gold*. London: Verso, 2003.

Sellwood, A.V. *Stand by to Die*. London: New English Library, 1961.
Shapiro, Harry. *Peking Man: The Discovery, Disappearance and Mystery of a Priceless Treasure*. New York: Simon & Schuster, 1974.
Shrader, Charles R., in John Whiteclay Chambers II, ed. *American Military History*. Oxford: Oxford University Press, 1999, p. 733.
Sides, Hampton. *Ghost Soldiers: The Forgotten Epic Story of World War II's Most Dramatic Mission*. New York: Doubleday, 2007.
Smith, Colin. *Singapore Burning: Heroism and Surrender in World War II*. London: Penguin, 2005.
Smith, Joseph. "Brazil and the Two World Wars." *Historian* (2004): pp. 16–24.
Smith, Robert. *With Chennault in China: A Flying Tiger's Diary*. Lancaster, PA: Schiffer, 1984.
Smyth, John George. *Percival and the Tragedy of Singapore*. London: MacDonald, 1971.
Spiller, Roger. *An Instinct for War: Scenes from the Battlefields of History*. Cambridge: Belknap Press of Harvard University Press, 2005.
Stick, David. *Graveyard of the Atlantic: Shipwrecks of the North Carolina Coast*. Chapel Hill: University of North Carolina Press, 1952.
Thomas, Lowell. *The Escape of the Treasure: These Men Shall Never Be Forgiven*. New York: John C. Winston, 1943.
Tolley, Kemp. *Cruise of the Lanikai: Incitement to War*. Huntington, NY: Robert E. Krieger Press, 1982.
_____. "The Strange Mission of the Lanikai." *American Heritage* 24, no. 6 (October 1973): pp. 1–8.
_____. *Yangtze Patrol: The U.S. Navy in China*. Annapolis: Naval Institute Press, 2000.
Tomaski, Mark. *Different Battles*. Manhattan, KS: Sunflower University Press, 1999.
Tsuji, Masanobu. *Singapore—The Japanese Version*. London: Constable, 1960.
Tullis, Thomas A. *Tigers over China: Aircraft of the A.V.G. Flying Tigers*. Hamilton, MT: Eagle Editions, 2001.
Underbrink, Robert. *Destination Corregidor*. Annapolis: Naval Institute Press, 1971.
Van der Vat, Dan. *The Atlantic Campaigns: World War II's Great Struggles at Sea*. New York: Harper and Row, 1988.
Van Patten, Robert E. "Before the Flying Tigers." *Air Force Magazine*, June 1999, www.airforce-magazine.com/magazinearchive/pages/1999/june%201999/0699before.aspx.
Warren, Alan. *Singapore 1942: Britain's Greatest Defeat*. London: Hambledon & London, 2003.
Whitley, M.J. *Destroyer! German Destroyers in World War II*. London: Arms and Armour Press, 1983.
Wilbanks, Bob. *Last Man Out: Glenn McDole, USMC, Survivor of the Palawan Massacre in World War II*. Jefferson, NC: McFarland, 2004.
"Willoughby Crashes Through." *Time*, May 25, 1942. www.time.com/time/magazine/article/0,9171,766565,00.html.
Willoughby, Charles Andrew. *Shanghai Conspiracy: The Scourge Spy Ring*. Boston: Western, 1952.
Winslow, W.G. *The Fleet the Gods Forgot: The U.S. Asiatic Fleet in World War II*. Annapolis: Naval Institute Press, 1982.
Wirth, John. *The Politics of Brazilian Development, 1930–1954*. Stanford: Stanford University Press, 1969.
Wrynn, V. Dennis. "American Prisoners of War: Massacre at Palawan." *World War II Magazine* (November 1997): 17–21.
Yahara, Hiromichi. *The Battle of Okinawa*. New York: John Wiley & Sons, 1995.
Zacharias, Ellis M. *Secret Missions*. Annapolis: Naval Institute Press, 1942.

Index

SS *Abberkirk* 128
Adair, Charles 18
Adelphi Hotel 177, 183
Admiralty Islands 189
Africa 51, 90
Air Advisor 116
Air Force 169
Alcantara, Aramdo 17
Alexander, Harold 89
Algerian 86
SS *Alicinious* 167
Alley, Norman 80
Allies 35, 37, 38, 49–53, 54, 61, 69, 73, 86, 87, 93, 102, 113, 118, 132, 136, 138, 145, 150–155, 157, 158, 161, 163, 164, 166, 169, 170, 182, 183
Allison, James W.M. 116
Almadin, Guzman Crispin 17
SS *America* 123, 130
American B-24 Liberator 161
American-British-Dutch-Australian Command (ABDA) 5, 26, 128, 170
American Defense Medal 129
American Revolution 95
SS *American Star* 130
Anders, Arthur 92, 186
Anderson, Oscar 134
SS *Annapolis* 124
Antilla, Cuba 135
Arabs 86
SS *Arar* 88
SS *Ararquara* 88
Aryans 32–35
IHN *Asashi* 27, 182, 184
Asiatic Fleet 5, 14, 16, 18, 20, 24–26, 75, 81, 166
Asiatic Squadron 188
ASW 126
Atlantic Charter 88
Atlantic Fleet 25
Atterbury, G.R. 51
USS *Augusta* 13, 78, 113
SS *Aurangi* 128

Australia 26, 67, 98, 103, 105, 115, 128, 141, 143, 147, 148, 150–153, 154, 155, 166, 171, 176, 179, 183
Australian Militia 51
RHMS *Australis* 130
Austria 36
Avengers 51, 54
SS *Awa Maru* 61
Axis 85, 86, 104

SS *Bacchus* 136
Baddeley, S. 182
Badung Strait, Battle of 27
SS *Baependy* 88
Baguio Gold Mines 45
Balchus, William J. 164
Bali 27
Baltic 35
Banka Straits 169, 173, 181, 182, 183
Barbernell, Larry 55
Barga 89
USS *Barker* 26
Barta, Joseph Fern 163
Bassett, James 3
Bataan 71
Batak (tribe) 159
Batavia 179, 181, 183
Battle Ground Atlantic 51
Bay of Biscay 52
Beary, Donald B. 122, 123, 128, 129
HMS *Bee* 79, 81, 83
Behind Bamboo 182
Behrendt, Petty Officer 51
Beijing, China 57, 61
Belarmino, Baldomero 17
Belgium 36, 103
Bellanea 29–90, 115
Bennett, John 174
Bergman, Ingrid 85
beri beri 160
Berthal Strait 129
"The Big Marnie" *see* USS *Massachusetts*
Billings, Richard N. 53

Binford, Thomas 26, 28
Bismarck (German ship) 124
Bismarck, New Guinea 189
Black, Davidson 57
Black Friday 179
Black Watch (British) 187
Black Watch (Canadian) 187
Blackburn F-2 111
Blackwood, Mike 107
Blakang Mati POW Camp 184
Bleichrodt, Heinrich 145, 148
blood chits 5, 117
Blood on the Sun 2
Bloody Foreland 144
Blue Funnel Line 167, 178
SS *Blumtt* 181
The Boat 108
Boaz, Thomas 2
Boeing Aircraft 110
Boeing P25 110, 114
Boeing 218 fighter 112
USS *Bogue* 51
Bogue, Douglas 157, 164
Bombay 104, 106, 107, 122, 126, 181, 183
Bonds 41
The Bonesetter's Daughter 3, 64
Boon, M.C. 106, 107
Bormann, Martin 38
Borneo 28, 159, 176
Bortinquen Field, PR 125
Bottcher, Herman 155
USS *Bowfish* 192
Boxer Rebellion 66
Boyd, Carl 1, 50
The Boys from Brazil 85
Bradbury, H.G. 124
Braun, Eva 54
Brazil 51, 73, 85–93
Brazilian Army 88, 89
Brazilian Expeditionary Force 88, 89, 90
Brazilian Navy 88, 90
Brazilian Soldier's Cemetery 91
British 12, 13, 14, 26, 67, 78, 83, 104, 105, 108, 112, 113, 120–125, 127–130, 132, 133, 148, 166, 168, 174, 176, 179, 180, 183, 199
British Admiralty 50, 127
British Commonwealth 102, 143
British Navy 167, 169
Bronze Star Medal 129
Brooke Point 163
Brotchie, Donald 78, 82
Brown, Trevor 59
Brunner, Alois 93
Brunswick, Georgia 134, 138
Buckeley, John Duncan 43
Buckeley Class 51

Bucker, Simon Bolivar, Jr. 193
USS *Bulmer* 26
Buna, Battle of 4, 47, 141, 156
Buna, New Guinea 150–155
Buna Mission 151, 155, 156
Buna Village 155, 156
Burmood, Cornelius 116
Burr, Elmer J. 156

Cabanatuan POW Camp 159
HMS *Caledon* 128
Camajore 89
Canada 86, 116, 142, 147, 148, 187
USS *Canopus* 16
Cape Canaveral 136
Cape Endaiadere 151
Cape Verde Island 51
Capetown, South Africa 122, 127
Capranh Bay 17
Caribbean 91
Carlson, Capt. 97
Cartwright, Cyril John 175
Case, Alfred L. 134
Caseley, John 178
Caseley, Katherine 179, 180
cash and carry 14
Cass, George 187
Casselton, ND 187
SS *Cassiando* 42
Castelnuovo 89
Castor Oil 176
Cave of Virgins 3, 9, 74, 192, 199
Cavite, Philippines 16
Cavite Naval Yard 18, 25, 163
C.C. Walefield and Company 176
Celebe 25
Central Aircraft Manufacturing Co. 5, 114
Central Aviation School at Chiao Airfield 113
Central Bank of China 115
Ceylon 183
Chaing Ki Shek 64, 69, 114, 118
Changi Buoy 128
HMS *Chang Teh* 182
Chefoo, China 25
Chen, Art 116
Chenglin, China 25
Chengzhi, Hu 59
Chennault, Claire 111, 115, 116, 117, 118
Chief of Naval Operations 121, 122
Chief of Staff 137
Child Overseas Reception Board 143
China 25, 56–62, 66–69, 77, 80–83, 98, 102, 110–118, 120, 168, 173, 186
China Air Task Force 118
China Fleet 188

Index

China Marines 3, 56
China Navigation Company 167
Chinese Air Force 3, 113, 115, 117, 118
Chinese Communist 25
Chinese National Air Corporation 116, 118
Chingwangtao, China 60, 61
Churchill, Winston 13, 14, 21, 121
USS *Cimarron* 125, 126, 129
Ciochon, Russell 2
SS *City of Benares* 142–148
Clark, Albert H 46
Clark, Annie 2, 4, 141, 176, 177, 179, 183, 184
Clark, Jack 184
Clark, John 183
Clark, Kathleen 176
Clark, Mark 89
Clark, Norman "Nobby" 176, 177, 183
Clemson Class 23, 25, 138
Close to Home 2
Coast Guard 99, 124, 132, 134, 135
Coast Watchers 5, 23
Cobb, Darian 8
Cobras Fumantes 89
Collyer Quay 177
Colombio 106, 182
Commander Prince 3
Commission for Aeronautical Affairs 115
Communism 62, 63, 64, 69, 70, 111
ComYangPat 68
Confiscated 35
Consolidate Mines, Inc. 47
Conspicuous Gallantry Medal 5, 113
USS *Constitution* 24
Convoy and Routing Section 137
Convoy Dm1 128, 129, 130
Convoy Hy71 105
Convoy William Sail 120, 128
Cooke, Lt. N. 169
Cooper, Gary 102
Cooper, Ronnie 146, 148
Coordinator of Inter-American Affairs 87
Coral Sea, Battle of 102, 103, 150, 151, 156
Corner Stone of Peace 199
Cornish, Mary 146, 148
Corregidor 12, 41, 42, 43, 46, 71
Corsair V92C 114
Countant, Seaman 174
The Crack in Space 3, 64
Craig, Col. 179
Creationists 59
HMS *Cricket* 78, 81
Cross, H.E. 51
Crowley, Dan 159, 163
Cryptology 53, 83
Cummings, Beth 147

Currency 41
Curtiss, Hawk 111
Cussler, Clive 64
Czechoslovakia 86

USS *Dahlgren* 138
Daichi Women's High School 144
Damsel in Distress 81
Daniels, Tommy "Pops" 164
Day, Lorraine 102
DD-224
Deal, Elmo V. 164
Deceit at Pearl Harbor 21
Deguchi, Sattaichi 165
SS *Delamore* 180
Dengue Fever 160
Denmark 36
Department of Defense 97, 99
Department of the Navy 97, 138
Department of War 97, 112, 124
Derbridge, Neil 173, 174
HMS *De Ruyter* 128
DESRON 29
USS *Detroit* 44
Dewoitine 150 115
Dick, Philip K. 3, 64, 82
Distinguished Service Cross 45
Distinguished Service Medal (British) 173, 174, 188
Doentiz, Adm. 51, 136
Dollars 41, 44, 49
Don Esteban 42
Doolittle, Jimmy 111
Doorman, Adm. Karl 26, 27, 103, 133, 176
HMS *Dorsetshire* 124, 127
Dorsey, E.D. 116
Douglas 2MC 114
HMS *Dragon* 181
Dragon Bone Hill 57
Dragon Bones 2
Duchess of Bedford 123
Dulles, Allen 53
Dunedin, NZ 189
DuPont, Joseph 159, 164
HMS *Durban* 128, 182
Duropa Plantation 11, 51
Dutch 12, 20, 29, 102–105, 108, 128, 136, 166, 181
Dutch Defense Forces 103
Dutch East Indies 102, 103
Dysentery 166

Earhart, Amelia 122
Eichelberger, Robert L. 154, 155, 164
18th Division 104, 122, 129, 155
USS *Electra* 82

Ellison, Harold H. 31
SS *Emerald* 128
Emmahaven, Indonesia 106
Empire of India 128, 129
Empire Star 128
Empire Star Convoy 179
SS *Empire State* 128
Empire State Building 63
Empress of Asia 117, 129, 176, 181, 182
HMS *Encounter* 128
The End of the Rainbow 45
Enigma Coding Machine 51
Entrance Creek 151
Eriksson, Albert 135
SS *Esparta* 133, 134, 138
Espionage 139
SS *Esso Baton Rouge* 132, 134, 138
SS *Esso Bayonne* 135, 136
Everett, Washington 117
Evergreen 3, 12, 48, 55
Executive Order 9066 136
HMS *Exeter* 124, 125
Extended Defense Office 179

F4U Corsair 31
F6F Hellcat 31
SS *Fanling* 183
Far East 13, 25, 120, 176, 182, 188
Farley, Richard Clarence 174, 175
Federal Malay States Volunteer Force 5, 184
Fenno, Capt. Frank 43–46
Ferguson, Niall 2
Fiat C-R-32 111
Fix 5, 51
Fifth Army, U.S. 88, 90
Fifth Special Naval Landing Force 151
59th Coast Artillery Regiment 163, 164
Filipino 17, 18, 21, 43, 159, 164
1st Fighter Group 91
1st Regimental Combat Team 89
First War Powers Act 41
Fish, Price 52, 54
Fitzpatrick, Joyce 179
Fleming, Thomas 18
Fletcher, Frank Jack 150
Flights, Blue 91
Flights, Green 91
Flights, Red 91
Flights, Yellow 91
Flood Tide 64
Florianopolis, Brazil 91
USS *Florida* 16
Flying Dutchman 23
Flying Tigers 3, 9, 74 111, 115, 116, 118
14th U.S. Air Force 118, 119

Flush Decks 5
Folmar, Cecil 116
Formosa *see* Taiwan
Fornovo 89
Forrest, Katherine 64
Fort Connaught 128
Fort Eustis 100
Fort Santiago 41
Four Stacker 5
4th Division 164
4th Marine Regiment 163
4th Marines 3, 25, 56, 59
4th U.S. Fleet 91
41st Infantry Regiment 154
France 36, 51, 53, 59, 90, 103, 112, 113, 115, 138
USS *Francis M. Robinson* 51
Free China 118
Fremantle, Australia 19, 180
French Moroccan 86
Froggatt, Engineer 182
HMS *Fu Wo* 169
Fuehrer *see* Hitler, Adolf
Fuerteventura Island 130
Fujian Rebellion 113
Fujimura, Yoshikazu 52, 53

HMS *G.85* 128
Galbraith, Douglas 83
Gall, James 172
Gallicano 88
Gallipoli 176
Gay, Franklyn 116
Geist, Lt. 81, 82
General Airplane Company 116
Geneva Convention 135, 137, 138, 139, 143, 145, 147, 148, 160
German Kid 36
German National Socialism 32, 33
Germanized 32, 33, 35
Gibbon, Elwyn Herbert 117
Gibson, Sgt. Walter 107, 108
Gilbert Islands 130
Girau River 151
Giropa Point 151
HMS *Glasgow* 128
Glassford, Adm. 68
Gluessing, Jens 92
Gold 3, 12, 41–45, 48, 53, 54, 55, 92
Gold Reserves (bullion) 41, 48
Goldgreen Hours 90
Gomez, Simplicio 17
Goosecreek *see* Casselton
Gordon, William 52, 54
SS *Gorgon* 179, 180
Government Gardens 151, 155

Government Rice Mills 176
Grant, Gary 85
Great Britain *see* British
Great Lake Ships 98
The Great Raid 165
Greece 86
Greenlaw, Harvey 116
Greennock, Scotland 147
Greiner, Joseph 92
Grey Ghost 123
Grover, David H. 100
USS *Growler* 29
Gruenert, Kenneth E. 156
Guadacanal 152, 156
Guam 26, 31, 44
USS *Guam* 66
Gulf Stream 125, 139
GulfAmerica 133, 134, 135, 138
Gunn, Frederick 43
Gunn, Rex 21
Gurkhas 86
The Guyand Project 92

HMS *H-10* 125
Hadley, James Bruce Douglas 173, 174
Haebaru Field Hospital (Japanese) 194
Haifeng, Yang 63
Hainan 17
USS *Hake* 28, 29
Halifax, Nova Scotia 121, 124, 135, 142
Hall, Jon 15
Hamburg, Germany 123
Hangchow, China 113, 116
Hankow, China 66, 69, 78, 117
Hansen, Krause Edouard 148
USS *Harde* 29
Hardegan, Reinhard 133, 135, 136
USS *Harder* 29
USS *Hardhead* 29
Hari-kiri 193
Harris, Andrew E. 67, 68
Hart, Carolyn G. 64
Hart, Thomas 14, 18, 20, 26, 42, 59
Hashimoto, Kingoro 82
Hastings, Max 7, 8
Hauaeh 77
Hausserman, John W. 45
Havana, Cuba 139
Haylor, Frank E. 23, 29
Heim, Albert 93
Heinean, P.R. 125
Heinkel HE 66Ch 114
Hell-Ship 5, 61
Hell's Angels 116
Hemingway, Ernest 139
Hemley, Edward 126

Henan Province 62
Henricks, Bill 2
Henshall, Phillip 53
USS *Hermes* 15
Hetzel Schoals 135
Hewitt, Kent 189
Higgins Company 97
Hilse, Rolf 145, 147, 148
Hilton, Stanley E 93
Himeyuri Monument 199
Himmler, Heinrich 33, 34, 35, 92
Hiro Bay, Japan 30
Hirota, Koki 79
Hirsbanner, Lt. 51
Hitler, Adolf 33, 34, 54, 85, 86, 132, 137, 143
Hobart, Alice Tisdale 76
Hoeksema, Capt. 105, 106
Hohsien, China 75, 78
Holbrook, Roy 116
Holland 36, 103, 106
Hong Kong 109, 167
Hongjiao Airport, Shanghai 111
Horrigan, John H. 128
hot zones 96
Houghton, Henry 57
USS *Houston* 16
Hu chau *see* blood chits
Hue 17
Huff Duffs 51
Hughes, Howard 116
Hughes, J.H. 75, 76, 78, 82, 186
Hull, Cordell 20, 148
Huntley, Cecil 174
HMS *Hurricane* 146, 148
The Hurricane 15
Hurricane Fighter 171

HMS *I-68* 198
Ibara Surgery Shelter 185
Imperial Japanese Army 56, 84, 168
Imperial Navy Attaché Air Unit 110
Imperial Navy of Japan 5, 19, 24, 28, 48, 50–55, 65, 84, 120, 167, 170, 183
Imperial War Museum 174
Inaho, Otani 65
India 86
Indian Ocean 25, 49, 128
Indo-China 17, 20
Indo China Steam Navigation Company 167
Indragiri River 106
Ingersoll, Adm. 20
Insect Class Gunboat 78, 79
Institute of Vertebrate Paleontology and Palenoantaropology 63

Insular Force 15, 16
International Air Squadron 15
Iron and Blood Corps 194, 197, 199
USS *Isabel* 14, 15, 17, 26
Isar River 37
Ishi Battalion (Japanese) 198
Isoble, Lt. 76
SS *Itacib* 88
Italia Division (Italy) 90
Italy 86, 88, 89, 90, 91, 98 112, 113

Jacksonville, Florida 134, 135, 137, 138
KPM *Jaetensfontain* 115
SS *Jalakrishna* 180
SS *Jalibar* 180
Jambock 91
USS *Jannsen* 51
Janus, Christopher 62, 63
Japan 14, 15, 19, 21–24, 26, 28, 29, 41–46, 48–50, 53, 56, 57, 60, 61, 62, 63, 69–73, 76, 78–83, 86, 88, 102, 104, 105, 107, 108, 110, 111, 117, 118, 120, 130, 150–157, 159, 166–173, 176, 177, 179–181, 186, 188–190, 193, 194, 196, 199, 200; aggression 7, 14, 20, 21, 25, 26, 65, 78, 192, 103–105, 113–116, 127, 141, 150, 157, 158, 173, 184; air action 82, 110, 111, 151, 168, 192; ambassadors 80, 81; military 102, 153, 155, 158, 159, 166; patrol boats 11, 24, 76, 187; planes 15, 19, 27, 28, 44, 75, 76, 77, 78, 82, 83, 110, 111, 115, 116, 128, 129, 167, 182; prisoners 30, 71, 160, 161, 184; submarines 1, 12, 48, 49, 50, 51, 53, 107, 132; troop ship 18, 172
Japanese Army 54, 75, 81, 84, 154, 166, 168, 169, 183, 193, 194
Japanese Harbor 24
Japanese Navy 20, 23, 24, 26, 28, 29, 44, 50, 51, 52, 65, 68, 71, 81, 84, 164, 170, 172, 183
SS *Jardine* 77
Jardine Matheson and Company 167
Jari River 92
Java 19, 23, 28, 103, 105, 166, 171, 179
Java Sea, Battle of 103
Jefferson Barracks National Cemetery 179
Jeffrey, Agnus Betty 179
Jew 32, 33, 34, 40, 86
Jisaburo, Ozawa 170
Jo Oka (soldier) 198
Johansen, J.E. (jr) 51
Johnson, Nelson T. 56, 78
Johor Straits 177
Johree Baharv 179
Johree Marine Department 181
SS *Joseph Dickman* 123–127, 130

Jouett, John H. 113
Jouett Mission 116
HMS *Juma* 128
Junkers K-47 111
HMS *Jupiter* 128

IJN *Kaga* 110, 118
Kagoshima 192
Kahrau, Helga 37, 38, 39
Kamikaze Planes 6, 193
Kampfhenkel, Schultz 92
Kanshi Medal 82
Kaohsiung, Taiwan 61
Karimata Straits 128
HMS *Kedah* 181
Kelley, F.H. 127
Kent, W.C. 117
Kiangnan Dock and Engineering Works 66, 75
Kidokoro, Lt. 110
Kiefer, Edwin 45
King, Adm. 51, 158
King Hotel 138
King's Commendation for Good Service 148
Kinjo, Shegeaki 198
Knamacher, Carl 116
Knight, M.R. 117
Knights Cross 137
Koblos, Ernest J. 164
Kojima, Nagayoshi 160, 165
Kokoda Tract 151
Kokoda Trail, Battle of 103, 154
Koninklhke Paketuarrt Maatsschappij (KPM) 6, 103, 104, 106
Korea 129, 199
SS *Korsholm* 133, 136
Kotani, Lt. 110
Kranji 184
Kraut Kids 36
Krigbarn *see* Kraut Kids
SS *Kuala* 182
Kuala Lajau Delts 179, 181
HMS *Kung Wo* 174, 183
Kunming, China 115
Kuomintang 115, 118; *see also* Nationalists
Kure 30, 48
SS *Kwang* 183

HMS *Ladybird* 18, 79, 81
SS *Lake Flagstaff* 135
Lamb, S.G. 24
Lamour, Dorothy 15
Lang, John Henry 2, 3, 141, 186, 187, 189
Lang, Walter Patrick, Jr. 189

Lange, Kurt 51
USS *Langley* 130
USS *Lanikai* 2, 3, 9, 12, 13, 15-21
HMAS *Lanikation* 19
La Serra 89
The Last Man Out 2, 165
Latin American countries 92
League of German Girls 34
Lebensborn 32-34, 36, 40
Lebensborn Eingetranger Verein 36
SS *Lee Sang (Li Sang)* 177, 178
Legion of Merit 45
Lemmon, Jack 95
SS *Leonard Wood* 123, 124-127, 129
SS *Leslie* 133, 135, 138
Levin, Ira 85
USS *Lexington* 150
L.G. Gal Co. 112
HMS *Li Wo* 2, 4, 9, 141, 166, 170-174, 181
Liberator B-24
Liberty Ships 98
Lidice massacre 35
Life Boat #5 146
Life Boat #10 147
Life Boat #12 146, 147, 148
Life Boat #14 147
Lily White Girls 3, 81
HMS *Lipes* 167
USS *Litchfield* 44
Liverpool, England 136, 142, 143
The Longest Day 8
Lorient, France 48, 50
Lost in Translation 61
Love Day 193
Low, Adm. 51
Loyang, China 117
Lugao 159
Lutheran 87
Luxembourg 36
USS *Luzon* 67, 68, 71
Luzon, Philippines 157
Luzon Stevedoring Co. 16, 19

MacArthur, Douglas 43, 45-47, 91, 115, 150, 152-154, 163, 165
MacKinnon, Adm. 142
Magtulis, Vincente 17
Makassar 26
Malacca Strait 106, 179
Malaria 160
Malaya 14, 102, 106, 127, 130, 166, 168, 173, 176, 177, 183
Malinta Tunnel complex 6, 42
The Man in the High Castle 82-83
SS *Manhattan* 123

Manila 19, 26, 47, 66, 67, 68, 70, 159, 160
Manning, Henry 122
Mantua 91
Marano Su Panaro 89
USS *Marblehead* 26, 95 103
Marciano, Matos Damero 17
Mariana Bay 177
Marines 25, 193
Maritime Commission 95, 96
Marshal 77
Marshall, George C. 137
Marshall Islands 130
Martin 139 115
Martyn, Donald Joseph 163
Marxism 32
USS *Maryant* 120, 125, 126
Mascarenhas, Gen. 90
Masonic Club 177, 183
USS *Massachusetts* 189
Master Race 40
SS *Mata Hari* 192
Mathewson, Christopher 116
Maureen (Clark) 183
May, John 117
IJN *Maya* 182
Mayell, Eric 80
McDole, Glen 2, 163, 165
McDonald, Angus 107
McDonald, William 116
Measa Matril, Egypt 81
Medal of Honor 156
Mediterranean Ocean 25
Mei An 77
Mei Hsia 77
Mei Ping 76, 77
Mei Yuan 71
Mengele, Josef 85, 86
Merchant Marine 101, 109
Merchant ship 122, 132, 135, 136
Metro-Goldwyn-Mayer (MGM) 15
Michaud, Edward 11, 45
USS *Michigan* 44
Michigan National Guard 152
Midway, Battle of 102, 107, 150
The Mighty Peking Man 64
Military Sea Transportation Service 99, 100
Milwaukee, Wisconsin 187
Mine Bay 155
USS *Mindanao* 16
Mindoro 159
Mint (U.S.) 44
Miranda, Carmen 87
Mitsubishi B1M 110, 118
Mitsubishi Corporation 48
Mitsura, Ushijima 193

Miyagi (student) 195, 197
USS *Moffett* 125, 126
Mokpo, Korea 30
USS *Molly Malone* 18
Molucca Island 28
Mones, Nicole 64
Monte Acuto 89
Monte Castello 89
Monte Prano 89
Monte Rosa Division (Italian) 90
Montese, Italy 89, 90
Morishita, Ruriko 195
Morrison, Samuel E. 91
Moscow, Russia 16
Mothballs 6, 25
Motomura (student) 196, 198
USS *Mount Vernon* 122, 123, 126–129
Moura, Nero 91
Mulock, G.F.A. 173, 182
Muntok (Indochina) 173, 182

Nabasan Bay 13
Nakajima fighters 76
Nakamura (student) 198
Nakazato, Toshinobu 200
Nanking, China 3, 25, 69, 75, 76, 78, 82, 84, 114, 115, 116
Nanxiangzhen, China 110
SS *Narkunda* 128
USS *Narwhal* 71
Nationalist Chinese 6, 25, 69, 75, 82, 111, 112
Naval Court of Inquiry 83
Navtico Corporation 48
Navy 16–19, 23, 28, 30, 42, 44, 45, 50, 54, 67, 73, 80, 84, 95–101, 117, 121, 123, 129, 132, 135, 137, 147, 150, 168, 184, 188, 189, 190
Navy Cross 189
Navy Department 20, 51
Navy List 6, 15, 28, 30
Nazism 7, 32, 34, 37, 39, 40, 85, 87, 89, 92
Nelson, Ricky 95
Netherlands East Indies 4, 19, 103, 106, 169
Neutrality A 141
New Port, Rhode Island 123
New Port News, Va. 100
New Strip 151, 155
New York 123, 135, 136, 163
New Zealand 86, 143, 147, 176, 177, 183, 184
Nielsen, Eugene 163, 164
IX Boats (German) 133
9 FM 2, 51

19th Bomber Group 164
92nd Infantry Division 86
9th Bomber Squadron 116
Norfolk, Va. 123
North Africa 189
North Dock 42
Northrop 2 Bomber 115
Norwegian (Norway) 34, 36, 37, 40, 103
Notorious 85
IJN *Nowaki* 182, 184
Nuremberg Laws 33
The Nursery *see* Casselton
SS *Nutmeg State* 124

USS *Oahu* 3, 16, 67, 68, 71, 78, 79
Oakley, T.B. 30
OB-213 142
Ogawa, Toru 165
O'Kane, Richad H. 137
Okinawa, Japan 141, 192–195, 197, 198, 200
Okinawa Shinhan Women's School 194
Okinawa Teacher's School for Women 200
SS *Oklahoma* 132, 133, 137, 138
Okumiya, Masatake 82
Old Strip South 151, 155
Oldendorf, Jesse B. 30
186th Infantry Regiment 164
144th Infantry Regiment (Japan) 151, 152
131 Airfield Battalion (Japanese) 165
128th Infantry Regiment 152, 154
126th Infantry Regiment 152
1043rd Regiment 90
Operation Drumbeat 133, 139
Operation Iceberg 193
Operation Pied Piper 143
Operation Plan 14.3 A 121
Operation Project Orca 48
Operation Rising Sun 55
Operation Torch 189
Operation Victor I 164
Operation Victor II 164
KPM *Ophair* 107, 109
Opium 54
Orange War Plan 17
HMS *Orcades* 124
Order of the British Empire 148
Order of the Chrysanthemum (Japan) 188, 190
Orejas, Tonette 23
USS *Orizaba* 123, 124, 127
IJN *Oshio* 21
O'Sullivan, Father 146
Ota, Mashide 199, 200
Owen Stanley Range 154

Index

P&O Office 177
Pacheco, Albert D 164
Padang 105, 108, 184
Palawan 158–161, 165
Palawan Massacre 74, 164
Palawan Penal colony 157
Palawan POW Camp 3, 141, 159
Paleoanthropology 57, 61
Paleolithic Age 57
Paleontology 6
Palestine 86
Palmer, George Archie 107, 174
Palmetto cemetery 138
KPM *Palopo* 107
Pamero, Mario 17
Pan American Airways 88
Panama 91
Panama Canal 91, 123
USS *Panay* 3, 9, 21, 74–78, 80–84, 116, 186, 188, 189, 192
Papua, New Guinea, 150, 152, 154, 156
Paraguay 89
Paravento 89
Parkins, Robert Sinclair 2
Parris, Archie 107, 108
USS *Parrott* 26
Parsons, Thomas Henry 170, 174, 174
Passchendaele, battle of 187
Patrol Boat #102 32 24, 28, 29, 30
Patrol squadron 32
Patterson, Allen 3, 116
Paukenschilag 50, 135
Pawley, William 117
Paxton, J. Hall 78
Peace Prayer and Memorial Museum 199
Pearl Harbor 12, 19, 21, 43, 46, 59, 60, 65, 82, 127, 141, 157
Peek, R.E. 51
Pei, W.C. 62
Peking, China 59
Peking Man 3, 12, 56–64
The Peking Man 64
Peking Union Medical College 57, 58
Peninsular and Oriental Steam Navigation Company 177
People's Republic of China 6
Pesos 41, 42, 44, 45
HMS *Peterel* 68, 69
Pether, Harold 176, 183
Pether, Kathleen, 183
Petherbridge, Seaman 174
Petillo, Porfessor 46
Petry, Edwin 164
Philippine Central Bank 41
Philippine Insurrection 97
Philippine Island 13, 18, 19, 25, 26 29, 41, 44, 46, 47, 98, 102, 130, 157, 159, 163, 166
Philippine National Treasury 41, 45
Philippine Scouts 42, 157
RTN *Phra Ruang* 23, 29
Pickings, Merle, CGM 16
USS *Pigeon* 45
SS *Pilar* 139
KPM *Plancius* 4, 104, 109, 181, 183
Plymouth argyles 168
Pointe de Camau 17
Poland 35, 86, 90, 93
Polikarpov 1–15/16 115, 117
Polkington, Stephen 68
Pom Pong Island 182
Port Arthur, Texas 135
Port Moresby 150–153, 156
Port Tampa, Florida 136
Portuguese 85, 90
Potsdam Conference 91
POWs 6, 54, 68, 74, 141, 158, 159, 160, 161
Pradoa, John 83
Prefectural Memorial Museum 199
Prefectural Senior Girl's High School 200
SS *President Harrison* 45, 59, 60, 61
SS *President Hoover* 113, 124
SS *President Madison* 59
SS *President Pierce* 124
SS *President Taft* 117
HMS *Prince of Wales* 12, 168, 169, 170, 174, 178, 189
Princesa Palawan 159
Princess Hotel 138
Profeta, Santiago Reyes 17
Prostitutes 34, 36, 39
Puerto Princesa 159, 162, 163, 164
Purple Heart 189, 190

Q-boats 139
Quartermaster 42
Quezon, Pres. Manuel Luis 21, 44, 46
USS *Quincy* 127
QWF Signal 54

Race and Settlement Office 33
Radar 6
radio receiver 17
Raffles Hotel 178
rainbow 17
Rains, Claude 85
RAMP 6, 31
USS *Range* 124, 126
SS *Rantau* 182
Ratai Bay, Sumatra 27
RAY (Rear Admiral Yangtze) 79

Ray, Mrs. 178
RCS 6, 67
Recife 91
Red Arrow Division *see* 32nd Infantry Division
Red Cross 183, 194
SS *Redang* 181
Reilly, Muriel 181
Reinburg, George 117
SS *Releau* 182
Relief Expedition to Peking 97
REN 63
Renavigation (RENAV) 54
Republic of China 71
Republic P-47 91
HMS *Repulse* 168, 169, 173, 174, 178, 183
Rickets 160
Rider, Morris 82
River, Roha 182
River Rats 6, 16
RNVR 6
Roberts, Charles 173
Rockefeller, Nelson 87
Rockefeller Foundation 57
Rockwell, Francis Warner 18
Rogers, Charles Halme 174, 174
KPM *Rooseboom* 106, 107
Roosevelt, Edith 123
Roosevelt, Franklin D. 12, 134, 16, 17, 19, 20, 21, 25, 80, 83, 87, 114, 120, 121, 122, 134, 136
Roosevelt, Theodore 123
USS *Rowan* 125
Rowland, Harry T. 116
Royal Air Force 168
Royal Highland Regiment 187
Royal Navy 172, 178
Rudolph, Anthony F. 126
Russia 90, 112, 113, 115, 118
Ryan, Annie 148
Ryukyus 192
IJN *Ryuujo* 118, 170

Sachiko, Uezu 198
St. Nicholas, Aruba 138
St. Simons Island, Georgia 132, 133
St. Simons Sound 138
Saipan 130, 189
Sakemago, Yoshir 110
Salewski, Michael 137
San Jose Bay 43, 45
San Juna 125
San Marco, Italy 90
San Quirico 89
Sansbury, Ronald 117
Sanur Road 27

Sasebo, Japan 49
Sato, Yoshikazu 161
Sawa, Tomisabura 165
Sawyer Robert 61
Sayre, Francis B. 41
HMS *Scara* 78, 81
Scarff, Elizabeth 178
Scarff, Jopin 178
Scarff, Dr. J.W. 178
Schmidt, Vincent 115, 116
Schulze, Petty Officer 51
Schweiter, John 117
HMS *Scorpion* 182
HMS *Scott Harley* 178–181, 183
Scurvy 166
USS *Sea World* 43
USS *Seadragon* 43
Sean Creek *see* Casselton
2nd Selangor Battalion 184
Secret Mission 2
Secret Room 6, 50, 51
Secretary of State 174
7th Fleet Headquarters 157
7th Infantry Division (Australian) 152, 154, 155
7th Material Squadron 164
7th Transportation Group 100
Shanghai 25, 56, 65–69, 71, 75, 82, 83, 111, 113, 116, 117, 167, 176
Shannon, Ellis 119
Shaw Brothers 64
Shearing, Paul 146
Sheehaw, J.M. 78
Shelter #20 195, 198, 199
USS *Shengking* 82
Shetlands 51
Shizuo, Fukui 28
Shoemaker, Harry E. 14
Short, Robert 110, 11, 112
Sibolga 105
Sicily, North Africa 130
Siegler, William 123
Silver (bullion) 41, 45
Silver Star 45, 46
Sime Road Camp #1 183
Simms, Hugh Crofton 148
Sinclair, J.L. 181
SS *Sing Kheng Seng* 182
SS *Sing Wo* 182
Singapore 26, 48, 49, 53, 81, 103, 104, 107, 122, 127–130, 141, 166–170, 173, 174, 176, 181, 183, 184
Singapore Cold Storage 179
Singapore War Memorial 184
Sino-Japanese War 111, 104
Sipora Island 109

Index 219

6th Regimental Combat Team 89
60th Coast Artillery Regiment 164
Skullduggery 64
Sleeping Bones 64
Slocum, Harry 20
Smith, Columbus Darwin 65, 68, 70, 71
Smith, Harold P. 26, 28
Smith, John 174
Smith, Rufus "Smitty" 164
Smoking Snakes *see* Cobras Fumantes
HMS *Snapdragon* 148
Snow, William Thomas 171, 172, 174
Sobibor Extermination Camp, Poland 93
Sonar 6, 19
Soochow, China 110
Soprassasso 89
South Africa 143, 147, 183
South America 88, 93
South China Sea 128, 168
Southwest Pacific Area (SWPA) 98, 103, 152
Soviet *see* Russia
Sparks, Ken 146, 147
Special Landing Force Troop (Japan) 65
Spencer, Victor 174
Spendlove, Albert 174
Standard Oil (Socony) Company 76, 77, 80
Stangl, Franz 93
Stanton, Lt. 173
Star Lily 195
Star Lily Corp 192, 194, 196, 197, 199
Star Lily Schools 192
Star Lily Unit 200
Stark, Adm. H.R. 20, 121
State Department 161
Steel, Fred 146, 167
Steinhoring, Germany 30
USS *Stewart* 3, 11, 24–28, 30, 31
Stewart, Charles 24
Stigler, Franz Joseph 123
Stimson, Harry 14
Stockade 4
The Story of Dr. Wassell 102
Straits Shipping Company 181, 182
Strip Point 151
USS *Stronghold* 174, 182
Subic Bay 6, 13, 18, 19
Sultan Shoal 167, 176
Sulu Sea 159
Sumatra, Indonesia 26, 105–108, 182, 184
Sunda Strait 28
Sunderland Flying Boat 147
Surabaya, Java 19, 27
Sutherland, Richard K. 153

USS *Swenning* 51
USS *Swordfish* 43
Szechuan 77

Tacoma, Washington 112
Tagbanua (tribe) 159
RCS *Tai Yuan* 69, 70
Taiwan 61, 79, 160, 199
Takahiko, Kiyota 30
IJN *Takao* 134
Taleon, Demetrio 17
Tamaoto, Col. 155
Tamotsu, Mizutani 28
Tan, Amy 3, 64
USS *Tang* 138
Tang-Shengzhi, CinC 75
Tanjung Proik 106
Tankers 76
Tarakan Roads, Borneo 26
Tarquinia 91
Taschajian, Clair 59
Task Force Casablanca 51
Task Force 14 122, 127
Task Force 45 89
Task Group 53 30
Tasueoa, Capt. 155
IJN *Tatara* 68, 69
Tatum, Sterling 117
Tau't Batu (tribe) 159
Taylor, E.A. 120
Taylor, Jesse D. 52, 54
Taylor, Thomas 116
Teilhard de Chardin, Pierre 58
Tengan 177
Tensing, China 60
10th Fleet 6, 50, 51, 138
Thai Navigation Company 181
They Were Expendable 43
13th Air Group 82
32nd Army (Japan) 193
32nd Infantry Division 152–156, 171, 173
Thompson, Arthur William 171–173
Three Caballeros 87
350th Fighter Group 91
Tianjin, China 62
Tidwell, Paul 48, 55
Tientsin, China 59, 60, 61
Tipay, Crispin Malto 17
Tjilatjap 19, 16, 18, 184
Tobruk 81
Tojo, Hideki 161
Tolley, Kemp 2, 3, 16, 17, 18, 20, 68
Tomoyoshi, Yoshima 179
Tormey, Col. 179
Torpedo Boat 43 43
Torraccia Range 89

Toscana, Italy 91
Tota, Antonio Pedro 87
Trinidad 91, 122, 125
Troopship Division 17
Troopships 121, 123, 127, 167
Tropical Ulcers 160
USS *Trout* 3, 12, 43, 44, 45, 46, 47
Truman, Pres. Harry 99
Tsurayuki, Okubo 87
Tsushima Maru 192
Tumbagahan, Prudencio 17
Tupolev SB 2 115, 117
USS *Tutuila* 16, 67, 71
12th Infantry Brigade (British) 107
XXII Tactical Air Command 91
200th Coast Artillery Regiment 164
216 Australian 155
233 Division (German) 90
Two Ton Tessie 147
Type IX Boats (German) 133
USS *Typer* 134
Tyskerunger (Kraut Kids) 36

U Boat *539* 51, 54
U Boat *532* 138
U Boat *48* 145, 148
U Boat *60* 144
U Boat *12* 132–135, 137, 138
U-Boats 6, 132, 134–137
Ukraine 35, 52, 58
Ultra 51
Underwater Demolition Team #2 52, 189, 190
United Fruit Company 134
United Nations Security Council 92
United States (citizens) 14, 21, 66, 70, 73, 74, 76, 77, 80, 83, 85, 86, 95, 190
United States (nation) 7, 9, 12, 12, 19, 20, 29, 31, 41, 42, 46, 56, 61, 62, 67, 69, 71, 80, 83, 84, 87, 91, 93, 99, 100, 102, 113, 114, 118, 120–27, 132, 136, 137, 141, 147, 164, 188, 183, 197, 198; armaments 24, 29; gunboats 3, 21, 75, 78, 186; military 59, 79, 87, 152, 154, 155, 159, 180, 192, 197, 198; planes 30, 110, 161, 177; prisoners 3, 68, 161, 162; ships 4, 14, 21, 23, 65, 80, 135, 192
United States Air Corps 13, 114–116, 118, 164
United States Air Transport Command 91
United States Airmen 111–113, 116–118
United States Army 7, 8, 81, 84, 95–100, 123, 168, 193
United States Army Reserves 110, 112
United States Army Ships and Watercraft of World War II 100

United States Congress 14, 122, 123, 133, 137
United States Diplomatic 69, 78, 79, 139, 148
United States Field Manual 98
United States Finance Corps 42
United States Intelligence Corps 41, 82
United States Transportation Corps 98, 100
United States Transportation Service 96, 97
Uno, Kanmero 48
Uranium 12

USS *Vampire* 128
Vance, Col. 42
Vancouver, BC 117
KPM *Van Imhoff* 104, 105, 106
HMS *Van Tromp* 128
Vargas, Getulio 86, 88
Velarmino, Hilario 17
Venezuela 125
Victoria Cross 6, 173, 174
Vietnam 17, 129, 199
USS *Vincennes* 126
Vines, Mr. 79
SS *Volendam* 124, 144, 145
Volta Redonda steel mill 87
Von Clausewitz, Carl 7, 8
Vosseller, Aurelius B. 51, 52
Vultee P-66 117
Vultee U-11 115, 117
Vultures 184
SS *Vyner Brooke* 179

The Wackiest Ship in the Army 95
USS *Wainwright* 126
"Wakare no Uta" (song) 200
USS *Wake* 3, 11, 15, 65–71
SS *Wakefield* 122, 123, 126, 127, 129, 130
Wantun, China 77
SS *Wantung* 78
War Cabinet 20
War Plan Orange 6
War Shipping Administration 98
Warrant Officer 190
Warren Force 154
SS *Washington* 122, 123
Waverell, General 103, 181
Weaster, Capt. 144
Weidenbach, Adolf Tscheppe 47
Weidenreich, Franz 58
Wenzhong, Pei (W.C. Pei) 57
Wermuth, Otto 54
Wernigerode, Germany 38
USS *Wesson* 31
SS *West Point* 123, 127, 129, 130

Western Naval Task Force 130
SS *Western World* 124
Whangpoo River 117
White Coolie 179
Whiting, Francis E.M. 189
Whitney, Courtney 47
Wiesenthal, Simon 93
Wilding, Dick 174
Wilkinson, Thomas 167, 169, 170–174
William Sail 12 X 120, 122, 126
Williams, Beth 147
USS *Willis* 51, 120, 122
Willoughby, Charles 2, 3, 4, 41, 42, 45, 47, 152, 153
Wilson, Pres. Woodrow 41
USS *Winslow* 124
Winston Special 4 130
A Winter in China 83
Wisconsin National Guard 182
Woelpel, Lyman 117
Wood, J.J. 126
Woollcombe, Geoffrey Charles Douglas 107
Wooten, George 154, 155
World War I 15, 25, 97, 116, 120
World War II 3, 7, 13, 19, 24, 25, 61, 73, 82, 92, 93, 95, 97, 111, 132, 141, 192, 201

Wright Whirlwind 112
Wuhu, China 25, 78

Xing, Gao 63

Yangtze River 6, 14–16, 25, 66, 67, 70, 71, 75, 79, 80, 81, 82, 83, 166, 167, 182, 184, 188, 192
Yanqing, Ji 59
Yarnell, Harry E. 79, 81
Yasuaa, Capt. 151
Yellow River 117
Yellow Sea 25
Yokosuka 25
Yokosuka bombers 76
Yokoyama, Col. Shizuo 117, 151
USS *Yorktown* 150
Yoshimatsu, Tamori 29 107
Yoshimi, Lt. 30, 165
Ypres 187
Yunnan Provnce 115

Zambale 18
Zero: The Story of Japan's Air War in the Pacific 82
Zocca 89

www.ingramcontent.com/pod-product-compliance
Ingram Content Group UK Ltd.
Pitfield, Milton Keynes, MK11 3LW, UK
UKHW041950140426
5217IPUK00014B/736